Shari`a, Citizenship, and Identity in Aceh

CONTENDING MODERNITIES

Series editors: Ebrahim Moosa, Atalia Omer, and Scott Appleby

As a collaboration between the Contending Modernities initiative and the University of Notre Dame Press, the Contending Modernities series seeks, through publications engaging multiple disciplines, to generate new knowledge and greater understanding of the ways in which religious traditions and secular actors encounter and engage each other in the modern world. Books in this series may include monographs, coauthored volumes, and tightly themed edited collections.

The series will include works that frame such encounters through the lens of "modernity." The range of themes treated in the series might include war, peace, human rights, nationalism, refugees and migrants, development practice, pluralism, religious literacy, political theology, ethics, multi- and intercultural dynamics, sexual politics, gender justice, and postcolonial and decolonial studies.

SHARI`A, CITIZENSHIP, *and* IDENTITY IN ACEH

Arskal Salim,
Moch. Nur Ichwan,
Eka Srimulyani,
and
Marzi Afriko

University of Notre Dame Press
Notre Dame, Indiana

Copyright © 2025 by the University of Notre Dame
Notre Dame, Indiana 46556
undpress.nd.edu

All Rights Reserved

Published in the United States of America

Library of Congress Control Number: 2024947146

ISBN: 978-0-268-20930-8 (Hardback)
ISBN:978-0-268-20931-5 (Paperback)
ISBN: 978-0-268-20933-9 (WebPDF)
ISBN: 978-0-268-20932-2 (Epub3)

GPSR Compliance Inquiries:
Lightning Source France, 1 Av. Johannes Gutenberg, 78310 Maurepas, France
compliance@lightningsource.fr | Phone: +33 1 30 49 23 42

CONTENTS

List of Figures — vii
List of Tables — ix
Acknowledgments — xi

Introduction — 1

PART I
Theoretical Frames

1 Politics of the Dominant Culture — 25

2 Dormant Citizenship — 40

PART II
The Shari`a State

3 Religious Bureaucratic Authority — 63

4 Non-Muslims in Shari`a Courtrooms — 79

PART III
The Causes of Interreligious Exclusions

5 Mutual Ignorance and Unreciprocated Relations — 97

6 Officializing Confessional Exclusion — 115

PART IV
Lived Experiences of Minorities in Aceh

7 The Negotiated "Space" of the Chinese Community   131

8 The Uprooted Identity of New Muslim Converts   147

9 The Limited Agency of Female Religious Minorities   165

Conclusion   180

Notes   193
Works Cited   215
About the Authors   233
Index   235

FIGURES

Figure I.1. Map of Bordering Districts between Aceh
    and North Sumatra   16

Figure 1.1. Map of Aceh and Aceh Singkil   33

Figure 8.1. Zakat and Allocation for Muallaf, 2009–2014
    (in Indonesian rupiah)   163

TABLES

Table 2.1. Pork Consumption in Three Areas in Aceh
(in kilograms)   54

Table 2.2. Number of Protestants and Catholics in
Aceh Singkil District in 2018   57

Table 3.1. Comparison of Competence among the
DSI Apparatuses in Aceh   75

Table 4.1. Non-Muslim Offenders and Jinaya Cases in Aceh,
2016–2019   83

Table 5.1. Top Five Lowest Scores of National Interreligious
Harmony Index (2017–2019)   111

Table 6.1. Religious Populations of Border Areas, 2018   117

Table 6.2. Religious Populations in Aceh Selatan and
Simeulue in 2018   119

ACKNOWLEDGMENTS

This work would not have been possible in this format without the support and assistance we received from many people in Indonesia and elsewhere. We must admit that gathering data and information across the province of Aceh required a big effort. Doing so while meeting a lot of challenges during the last four years has not been a simple task. In fact, the authors of this book, who live in different places in Indonesia, have had to struggle not only to travel to the research sites in different regions of Aceh but also to find time to prepare the manuscript for review and publication.

We are thankful to a number of our local assistants, including Muhajir Al Fairusy in Aceh Singkil and Putra Lastika Bruh in Aceh Tenggara, who provided support in different ways. Their knowledge of the region has greatly facilitated interviews with key informants, contributing significantly to the data presented in this book.

Our extended gratitude also goes to all of the informants we spoke with from government institutions in Aceh at the provincial and district levels—Mahkamah Syar`iyah, Dinas Syariat Islam (including dai perbatasan or preachers at the borders), Dinas Dayah, Baitul Mal, Satuan Polisi Pamong Praja and Wilayatul Hisbah, Kejaksaan Negeri, and Kementerian Agama offices, who took the time to respond to our inquiries, especially regarding various legal issues and religious policies.

We feel so fortunate to have had a chance to meet and talk with various community leaders in Aceh (Muslim, Protestant, Catholic, Hindus, Buddhist, and Confucians). We really appreciate the friendly support we received from leaders of Forum Kerukunan Umat Beragama (FKUB) of Aceh (in Banda Aceh, Aceh Singkil, Southeast Aceh, Aceh Tamiang, Lhokseumawe, and Central Aceh) as well as from the heads of civil society organizations: Ko Kie Siong of Hakka, Abdul Rasyid of FORMULA, Head of Laksana Kampong, Fatimah Azzahra of PMAS,

A. Kim of Buddhist community figure in Tamiang, Sabar A. Simbolon of HKBP, and Boas Tumangger of FORCIDAS. Desk officers of Protestant and Catholics at both the provincial and district Offices of Ministry of Religious Affairs in Aceh also welcomed and provided us with deep insights into the issues under investigation. All of their kind assistance has been tremendously useful for our understanding of the local dynamics of majority-minority group relations in Aceh.

This study was enriched by a series of disseminations of both our initial findings and the policy brief of Contending Modernities in Banda Aceh. We deeply thank the director of UIN Ar-Raniry's Graduate Program for organizing the seminar events, as well as active participants of Sehat Ihsan Shadiqin, Anton Widyanto, Arfiansyah, Cut Dewi, Saiful Akmal, Saiful Mahdi, and Teuku Zulfikar; M. Saleh Sjafe`i, Khalida Zia, and Adil Abdillah (PPISB Unsyiah); Safrida, Huliatul Adnin, Dian Rubianty, Era Maida, Evi, and Afif (the ICAIOS Management Team). These events helped circulate the findings of our research and enhanced its recognition among the people in Aceh.

We also offer our appreciation to several prominent Aceh Muslim scholars such as Muslim Ibrahim, Alyasa` Abubakar, Rusjdi Ali Muhammad, Yusni Saby, Hamid Sarong, Misri A. Muksin, Syahrizal Abbas, Muksin Nyak Umar, Agusni Yahya, A. Rani Usman, Fuad Mardhatillah, and Aslam Nur for their advice on and important insights into different topics discussed in this book. Likewise, we also thank a number of young Muslim intellectuals in Aceh and North Sumatra: Salman Abdul Muthallib, T. Lembong Misbah, Rosnida Sari, and Reza Idria (Banda Aceh); Muhammad Ansor, Muhammad Alkaf, Ismail Fahmi, and Noviandy (Langsa); and Jakfar, Zulkarnain, Jufri, Johaini, and Dahlia (Medan) for sharing with us their experiences of interacting with non-Muslims in everyday life in both Aceh and North Sumatra.

Our sincerest gratitude goes to Mun`im Sirry and the staff of the Contending Modernities Program of Notre Dame University (Dania Maria Straughan in particular), who have been so kind, patient, and supportive in keeping us on track and facilitating this project through to its final stage. Special thanks go to Anisa Ja'far, who provided support for all operational and logistical matters in Indonesia during the course of this study, and Arnis Silvia, who helped provide language-related feedback on some parts of the earlier draft of this manuscript. Likewise, we would like to thank Ruth Homrighaus for her professional assistance in copyediting the final manuscript before submitting it to the University of Notre Dame Press. Our big thanks obviously go to the staff at the University of Notre Dame Press for accepting and preparing this manuscript for publication. Last but not least, we sincerely thank the anonymous reviewers for careful reading of our manuscript and their effort to provide this book with insightful comments and very useful suggestions.

Finally, we must acknowledge that three chapters included in this book have previously appeared in the following publications:

1. Chapter 2 was published as a journal article, "Islam and Dormant Citizenship: Soft Religious Ethno-nationalism and Minorities in Aceh," *Islam and Christian-Muslim Relations* 31, no. 2, (2020): 215–40. Copyright © 2020 University of Birmingham, reprinted by permission of Taylor & Francis Ltd., https://www.tandfonline.com on behalf of 2020 University of Birmingham.
2. Chapter 3 was published as a book chapter, "Aceh's Sharia Office: Bureaucratic Religious Authority and Social Development in Aceh," in *The New Santri: Challenges to Traditional Religious Authority in Indonesia*, edited by Norshahril Saat and Ahmad Najib Burhani, 64–82. Singapore: ISEAS, 2020. Reproduced here with the kind permission of the publisher, ISEAS-Yusof Ishak Institute, https://bookshop.iseas.edu.sg.
3. Chapter 7 was published as a journal article, "Diasporic Chinese Community in Post-conflict Aceh: Socio-cultural Identities, and Social Relations with Acehnese Muslim Majority," in *Al-Jami`ah Journal of Islamic Studies* 56, no. 2 (2018): 395–420.

We thank the editors of the respective publications for granting us permission to reproduce those works in more polished form in this book.

Introduction

Historians, anthropologists, sociologists, political scientists, and jurists have written numerous works about non-Muslim minorities who live under Muslim rule. A number of these scholars discuss aspects of the economic life of non-Muslim minorities, such as property ownership and taxation,[1] while others focus on the protection of the rights of minorities,[2] including restrictions on these rights.[3] In addition, some authors have paid attention to the emerging concept of citizenship for non-Muslim residents in Islamic countries.[4] More interestingly, a number of works have sought to look at the viability of integrating modern concepts, such as citizenship, into Islamic legal traditions, arguing for the relevance of these traditions in modern times.[5]

Discussion of citizenship in the context of non-Muslim minorities who live under Muslim majority rule raises questions about identity formation among different communities. From the perspective of equal citizenship, the extent to which both majority and minority groups readily claim a common identity remains problematic. Which and whose identity should be displayed and promoted in the public sphere? Should minority groups' cultures be absorbed into the dominant majority culture, or should they be provided with autonomous jurisdictions for an identity-making process within their respective spaces?

In the case of Aceh, the issue of minority rights has been intensely discussed over the past two decades, especially following the implementation of shari`a in the region. A number of works have considered the experiences of non-Muslims living under the authority of shari`a rules.[6] Whereas some scholars have explored the views of the Acehnese regarding the application of shari`a rules to non-Muslim residents,[7] others have focused on the impact of Aceh shari`a rules on religious freedom.[8]

Among works discussing non-Muslim minorities in Aceh, two are particularly relevant to the central concerns of this book. Makin, by providing a narrative of an attack on a Christian church in Banda Aceh, argues that the implementation of shari`a constructed a new identity formulation, "Islamic Acehnese," by means of which the dividing line between "Muslims" and "non-Muslims" has been further stressed and Acehnese sentiments against non-Muslims nurtured.[9] In addition, Ansor, by considering the way in which Christian female residents of Aceh deal with complexities of everyday life that result from the formal implementation of shari`a in Aceh, has considered how the public sphere is framed in religious values and identity through the formalization of Islamic law, and the implications of this development for the dynamics of Christian women's agency as minorities in Aceh.[10]

The work of both Makin and Ansor demonstrates that the process of identity making for minority groups in contemporary Aceh has to adapt to—or to blend with—the identity-making process of the Muslim majority. Although the public sphere in any democratic country is always an arena of contestation for each group to express its identity and interests, the case of Aceh suggests how Islamization alters and affects this process. Yet, as noted by Ansor, efforts toward Islamization in Aceh do not necessarily succeed in unifying the performance of public spaces. In fact, the implementation of shari`a in Aceh has triggered the emergence of a counterpublic sphere that serves to consolidate and reproduce, as well as to disseminate, subaltern groups' voices.

Although few studies have discussed the contemporary process of identity making by both Muslim and non-Muslim communities in light of the current implementation of shari`a in Aceh, no scholarship has attempted to look further at the relationship between the Muslim majority population and groups of minorities by bringing into consideration these minorities' struggle for recognition of their dignity in a predominant Muslim region.

While this gap has been the focus of this book, it also pays attention to the process of mutual recognition of majority and minority groups. This study therefore deals with how both Muslim majority population and non-Muslim minority groups in Aceh have been struggling for having their respective identities recognized in their own ways. Rather than simply assuming that it is minority groups alone that are seeking such recognition, this book argues that the specific communitarian traditions on which Indonesia's organization of religion stands depends very much on members of the majority religion seeking recognition (within unequal power hierarchies) from minority groups. Thus, there is a common insistence throughout the archipelago that minority religions recognize the prerogatives of the majority and stay in their place, in return for their own recognition as good citizens in a particular region.

It is necessary to make a disclaimer here that this study does not concern a sexual minority population in Aceh. It is worth noting, however, that a sexual orientation as such has been present since colonial times. As observed by Christiaan Snouck-Hurgronje, a Dutch orientalist-cum-colonial servant, the existence of same-sex relations (homoeroticism) was reflected in the Seudati, an Acehnese traditional dance. One of the authors of this book (Ichwan 2021) has discussed the presence of sexual minorities movement in contemporary Aceh.[11] After 2008, the emergence of the queer movement (comprising of lesbian, gay, bisexual, transgender) has been more organized in the form of nongovernmental organizations, such as Violet Gray and Putroe Sejati. This movement once caused controversy when they held the Aceh Transgender Festival in 2010. The media coverage following this event invited a strong reaction from the ulama and Islamic organizations. The backlash came when the Aceh's legislature passed the *Qanun* on *Jinayat* (Islamic penal code) in 2014, which includes a corporal punishment of one hundred lashes for those who are found guilty in same-sex activity. Soon after the enactment of such *jinayat qanun*, those queer organizations declared their dissolution. Even though the issue of sexual minorities is interesting, it is beyond the scope of this book.

Approach of the Book

This book presents both an ethnographic and a sociohistorical account of identity making among both the Muslim majority population and different minority groups in Aceh. As identity making is often shaped by complicated sets of social relations in a particular space, this study sought to uncover how Islamic identity, as well as Acehnese identity, have been interactively conceived of—mostly by Muslim residents—and responded to—primarily by non-Muslim residents—in the region in certain periods and especially in the period since Aceh was granted autonomy in the implementation of shari`a. Our discussion considers how the concepts of identity and citizenship have been intertwined within the dynamics of the relationships between various ethnic groups as well as different religious adherents.

Given the Muslim majority population and the long-standing presence of non-Muslim minorities in Aceh, this study seeks to account for the process of identity- and community making for both the Muslim majority population and for non-Muslim minority groups by looking at why and how the process has been in conflict, or aligned, with the concept of citizenship in a region that applies shari`a rules.

This study debunks the concept of citizenship by way of deploying the concept of the politics of recognition in the juxtaposition of the politics of the dominant culture theory in Aceh social contexts. The politics of the dominant culture certainly does not go along with the politics of equal recognition. As the former has been reinforced in many ways especially after shari`a has been implemented officially in Aceh since the beginning of this century. The repercussion of such politics has inflicted damages on the equal citizenship of non-Muslim minority groups. Their equal dignity as well as unique identity have been hardly acknowledged or accommodated in a formal way.

As pointed out by Taylor, the politics of equal recognition becomes more central thanks to identities that are formed in open dialogue.[12] In his view, recognition plays an essential role in the culture to form or deform an identity. It needs, or is vulnerable to, the recognition given, or withheld, by significant others. In other words, the granting of recognition implies an emancipation, while the withholding of recognition can be a form of oppression. The content of the politics of recognition, according to Taylor, has been the equalization of rights and entitlements.[13] This kind of politics refuses the typology of "first class" and "second class" citizens. All citizens are equal.

This book explains the problematic relationship between the politics of equal recognition and the politics of identity as expressed through the dominant-culture politics. It highlights that equal citizenship as well as feeling a sense of shared ownership has been largely deficient and vague, thanks to the politics of dominant culture applied in Aceh. Since their rights to participate as a legitimate and full member of society have been limited and less acknowledged, the citizenship of non-Muslim minority groups has been dormant in some ways. To substantiate this point, this study sought to answer the following questions:

(1) As citizenship puts diverse groups on an equal footing and requires everyone to feel a shared sense of ownership in society, to what extent do minority groups feel that they belong to Aceh's communal identity, which is mostly Islamic?
(2) Under current formal implementation of shari`a in Aceh, to what extent do minority groups feel that they are included and accepted (not merely as "guests")?
(3) How do minority groups in Aceh mitigate discrimination as well as denial to their particular identity?
(4) What kind of citizenship is in place when minorities feel marginalized living under Aceh's Islamic rules?

Defining Citizenship

It is important to understand citizenship as a multilayered construct that is affected by local, ethnic, national, and state dynamics.[14] To comprehend this, we should take into account the role not only of the history of Indonesian nation building, as suggested by Gerry van Klinken and Ward Berenschot, but also of local history, political processes, religious ethnonationalism, and shari`a politics in (re)constructing citizenship.[15] We argue that the synthesis of religion and local memories of Aceh as a "civilization" and "nation" (*bangsa*) has formed Acehnese "religious ethnonationalism." During the colonial period, religious ethnonationalism manifested in its hard face, as reflected in the Prang Sabi (war in God's path) movement, and in the postindependence period it was seen in the independence movement of Darul Islam (1953–63). After the collapse of Suharto's regime, and especially after the Helsinki memorandum of understanding between the Gerakan Aceh Merdeka (Free Aceh Movement) and Jakarta in 2005, which signified the end of the conflict between the two parties, Acehnese religious ethnonationalism has been manifested in its soft face, as embodied in contemporary shari`a politics. Aceh is not a liberal society, so applying liberal notions of citizenship would be inappropriate. Aceh is certainly a communitarian society that considers community above individuality. In such a society, rights belong not only to the individual but also to the ethnic group and the religious group (the

Islamic *ummah*), collectively. The common good is mostly considered more important than individual rights. Given all this background, communitarian and multilayered approaches should be used to understand citizenship in Aceh in the postconflict period.

Citizenship can be defined in relation to two things. First, it constitutes membership in a polity, and as such, it inevitably involves a tension between inclusion and exclusion, between those deemed eligible for citizenship and those denied the right to become members. Second, membership brings with it a reciprocal set of duties and rights, both of which vary by place and time, though some are universal.[16] Citizenship is related to membership in a particular political community and involves a relationship between core features of citizenship: rights, duties, participation, and identity.[17] Emphasis on some core features, rather than others, reflects different approaches to citizenship, either liberal, republican, or communitarian. The liberal approach emphasizes rights, the communitarian duties and identity, and the republican participation. The liberal approach examines the legal status of the individual and the importance of achieving civil and political rights. The communitarian approach deals with the management of societal diversity, aiming to maintain peace and harmony while respecting minority rights. The republican approach focuses on the role of an active and informed citizenry. Robert Hefner argues that communitarian citizenship has relevance to Indonesia,[18] whereas Van Klinken and Berenschot argue that republican citizenship is more relevant to Indonesia's democratization,[19] although the latter also acknowledge that it is due for renewal. In the context of Aceh, communitarian citizenship is more relevant.

As pointed out by T. H. Marshall, there are three types of rights: civil, political, and social.[20] Civil rights include individual freedoms, such as free speech, freedom of religious expression, and the right to engage in economic and civic life. Political rights involve those rights that ensure the ability to actively participate in the realm of politics. Finally, social rights involve rights to various welfare provisions designed to guarantee, to everyone, a minimum standard of living necessary for the other two rights to be meaningful. Included in this type of right are guarantees of educational opportunities, health care, decent and affordable housing, pensions, and so forth.

Citizenship assumes an inclusionary nature because it promises the protection of human rights, including social, political, civic, and economic welfare rights. In practice, however, citizenship may be inclusionary or exclusionary.[21] The majority, along lines of nationality, ethnicity, gender, class, age, disability, and sexual orientation, define the inclusionary or exclusionary nature of citizenship.[22] Some scholars, such as Ruth Lister,[23] Gail Lewis,[24] and Lena Dominelli, have shown that various forms of exclusion through state or social practices are related to social divisions—namely, gender, ethnicity (including indigeneity), ability, age, class, and sexual orientation—and we should include religion, too.[25]

It has been argued that religion, including religious symbols and issues, is also a cause of social division and, as Barbara Metcalf puts it, "a language for issues of citizenship."[26] Hefner has argued that the increasing visibility of religion and its importance in public debates across Southeast Asia, including Aceh, has affected the nature and interpretation of citizenship.[27] Consequently, the interpretation and practice of citizenship is closely tied to religious interpretations and practices[28] as well as, to use David Kloos and Ward Berenschot's term, to "the construction of religious discourse."[29] This is also true in the case of Aceh, but the question is, why do certain religious symbols and issues, the visibility of religion and its importance in public debates, religious interpretations and practices, and the construction of religious discourse result in both inclusive and exclusive citizenship? First, religion is not monolithic and static but dynamic; it cannot avoid cultural, social, economic, and political influence. Second, the term "religion" may refer to its norms (laws) or its values. Norm-oriented religion would naturally lead to a formalist-scriptural understanding of religion, whereas value-oriented religion would lead to substantive understanding of religion; the former would usually lead to an exclusive citizenship and the latter to an inclusive one. Aceh provides an example of how religious Islamic norms influence the interpretation of citizenship.

The Islamic Context of Aceh

The Indonesian province of Aceh is a predominantly Muslim region with a very strong Islamic identity. It is located in the westernmost part of Indonesia, situated at the northern tip of Sumatra island. As early as the twelfth century, the first Muslim sultanate was established in Aceh, well before other Indonesian islands—among them Java, Kalimantan, and Sulawesi—became predominantly inhabited by Muslim believers. Today, nearly 99 percent of the inhabitants of Aceh are Muslim. The

Acehnese are proud of having accepted Islam earlier than other Muslim ethnic groups of Indonesia. As the first region of Indonesia to embrace Islam and to host a Muslim kingdom, Aceh has a long history of implementation of shari`a—the sacred law of Islam—compared to other areas of Indonesia.[30] The Acehnese are proud of this history, which forms the basis of a strong sense of shared identity.

The first years after Indonesia attained independence from the Dutch in 1945 found the ulama controlling political positions in the Acehnese regional government. Their primary mission was to restore the entrenched identity of the Islamic Acehnese, which had been suppressed by the colonizing Dutch. As the first step, the ulama demanded that Aceh's territory be made a province, not only as a basis of their authority but also as a means of protecting the Islamic identity of the region.[31]

This attempt to construct a strong Islamic identity for the region of Aceh was opposed by the national government in Jakarta, however. Consequently, for almost ten years, the ulama rebelled against Jakarta by declaring Aceh a separate state, Negara Islam Indonesia (Islamic State of Indonesia). This rebellion was defeated in the early 1960s.[32] Under the New Order regime that followed (1966–98), all forms of Islamic identity expression in Aceh were undermined. An effort to enact a regional regulation (qanun) implementing shari`a (Regional Regulation 6 of 1968 on the Implementation of Shari`a Law in Aceh) was refused, and in the midst of central government suppression, the robust ideological stance toward strengthening the Islamic identity of Aceh that the ulama had expressed since the 1950s moved underground for three decades.

In the post–New Order era, the ulama were once again offered a chance to (re)shape Aceh based on Islamic identity. Thanks to two national laws, Law 44/1999 and Law 18/2001, Aceh was granted special autonomy to apply shari`a. This privilege extends to religion, local custom, and education in which the council of ulama is required to be actively involved. Aceh's Muslim religious leaders have been authorized to reshape Aceh through their exercise of a number of political roles and responsibilities, including issuing legal opinions (fatwa) on governance, economy, and cultural life; giving feedback, consideration, and suggestions to the government of Aceh and the provincial legislature in the lawmaking process, particularly regarding shari`a regulations; and supervising governance and the implementation of regional policy in accordance with Islamic shari`a.

In addition to the ulama, two new regional Islamic institutions have helped to restructure and strengthen Islamic identity in Aceh since 1998. The first is the religious bureaucracy, the Department of Islamic Shari`a (Dinas Syariat Islam, DSI). This office has substructures within all districts of Aceh. It plays an active operational role in enforcing shari`a rules enacted in the form of qanun, or regional regulations. The office employs young people for its task force in the field, the Shari`a Police, or Wilayatul Hisbah. The second is the transformed religious court, the Mahkamah Syar'iyah, or Shari`a Court. This court has more extensive jurisdiction than do religious courts elsewhere in the Indonesian provinces. Whereas the Mahkamah Syar'iyah initially only dealt with personal or family issues, its jurisdiction has been expanded to cover some criminal acts, including cases involving non-Muslim offenders.

Other than regional Islamic institutions above, a nationally vertical organization of Ministry of Religious Affairs is also present in Aceh. While the headquarters of the ministry is located in Jakarta, the capital of Indonesia, its area offices are found at the provincial, district, and subdistrict levels all over Aceh. Although all these branches are called Offices of the Ministry (Kantor Kementerian), they differ slightly from one another depending on their territorial scopes. These offices of the ministry in Aceh, like in other Indonesian provinces, merely focus on common religious issues such as Islamic education, hajj, zakat, waqf, and so on.

Through these political developments, Muslim leaders in Aceh believed they could revive their historical authenticity and the region's unique Acehnese identity. The presence of these newly established or transformed Islamic institutions in Aceh, and of their respective authorities (advisory, bureaucratic, and judicial), remains mostly symbolic, however, as the influence of Aceh's Muslim leaders on policymaking processes in the region has been relatively limited.

Minority Groups in Aceh

While Muslims in Aceh take pride in the region's ingrained Islamic identity, non-Muslim groups also feel a strong sense of being an embedded part of Acehnese identity—although they consist of only about 1 percent of the region's total population of 5.4 million people. As a general rule, these non-Muslim communities coexist happily side by side with their fellow citizens, and areas at the provincial borders host mixed populations of Muslim and non-Muslim residents.

Non-Muslim minority groups in Aceh include Protestants, Catholics, Buddhists, Hindus, and Confucians. They live in different cities and districts of Aceh but are concentrated in the regions bordering North Sumatra, including Singkil, Subulussalam, Kutacane, and Tamiang, as well as in urban areas of Lhokseumawe, Langsa, and the provincial capital of Banda Aceh.

Of the cities where non-Muslims concentrate in Aceh, Kutacane and Singkil have the largest Christian populations. Located at the provincial border, these cities are culturally and demographically affected by North Sumatra, which has a large Protestant population. In Kutacane, people of different religious backgrounds demonstrate relatively robust social cohesion, while the different peoples of Singkil tend to be socially segregated. The residents of Singkil have marked difficulty comprehending and presenting their social identity. The question of whether Singkil is Acehnese or how much it has been "Acehnized" remains unresolved. This question implies that to be Singkil is not necessarily to be Muslim; the identity of the city does not cover both ethnic and religious categories at the same time. This is because Singkil is understood also to include the Batak ethnic group of North Sumatra. While some Batak are Muslim, Batak Pakpak are quite strongly identified as non-Muslim. Some of those we interviewed for this book suggest that Singkil is one thing, and Aceh is quite another. Thus, the current term "Aceh Singkil" suggests an attempt on the part of the state to forcefully blend two identities that have not yet been collapsed into one.

By contrast, people in Kutacane easily define their proper identity as being Alas, the predominant ethnic group of the area for centuries. "Alas" is not equivalent to "Acehnese," but like the Acehnese, almost all Alas people are Muslims. If an individual from Alas happens to convert to other religions, she or he would conventionally be regarded as a non-Alas person and would not be allowed to use any surname belong to Alas ethnic group. For this reason, Alas people are easily able to integrate with the prevailing political culture of the province, including the implementation of shari`a. Non-Muslims living in Kutacane are mostly considered "outsiders" who migrated from North Sumatra. Nonetheless, they are able to find opportunities to build their own distinct community and strengthen their particular identity even under the authority of Islamic shari`a.

The largest non-Acehnese as well as non-Muslim group in the capital city of Banda Aceh is Chinese, who mostly adhere to Buddhism and Confucianism. Some of them are Catholics or Protestants. A quite significant number of Chinese people are also found in Tamiang, a district neighboring the province of North Sumatra. Ethnic (or "diasporic") Chinese have been present in Aceh for centuries. They arrived mostly as merchants in the sultanate period as early as the seventeenth century. With the sultan's approval, the Chinese built a settlement not far from the palace in Kutaraja, which is currently Banda Aceh. This settlement is close to a river that allows access to the seaport. It remains today and is called Peunayong, which refers to the local word *payong*, or "umbrella," describing a place that receives a cover of protection. For many years, Peunayong has been mostly inhibited by ethnic Chinese, and thus it is a "Chinatown" of Banda Aceh.

Identity Politics

To help explain why and how the process of identity making of both Muslim majority and non-Muslim minority groups in Aceh has taken place, this study utilizes the work of Francis Fukuyama on identity politics and the struggle for recognition in modern democracies.[33] In Fukuyama's view, the rise of identity politics has largely to do with the demand for recognition. Referring to G. W. F. Hegel's work, Fukuyama contends that the struggle for recognition—specifically, mutual recognition of shared human dignity—is the ultimate driver of human history.[34] According to Fukuyama, beginning in the twentieth century, the democratic upsurge has been driven by people demanding recognition of their political personhood and their capability of sharing in political power.[35]

Why has identity politics been a large part of the political struggle of the contemporary world? Borrowing a phrase from Charles Taylor, Fukuyama points out that identity is the "powerful moral idea that has come down to human beings."[36] This moral idea has led human beings to focus on their demand for recognition of dignity. The term "identity politics" emerged in the 1980s and 1990s and is widely understood to refer to social categories, social roles, or information about oneself. Identity in contemporary politics is significant because it grows out of a distinction between one's true inner self and an outer world of social rules and norms. The inner self is the basis of human dignity, which seeks recognition. Because human beings naturally crave recognition, the modern sense of identity quickly evolves into identity politics in which individuals demand public recognition of their worth.[37]

The demand for recognition of one's identity is a master concept that unifies much of what is going on in world politics today. This demand for recognition often takes a more particular form, centering on the dignity of a particular group that has been marginalized or disrespected. For this particular group, the inner self that needs to be made visible is not that of a generic human being but of a particular kind of person from a particular place who observes particular customs, which can be based on nation, religion, sect, race, ethnicity, gender, or by individuals wanting to be recognized as equal or even superior. When this particular group demands recognition of its own dignity, its demand turns into a political movement.[38] Here, the universal recognition of the dignity of every human being has been challenged by other partial forms of recognition.

Fukuyama further argues that the politics of recognition has two forks.[39] One fork led to the universal recognition of individual rights, while the other fork led to assertions of collective identity. In the contemporary Muslim world, such collective identity often seeks recognition of a special status for Islam as the basis of political community. This demand, which is either overtly or covertly expressed, has been a hidden or suppressed identity that seeks public recognition of Islam. It extends to broader phenomena, including politicized Islam, much of which is rooted in the demand for recognition of Islamic identity. Political Islam, as broadly defined by An-Na'im, is "the mobilization of Islamic identity in pursuit of certain objectives of public policy both within an Islamic society and in its relations with other societies."[40]

Whereas Fukuyama employs the politics of recognition as an approach to interpreting contemporary identity politics in which he observes different demands for the equal recognition of dignity, or the so-called revolutions of dignity in the modern world, this study uses the concept of the politics of recognition as an analytical tool to examine the particular case of the relationship between the Muslim majority and non-Muslim minority groups in Aceh. Precisely, this book puts the concept of the politics of recognition in the juxtaposition of the politics of the dominant culture theory in the contemporary sociopolitical contexts of Aceh. Within such a framework, this book pushes the analysis further by looking at how equal citizenship in a democratic political system has been negotiated and compromised.

In Search of Recognition

Modern democracies promise and deliver a minimal degree of equal citizenship. Yet, as Fukuyama points out, the rights of people from different backgrounds cannot be guaranteed to be equal in the everyday life of a democracy, particularly for those minority groups with a history of marginalization.[41] Everywhere in the contemporary world, marginalized minority groups share similar experiences of being forced by the government to integrate into a society very different from their own. Their unique identities often become a target of unification policy. Their fundamental rights are largely ignored, and they are subject to discrimination.

The enforcement of a uniform singular character for people of multifaceted identities is likely to cause either tension or resistance. Tension and resistance arise where there are conflicting identities, and these different senses of identity, as noted by Hughes,[42] lead to different ideas of law, politics, and the state. This is the case not just between differentiated groups but also between separate powers. In the case in question, while tensions frequently arise between the Muslim-majority community and non-Muslim minority groups in Aceh, resistance and even confrontation occurred between the provincial government of Aceh and the national government of Indonesia during the first decades after Indonesian independence.

Aceh was a virtually autonomous imperium in imperio under the banner of a distinctly Islamic local and ethnic patriotism when it started to become a part of the independent Indonesian state in 1945.[43] As Morris has described, however, there was a conflict of conceptualization between the Acehnese and the national government regarding the regional identity of Aceh.[44] Having been challenged to make a choice between national integration under the ideal of Islamic solidarity and Islamic expression within regional identity, the Acehnese chose the latter, opposing the power of a majority Muslim country ruled by a nominally secular state. Thus, the revolt of Aceh took place in the 1950s not only because many Acehnese felt the national government's policy was inappropriate but also, and mostly, as an expression of Acehnese resentment that recognition of their Islamic identity was not forthcoming.[45]

The demand for recognition of Aceh's Islamic identity continued and only received a positive response following the collapse of the New Order regime in 1998. The post–New Order governments responded to Aceh's request for formal implementation of shari`a during the years of political transition. Thence, the recognition of Islamic identity for Aceh region has been intensively and extensively observable, primarily through the passage of Islamic legislation. As this recognition is legalistic in nature, the demand for the recognition of Islamic identity in Aceh accordingly includes acceptance of and submission by Muslim and non-Muslim residents to all rules stipulated in the qanun on shari`a.

How do Muslim and non-Muslim residents in Aceh make claims for the recognition of their own identity? On the one hand, some Muslim leaders in Aceh were satisfied with the national government's offer to allow Aceh to apply shari`a rules in the region, a reform they felt was long overdue. For these leaders, the shari`a offer became a symbol of the recognition of their identity by the national government. Yet for others, this official recognition was not enough. They also wanted grassroots recognition from each component of society, including recognition from non-Muslim minority groups living in Aceh. One of many ways in which non-Muslims demonstrate that recognition is through their compliance with the shari`a rules stipulated in the qanun.

Non-Muslim inhabitants who live under shari`a rules in Aceh have their own need for recognition of their particular identity. Although they might acknowledge that they cohabit a region dominated by others who, due to the greater size of their population, think of and define themselves as hosts, the non-Muslim inhabitants of Aceh are not reluctant to claim recognition of their rights and dignity as well. They do so by requesting the authorities treat them fairly and equally regardless of their religious affiliation. As observed by N. Ghanea, religious minorities living in Muslim Middle Eastern countries have challenged their inferior status as well as their inequality before the law.[46] They have asked for equal participation in various aspects of life so that they would be able to contribute to the outcome of events and structures that influence their conditions, whether in the legal, political, or cultural spheres.

Why do minority groups demand recognition of their identity and dignity? What is the underlying cause behind it? Their motivation to struggle for recognition stems from what Fukuyama identifies as *thymos*.[47] Thymos is a part of the human soul that craves recognition of dignity; its extended term is *isothymia*, which means a demand to be respected on an equal basis with other people. In the view of Fukuyama, thymos is the seat of judgments of worth.[48] These judgments can come from within, but they are most often made by other people in the surrounding society. Positive judgment results in feelings of pride, and negative judgment leads to shame or anger. With this in mind, it can be said that both the majority population *and* minority groups zealously demand recognition of their own rights, identity, and dignity—even if gaining this recognition requires them to take big risks.

The legal basis for non-Muslims in Aceh to claim their own (religious) rights is the Bylaw No. 05/2000 on the implementation of Islamic Shari`a law. Article 2 (2) of this bylaw stipulates that "other religions outside of Islam will continue to be recognized in this region, their religious teachings can be practiced by their respective followers." This obviously recognizes and welcomes non-Muslims to live and practice their religion in Aceh.

However, despite this clear stipulation of their rights—respecting, protecting, and granting them the freedom to worship according to their religious teachings—a number of regional legislations in recent years have raised concerns among non-Muslims. These concerns are particularly related to the strengthening of Islamic identity in Aceh. As Ansor points out, non-Muslims are especially concerned with issues of equality and justice, as they face limited access to expressing their collective identity in public spaces.[49]

Methods and Sources

This is a three-year qualitative study that began in early 2016. It consisted of fieldwork as well as library research. For the first time, in March 2016, we visited research sites at bordering districts between Aceh and North Sumatra provinces. Instead of starting our trip from Banda Aceh, we departed from Medan, the capital of the North Sumatra province. We did so not only because of Medan's relative proximity to the destination but also to see and feel how much districts at the provincial border are culturally and demographically affected by North Sumatra, which is quite different from Aceh. While Aceh is primarily a Muslim province, North Sumatra is a province with a significant number of Protestant population.

Over three years, we paid a recurring visit to eight cities for this study, which include Kutacane, Subulussalam, Singkil, Tamiang, Langsa, Lhokseumawe, Takengon, and Banda Aceh. In each of these cities, we stayed almost a week and met more than a hundred people altogether and had many long conversations with key informants. They were leaders of different (religious) groups, officials of district as well as provincial

Figure I.1. Map of Bordering Districts between Aceh and North Sumatra

governments, judges, attorneys, lawyers, and prominent academic figures. Also, we conducted observations over a number of social and religious events held indoors as well as outdoors all over those cities. In addition, we organized several focus group discussions and coordination meetings in Jakarta and Banda Aceh whereby we invited independent scholars as well as representatives of mass religious organizations to have their feedback to our study.

As an ethnographic study, the inquiry that led to this book is largely informed by interviews as well as documentary analysis. Interviews were recorded and transcribed. Data from these interviews were then collated and thematically analyzed based on key issues. Analyses and interpretations derived from this process were further reconstructed and triangulated with other information from different sources including from archives and relevant documents. To verify collected data from the field and reconfirm our analysis and interpretation, a number of limited discussions with prominent Acehnese scholars were held.

The writing process of this book was a real challenge. As we live and work in different cities in Indonesia (Arskal Salim in Jakarta, Moch. Nur Ichwan in Yogyakarta, and both Eka Srimulyani and Marzi Afriko in Banda Aceh), it was not easy to bring us together for the completion of the full manuscript. We assigned each of us to write different drafts chapters of this book. Introduction, chapter 1, and the second part (chapters 3 and 4) were finalized by Arskal Salim. Chapter 2 and the third part (chapters 5 and 6) were completed by Moch Nur Ichwan, while the fourth part (chapters 7–9) were prepared by Eka Srimulyani. The concluding chapter was jointly written. Marzi Afriko provided great assistance one way or another to the writing of some chapters of this book, including the full bibliography. To synchronize our drafted chapters, we not only exchanged them via email and discussed some related issues through online meetings or WhatsApp messages, but we also met in person twice in 2018 and once in 2019 to discuss the writing progress of the manuscript and to make the whole draft of the book ready for submission to the publisher.

Plan of the Book

The first part of this book addresses how authority and the identity-making process of the Muslim majority population in Aceh are interwoven. Its two chapters seek to demonstrate how Islam, as a religious identity of the majority group in Aceh, has been strengthened by both the political and the legal authorities. Drawing on dominant culture theory, chapter 1 confirms a process of identity making that has taken place in Aceh over time, especially in the northern and eastern parts of the province including districts in and along the provincial border. For the multifaith and diverse society of the border, dominant culture theory is a problematic approach and is unlikely applicable because the construction of Islamic identity as the dominant culture in the borderlands affects the rights of non-Muslim minority groups who have traditional ties with Christian people in the neighboring province of North Sumatra. Since religious minorities have difficulty identifying themselves with and complying with shari`a rules in Aceh, the politics of dominant culture—by way of introducing and implementing Islamic rules in the region—often causes them to feel like outsiders or half citizens, as well as to feel that their religious liberties are being violated. Given that the politics of dominant culture is observed in Aceh, non-Muslim minority groups lack a feasible means to resist decisions or regulations that disadvantage them. Doing so would only result in causing themselves to be portrayed as disrespectful to the Islamic identity of shari`a in Aceh.

As religious identity has become an important marker of citizenship, chapter 2 looks at how the implementation of shari`a in Aceh affects the state of citizenship. Here, the issue of accepted identity is crucial. Being Indonesian is not enough to enjoy full citizenship in Aceh; one must also be both a Muslim and Acehnese, or at least belong to an Aceh Indigenous ethnic group. Indeed, over time Aceh has created its own notion of citizenship defined by religious affiliation and strengthened by religious ethnonationalism. Given that the state of citizenship in Aceh departs from national citizenship, chapter 2 identifies the citizenship of minority groups as "dormant citizenship," indicating that a (re)construction of citizenship is taking place in which the implementation of shari`a has deactivated the full freedom and equal rights formerly enjoyed by non-Muslim minorities in the province of Aceh.

Equal rights for citizens who have different religious backgrounds and who coexist under shari`a has been a topic of substantial concern in recent scholarship. This issue is the focus of the second part of this book. This part is a demonstration of how the politics of dominant culture in Aceh is on the move. Chapter 3 explores the way in which an Islamic authority has evolved and transformed recent social developments in Aceh. It discusses the institutionalization of religious bureaucracy in Aceh through the establishment of Dinas Syariat Islam in 2001. While one of its primary tasks is to develop and formulate shari`a norms into regional regulations, the office has also been directed to provide both Muslim and non-Muslim residents of Aceh with guidance on how to appropriately live and behave in a shari`a territory. In spite of this, the religious bureaucracy in Aceh has not been successful in establishing its authority. As it remains a weak institution, many of its core tasks are poorly performed.

Chapter 4 deals with the way in which the politics of dominant culture have been imposed in the legal sphere, especially through the adjudication of non-Muslim offenders at the shari`a court of Aceh. While chapter 4 generally discusses how non-Muslims in Aceh have been treated under the qanun, or shari`a regulations, it highlights the fact that some non-Muslim offenders do subjugate themselves to Aceh's shari`a regulations. By looking at this particular process and examining legal options available to non-Muslim offenders at the court, chapter 4 explores and clarifies the citizenship status of non-Muslims in the biggest Muslim majority country in the world. Because the constitution of Indonesia grants equal rights to every individual regardless of his or her religious background, Indonesia faces a serious challenge in implementing shari`a rules for non-Muslim residents in one of its provinces, Aceh.

The third part of this book covers the relationships between different religious communities in Aceh. Chapter 5 explores their interactions, which are marked by mutual ignorance and nonreciprocal relations. In fact, as chapter 5 argues, the absence of interfaith education and genuine societal interfaith institutions have been key factors leading to the deepening of ignorance between the Muslim majority and non-Muslim minority groups. Despite national government efforts to compel schools and universities to offer civic education as a part of national curricula (including students in Aceh), the structural and cultural biases of the majority have hindered open dialogue and equal interaction with minority groups. Such biases are discussed further in this chapter in relation to the establishment of the Forum for the Harmony of Interreligious Communities (Forum Kerukunan Umat Beragama, FKUB) at the provincial level and its ramifications for related interreligious issues in Aceh.

By focusing on the border areas of the province, chapter 6 discusses government efforts to protect and strengthen Islamic identity against different kinds of threat and intrusion. These include the emergence of a defiant social movement from within Muslim communities, as well as Christian missionary activities conducted by evangelists from the neighboring province of North Sumatra. All this confirms that the politics of dominant culture plays a key role in maintaining Islamic identity (including refusal to allow churches to open in the region) and renounces anything that may endanger the implementation of shari`a. As the Islamic identity has been deeply emphasized, non-Muslim minority groups inevitably feel excluded. These groups perceive that both provincial and district leaders tend to side with the interests of the Muslim majority.

Such a political approach not only fails to ensure minorities are treated equally; it also generally works against their interests.

As far as the book's main focus is concerned, the final part of the book discusses three different communities or groups of people: diasporic Chinese, new converts or *muallaf*, and non-Muslim women. Chapter 7 examines the notions of identity being developed and projected by a minority group of diasporic Chinese in Banda Aceh. This chapter demonstrates how the implementation of shari`a rules affects the way in which those of Chinese descent interact with, respond to, and act in their relationship with the Muslim majority population. Other factors that also become responsible for such relationships are sociopolitical situations at the macronational level of the policies on minorities and political changes at the microregional (provincial and municipal) levels. The diasporic Chinese in Banda Aceh have worked consistently with the local Muslim majority to eliminate tensions and conflicts between different communities. In fact, in their efforts to claim proper recognition for their long presence in Aceh, the Chinese of Banda Aceh communicate that they are an integral part of the diverse Acehnese people dating back several centuries.

Chapter 8 looks at the transformation of identity of new converts, or muallaf—who are mostly female—especially in the districts of Aceh near the provincial border. Religious conversion from being a non-Muslim person to a Muslim offers a notable example of how the demand for recognition is increasingly phenomenal. Although being a muallaf is not easy, as it may generate family rejection, job loss, and financial hardship, religious conversion is common in Aceh. To recognize the muallaf as a part of the wider Muslim community, zakat (alms) has often been deployed by the government as a practical strategy to welcome and win the hearts of these religious newcomers. Chapter 8 analyzes the dynamics of being muallaf in the shari`a land by looking at the way newcomers to Islam organize themselves and their polarization.

Chapter 9 unveils the way in which non-Muslim women have sought to be visibly recognized within their own communities. It explores their efforts to construct agency vis-à-vis their male counterparts in the public space. In laying claim to recognition of their agency, these female actors pursue a number of social activities, including advocacy for children's education, serving their churches, and humanitarian volunteer work. Through these activities, women of non-Muslim minority groups are able to build a positive image for themselves in society and thus earn public recognition among the dominant culture of Aceh's shari`a.

Finally, unlike previous studies on majority-minority group relations in a predominantly Muslim country that tend to engage solely with one group's experiences and disengage the other, this study provides not only a narrative of majority-minority group encounters in a variety of issues but also a wide-ranging account of struggles from each of both Muslim majority and non-Muslim minority groups for recognition of their own identity in the public space. The book reveals that politics of identity recognition in Aceh have been interactively and mutually conceived by both groups of majority and minorities. The results of this endeavor in many cases unfortunately led to the uncomfortable relationship between majority and minority groups, which has been characterized by exclusion, ignorance, and even resistance.

PART I

Theoretical Frames

CHAPTER 1

Politics of the Dominant Culture

In Indonesia, cultural differences often become a barrier to the coexistence of people with different traditions or beliefs. To explain and work toward a resolution to this problem, a number of scholars have proposed applying dominant culture theory.[1] Parsudi Suparlan utilized this theory to study the interaction between different ethnic groups in the cities of Bandung, Sambas, and Ambon.[2] Inspired by E. M. Bruner's work,[3] Suparlan investigated guest groups—the Javanese in Bandung, the Madurese in Sambas, and the Buginese/Makassarese in Ambon—in terms of how they encounter the "host" culture in their respective locations. In his view, those "guest" groups who live in accordance with local wisdom are able to coexist harmoniously. Those who show little appreciation for the host culture and instead enforce their own traditions, by contrast, may end up in hostilities and ceaseless conflict.

In this chapter, we take issue with the sweeping and indiscriminate use of dominant culture theory as a tool to explain the peaceful coexistence of different identities or communities. We maintain that a complex set of social relations must be taken into account before considering the applicability of dominant culture theory to any given social conflict. Dominant culture theory tends to adopt the approach of majoritarianism to determine the best paths for social policy. This chapter points out the shortcomings of that approach through an examination of how the intertwined identity of Islam with Aceh has become the dominant culture of Aceh and the extent to which the government's construction of this regional identity has affected areas along the Aceh–North Sumatra provincial border.

The social experience of borders encompasses formal and informal ties between local communities and larger polities.[4] Borderlands thus constitute an interesting site for analyzing multiple dimensions of contested identities. This chapter compares three bordering districts—namely, Aceh Tamiang, Aceh Tenggara, and Aceh Singkil. While the first two districts have their own version of the dominant culture, the district of Aceh Singkil is culturally different: the people who live there are uncertain as to how to present their core identity. Following a discussion of how the dominant culture works in Aceh Tamiang and Aceh Tenggara, the third section will demonstrate that dominant culture theory is not a tenable explanatory theory for Aceh Singkil. The central questions here are (1) who are Singkil people, (2) whether the Singkil are part of or within the framework of Acehnese identity as well as within the Acehnese ethnic group's zone of influence, and (3) how much the people of Singkil have been "Acehnized."

The Construction of Aceh's Dominant Culture

According to the 2010 census, Muslims make up 98.81 percent of the total population of Aceh province. The rest of the population (1.19 percent) includes Christians, Buddhists, Catholics, Hindus, and Confucians. This non-Muslim minority largely lives in towns or districts along the provincial border with North Sumatra, including Aceh Singkil, Aceh Tenggara, and Aceh Tamiang. While the Acehnese are widely considered the staunchest Muslim adherents among Muslim ethnic groups in Indonesia, their population is far from homogeneous. Rather, it is culturally and ethnically diverse, and its religious practices are fundamentally plural.[5]

In the post–New Order period, the province of Aceh has exercised a special status, with autonomous governance in certain dimensions, including the implementation of shari`a. This chapter argues that the implementation of shari`a in Aceh needs to be understood in a broadly historical perspective that relates to the politics of the dominant culture. Here, "the politics of the dominant culture" refers to the attempts of the past and present government of Aceh to establish a dominant culture in which both Islam and the Acehnese were promoted and strengthened as an intertwined regional identity in most aspects of social and political life.

As Jillian Schwedler has pointed out, identity is largely based on location within complex sets of social relations.[6] Many Acehnese acknowledge that their (cultural) identity is a religious one. This view is strongly based on provincial history in many ways—namely, (1) the first Islamic kingdom founded in Indonesia, (2) the key role of the ulama in the modern history of Aceh, (3) holy war or *perang sabil* against the Christian Dutch (1873–1903), and (4) a traceable path of the implementation of shari`a in the region. All these have strengthened a sense of intertwined regional and Islamic identity among the Acehnese.[7]

In the view of Eric Morris, people in this northern tip of Sumatra have a heightened consciousness of their particular identity (Acehnese as well as Muslim) that transcended kinship, village, and territorial identities.[8] In fact, Islamic symbols and appeals became, and are still, the most effective instrument of social mobilization.

Thus, Islamic identity has long been embedded in the minds of the Muslim Acehnese, and the ulama played an important role in the translation of Islamic identity into sociopolitical action in Aceh. In fact, following the independence of Indonesia in 1945, the ulama held key positions in Acehnese regional government. With power in their hands, the ulama then set out to shape Acehnese identity in accordance with Islamic doctrines. For the ulama, the time had come to realize "their primary aim[, which] was to apply as much Islamic law as possible in Acehnese society." The national revolution became the ulama's "opportunity to restore the validity of Islamic law in the region."[9]

Less than a decade after independence, Acehnese leaders sought to build regional identity around the idea of an Islamic society with a strong religious expression.[10] By contrast, the national leadership in Jakarta promoted a religiously neutral state with Pancasila—an Indonesian philosophical theory with five foundational principles—as its principal ideology. This situation challenged the ulama either to bring Aceh under the national umbrella in solidarity or to maintain regional identity enshrined in the strong religious expression of shari`a. The ulama eventually preferred the latter, which led to open rebellion under the leadership of Teungku Daud Beureueh. The province of Aceh was soon declared separate from the Republic of Indonesia and part of the Negara Islam Indonesia led by Sekarmadji Maridjan Kartosuwiryo in West Java.[11] This revolt lasted until the early 1960s.

Another revolt broke out in December 1976. Under the leadership of Teungku Hasan M. Tiro, the struggle was known as Gerakan Aceh Merdeka (GAM), or the Free Aceh Movement. The motive for this revolt was different than the previous one. Instead of appealing to

Islamic identity, the rebels developed a discourse of Javanese colonialism and economic deprivation to justify their demands for the right to self-determination.[12] This motive was regarded as a much more viable means of gaining national and international sympathy. The rebels sought full independence. Their armed movement survived even after the collapse of the New Order regime in 1998.

Ironically, at a time when Islamic identity was discounted by Aceh's rebel movement, the Indonesian government began to provide wholehearted support for the consolidation of Aceh's Islamic identity. The Indonesian government offered two laws on regional autonomy, Law 44/1999 on the Administration of Aceh as a Special Province and Law 18/2001 on Extensive Autonomy for the Special Province of Aceh as Nanggroe Aceh Darussalam. The leaders of the rebellion viewed these offers as a means of co-opting and dividing the movement for independence and particularly as a way of driving a wedge between the rebels and the ulama.[13] By enacting long-overdue laws that granted greater regional authority over religious life, customs, and education to the province and strengthened the role of the ulama, the Indonesian government hoped to overcome the widespread resentment in Aceh and encourage the province to remain happily within the fold of the unitary state of Indonesia.[14]

In addition to the laws mentioned above, a special enactment later followed the 2005 Helsinki Peace Agreement between the rebels and the Indonesian government. A year after this agreement, Law 11/2006 on the Governance of Aceh was promulgated. This law is considered a "constitution" of Aceh within the unitary state of the Republic of Indonesia. It not only regulates aspects of general governance in Aceh but also specifies how shari`a is to be officially implemented in Aceh. The law makes stipulations for the creation of a number of shari`a-related institutions, such as Islamic local legislation, a shari`a court, a ulama council, and an office of shari`a. The details of how all of these institutions would work were to be worked out in regulations passed by Aceh's legislature.

Shari`a as a Singularized Identity

As pointed out by Douglas Pratt, basic Islamic identity is comprised of six factors: (1) ummah, or united community, (2) Sunnism or Shi'ism,

(3) the Qur'an and the Sunna, (4) the five pillars of Islam, (5) the geographic location where identification of ethnicities with religious identity occurs, and (6) the shari`a, which structures relationships in Muslim life. Of these six factors, shari`a, or Islamic law, is the encompassing term that covers belief and practice, creeds and symbols, and tradition and history.[15] Thus, it is not surprising that the implementation of shari`a is central to the agenda of contemporary political Islam in many Muslim regions. In fact, R. Michael Feener demonstrates that shari`a has become an instrument for social engineering, shaping the future definition of Acehnese society.[16] In other words, shari`a is a political tool of the dominant culture in Aceh.

As Dorota Gozdecka notes, the legal application of the principle of religious pluralism has strengthened dominant cultural and religious identities.[17] As far as the construction of the dominant culture in Aceh is concerned, it can be argued that all shari`a legislation was meant to create a framework for a singular Aceh cultural identity. Between 2002 and early 2017, numerous qanun on shari`a rules were legislated, covering varied structures of governance and social life. The institutions affected included not only the ulama, the bureaucracy, the courts, and the task force unit but also local village leadership right through to the state legal auxiliaries at the provincial and district levels. Moreover, the qanuns cover rituals, family issues, education, public decency, halal food, religious creed, Islamic economy, and Islamic crimes or jinayah.

The construction of a singularized cultural identity has been deepened by extending the application of shari`a to non-Muslim residents of Aceh. The qanun of jinayah rules (Qanun 6/2014) applies to non-Muslims as well. They are required to comply with certain Islamic injunctions applicable locally in Aceh, such as prohibitions on consuming or selling liquor, engaging in gambling, and committing *khalwat* (illicit proximity or intimacy) between two unmarried adults, and women are also required to adhere to the Islamic dress code. Any violation of these injunctions by perpetrators who are Muslim or non-Muslim, Acehnese or non-Acehnese, and Indonesian citizens or foreign citizens, that is committed within the boundaries of Aceh became subject to prosecution by the Shari`a Court. These rules have established Aceh's Islamic identity throughout the region. This shift was problematic, however, since it produced a very particular sort of displacement, particularly for non-Muslims who live in the border districts.

Cultural Identities along the Border

As there is always a link between identity and space,[18] this chapter asks, Who are the people inhabiting the border areas of Aceh? How can we best culturally identify them? In what ways do culturally unitary groups (tribes or peoples) of the borders associate themselves with their own territories? What is the dominant culture of those border-crossing people or the people who live on the border? Given the cultural differences that most likely exist along the border, is there a recognized "subculture" that coexists with the dominant culture in the same geographical and territorial space? All these questions are adopted to investigate the politics of the dominant culture along the Aceh–North Sumatra provincial border.

Aceh Tamiang

A field visit in 2016 to the three bordering districts—Aceh Singkil, Aceh Tenggara, and Aceh Tamiang—revealed an interesting contrast. Unlike other districts in the province of Aceh, all three districts have a strong presence of non-Muslims in terms of both population and the public presence of worship places and religious symbols. In Aceh Tamiang, Buddhist believers who are mostly Chinese constitute a significant non-Muslim population. In both Aceh Singkil and Aceh Tenggara, a large number of Protestants, predominantly of Batak ethnic background, make up a substantial group of non-Muslim residents. The Batak ethnic groups are not uniform. While Karo Batak people are mostly found in Aceh Tenggara, Pakpak Batak people can be found in Aceh Singkil.

Non-Muslims in both Aceh Tamiang and Aceh Tenggara have their own, different identities that do not necessarily correspond to the places where they live. Although the forebears of the Chinese Buddhists in Aceh Tamiang have been present since long before the Dutch occupied Aceh in the late nineteenth century, contemporary diasporic Chinese in the region identify themselves as a "migrant" group. Rather than establish a strong subculture like those of many Chinese diasporas in the world, they adjust to live in, or most likely to isolate from, the dominant culture of Aceh in general and the Malay culture in particular.

Aceh Tenggara

In Aceh Tenggara, the Karo Batak Christian believers who migrated from North Sumatra feel like guests in Aceh's territory. Their presence in the region was welcomed by the host ethnic group, the Alas, who have lived in Aceh Tenggara for centuries. The interaction between host and guest groups has been positive in some ways. They are bound by a variety of social relations, including interethnic marriage. Non-Muslims in Aceh Tenggara mostly live together in clustered villages, forming a communal identity. Of sixteen subdistricts in Aceh Tenggara, the Christians are observable in ten. Two subdistricts, Lawe Sigalagala and Babul Makmur, accommodate more than five thousand Christians, who constitute almost half of the Christian population in each of the two subdistricts. Altogether, non-Muslims in Aceh Tenggara constitute around 30 percent of the total population.

On several socioreligious issues, the Batak Christians in Aceh Tenggara have problems in adapting into social life to the dominant culture of the region. Interviews with local religious leaders reveal that problems arise out of cultural differences. What Batak Christians complain about most regarding their Muslim neighbors are those things prohibited in Islam, such as alcoholic drinks and the public sale of pork. Pig farms often create a problem, as these farms are not located far from Muslim neighborhoods. In the eyes of some Muslim leaders in Aceh Tenggara, alcohol and pork consumption are in conflict with the cultural identity of Aceh. For the Batak Christians, however, it is a part of their tradition to serve alcoholic drinks and pork roast at their parties as well as in some religious ceremonies.

Seen in light of dominant culture theory, the extent to which Batak Christians in Aceh Tenggara are able to address the social constraints under Aceh's Islamic shari`a rules should determine the possibility of peaceful coexistence between the cultural differences of the communities that live in the region. It is inevitable that non-Muslim communities living under shari`a rules in Aceh will be displaced, as they have no chance to construct their own identities based on both territory and culture. It may be unfair to insist the Batak Christians in Aceh Tenggara give up their eating and drinking culture in compliance with the dominant culture so that they might live harmoniously alongside their Muslim neighbors. Nonetheless, as Edwin Wilmsen has argued, the production of cultural difference occurs in a continuous, connected space, traversed by economic and political relations of inequality.[19]

Aceh Singkil

Unlike in Aceh Tamiang and Aceh Tenggara, the application of dominant culture theory in Aceh Singkil has been irrelevant. How can we explain this fact? Studies on Singkil people are very few. Among those few are works by Muhajir Al Fairusy.[20] His explanation of the history of the Singkil people helps us understand the social dynamics and cultural barriers that prevent plural communities of different backgrounds from occupying a coexisting space. Through its long history, Singkil, located in a border zone, has been politically, economically, and culturally marginalized. Yet, at the same time, Singkil has been praised and commended for its famous figures, Hamzah Fansuri and Abdur Rauf al-Singkili, both widely respected scholars during the sixteenth- and seventeenth-century sultanate of Aceh.

Cultural differences in Aceh Singkil have a long pedigree and can be traced back to the historical development of the region and the periodic transformation of its people. A number of historians have noted that Sumatra's west coast from Aceh to Minangkabau was under Sultan Iskandar Muda.[21] Singkil was most likely a part of his territorial expansion in the seventeenth century. Nevertheless, Singkil was not continuously ruled by the kingdom of Aceh. Because Singkil and its nearby coastal towns were important trading ports frequented by Chinese, Indian, and European merchants, complete control over these ports proved to be difficult. This made Singkil a "borderland" even before the nineteenth century. Thus, politically, Singkil was not treated as a part of Aceh, although culturally it was understood to be the southernmost part of Aceh.[22]

As far as whether Singkil's people are part of the Acehnese ethnic group (or how far the Singkil have been Acehnized), it is important to note that the association of place with memory and nostalgia plays a key role in the politics of dominant culture. Both evidence that Sultan Iskandar Muda ruled the west coast of Sumatra, including Singkil, and the role of two important figures who came from this region (Hamzah Fansuri and Abdur Rauf al-Singkili) in Aceh's history have been considered legitimate claims to the incorporation of Singkil into Aceh's territory. Many Acehnese leaders feel it is legitimate to claim that Singkil

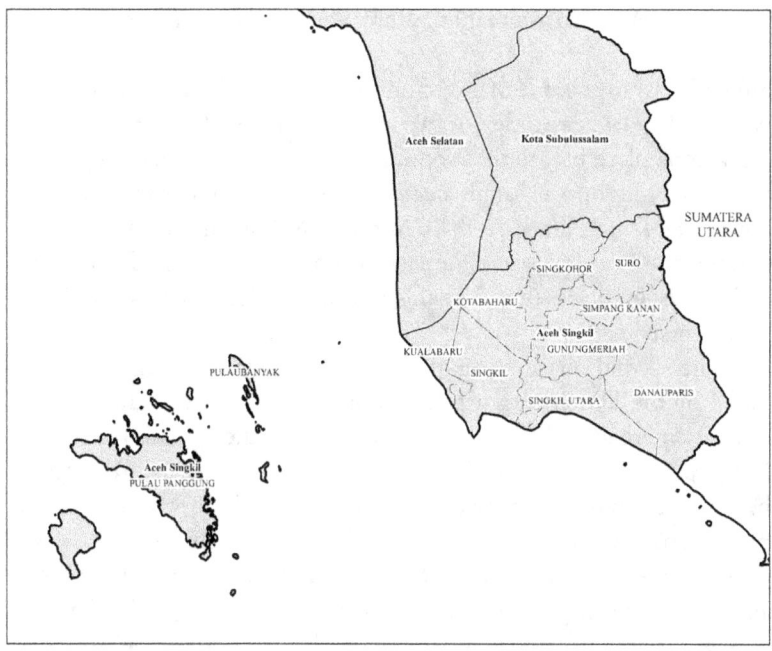

Figure 1.1. Map of Aceh and Aceh Singkil

constitutes a part of modern Aceh, given its strong Islamic identity. Muhajir Al-Fairusy writes that the first governor of Aceh after independence, Daud Beureueh, who led a rebellion against the government of Indonesia, is reported to have said, "No religious activity is allowed in Singkel other than Islam" (Tidak boleh ada aktivitas agama selain Islam di Singkel).[23] In fact, when he had a chance to visit Singkil after the end of the rebellion in 1968, Daud Beureueh gave a public oration warning against the Christianization of Singkil. He called for the eviction of Christian residents who came from Nias Island.[24]

Despite the elites' claim that Singkil has long been a part of Aceh, the formation of regional identity in the border region, as P. Sahlins has noted, is a two-way process in which the government cannot simply impose identity from the above.[25] Local communities and their inhabitants can draw on the criteria of their preferred identities and share the same consciousness within their (sub)groups. It is for this reason that the historical composition of the local population of Singkil needs to be considered in more detail.

Why Is Dominant Culture Theory Problematic?

Singkil's narrative is one of discontinuous identity, of peoples trapped between old and new realities, or two historical phases.[26] The Singkils' first phase took place before the Netherlands East Indies seized Singkil and incorporated it into Tapanuli *afdeeling*, one of North Sumatra's districts, during the Dutch times, in 1840. At the time, Singkil was mostly a borderland on the west coast of Sumatra where travelers and migrants from various distant places (e.g., Minang, Batak, Alas, Melayu, Nias, Aceh, and Java) crossed paths.

The second phase of Singkil took place when the region was annexed by the Dutch authority in the nineteenth century and administratively merged with the highland area where the Pakpak Batak lived. In this period, the criteria of who could be identified as "Singkil people" began to expand. The Singkil came to include those who mainly live on the coastline, along the riverside, or in the highlands; those who have surnames and those without family names; those who speak Baapo and those who speak Kade-kade; and those who are Muslims or non-Muslims. Earlier, the Singkil people had been identified only as those who lived on the coastline, who mostly speak Baapo, who were Muslim, and who did not have family names.

In the aftermath of Indonesia's independence in 1945, Singkil was part of South Aceh district for more than fifty years. In 1999, it was transformed from a subdistrict into a district. All areas along the southern provincial border of the previous district now became the district of Aceh Singkil. This district was split in 2006 with the creation of Subulussalam City, which is located in the northern highland area of Aceh Singkil district. According to the 2010 census, the non-Muslim population of Aceh Singkil constituted no less than 15 percent of the total. In this population, more Christian Protestants are represented than Catholics, Hindus, or Buddhists. The majority inhabitants of the district are Muslims who share similar ethnic backgrounds with the Christian Pakpak.

In light of changes in the district's demographic composition, it is difficult to say that the current Singkil identity is rooted in any particular culture or religion. In fact, "Singkil" is a category of ethnic groups with cultural differences. Each group or subgroup possesses symbolic boundaries of identities and cultures. Thus, the dominant culture remains vague. This has partly to do with the wide spread of Pakpak Batak culture, especially in the highlands and outskirts—that is, the subdistricts of Suro, Simpang Kanan, and Danau Paris.

The cultural identity of the Pakpak Batak differs significantly from Aceh's Islamic identity. Although some Pakpak Batak are Muslim, their ethnic identity is independent of their Muslim identity. Many Pakpak Batak are non-Muslim, however. Non-Muslim Pakpak Batak were the majority population across the Singkil region prior to Indonesia's independence in 1945. The provincial division after independence made non-Muslim Pakpak Batak a majority population in North Sumatra province, while across the border in Singkil, Aceh province, the majority of Pakpak Batak are Muslim.[27] For the Pakpak people who live in Aceh Singkil, religious differences do not disconnect bonds of solidarity or fraternity that have continued from earlier times. It is for this reason that non-Muslim Pakpak Batak who currently live in Aceh Singkil refuse to be identified as migrant outsiders.

The problem with dominant culture theory insofar as it applies to Aceh Singkil lies in the fact that in the borderlands, as noted by V. Konrad, identity is formed and reformed among those who claim indignity and others who cannot.[28] Pressures toward homogeneity in cultural identity compete with more extensive forces of heterogeneity to diffuse identities. Despite the fact that Aceh's Islamic identity is overwhelming and Muslims are the majority of the population in Aceh Singkil, there is no singular defining identity in the district of Aceh Singkil.

One of our informants contends that there are two majorities coexisting in Aceh Singkil. The majority is not necessarily religious—that is, not necessarily Muslim—because there is another majority that is cultural. The cultural majority are those who have a family name after their given name. This kind of majority consists mostly of people, both Muslim and non-Muslim, who have Pakpak Batak ancestors. The informant explained, "I don't understand who are the majority or minority population in Aceh Singkil. In Banda Aceh, we all know who are the majority, but in Singkil, whose community would be identified as the majority? I assure you that no one in Singkil dares to acknowledge 'I am part of the majority' or 'I am part of the minority group.' Can you imagine that almost 70 percent people of Aceh Singkil have surnames [*bermarga*]? A thing that differentiates them is merely a creed."[29]

The other problem is that the dominant culture approach to cultural differences like those of Aceh Singkil tends to segregate communities socially and politically and only advantages the majority group, either religiously or culturally. Disadvantaged people feel uncertain about how to present their social identity and, in particular, whether their status is that of insiders or outsiders in relation to the primary ethnic group. In sum, to be from Singkil implies identity elements that do not easily coexist with Aceh's cultural identity. The coexistence of equal cultural differences makes the politics of the dominant culture irrelevant to borderlands like Aceh Singkil.

The Dominant Culture, Discrimination, and Violence

The dominant culture in the borderlands faces challenges from a variety of unexpected external influences. In Aceh Singkil, the integrity of Aceh's Islamic identity has not only been under threat from Christianization brought by North Sumatra border crossers but is also confronted by inherited colonial ideas about what kinds of people and religions should exist in a particular territory.[30] It is for this reason that discrimination and violence have often been observed in the border.

When the coastal area of Singkil was merged in the nineteenth century with the highland area, where the Pakpak Batak mostly resided, the Pakpak Batak became the majority population of Aceh Singkil. Most are now Muslim, though some remain Christian adherents. Despite the fact that Christians and Muslims in Aceh Singkil have common ancestors, Christian-Muslim relations in the district are characterized by social discrimination.[31] As noted by Mujiburrahman in his study on Christian-Muslim relations in Indonesia, each group feels threatened by the other.[32] On the one hand, Muslims see the increase of churches in the district and the growth of the Christian population as being due to the arrival of border crossers from North Sumatra. On the other hand, the Pakpak Christians consider that a long period of social harmony in Aceh Singkil has been disrupted by the presence of the local radical Muslim group the Islamic Defenders Front (Front Pembela Islam, FPI),[33] a branch of the same organization at the national level, which in early 2021 has been nationally banned.

The discrimination is felt mostly by Christians. This has largely to do with restrictions on permission to open new churches, obligations to conform to Muslim dress regulations, and restricted access to Christian education and community representation in public spaces. The discrimination was escalated and exacerbated by the 2012 election of Aceh Singkil's head of district. Candidates in the local election are reported to have utilized the rivalry between the Christian and Muslim populations for their own political benefit. Their maneuvers included a promise to approve the establishment of churches in Aceh Singkil.

A license to open a church is very difficult to obtain in Aceh. A 2007 governor's regulation (no. 25) put even more criteria and prerequisites in the way of obtaining a license than had existed under an earlier national-level regulation. Of more than twenty churches in Aceh Singkil, including *undung-undung*, or small churches/chapels, very few have official licenses issued by the government. Most operate without a proper government permit and thus become targets of Muslim groups that undertake to raid Christian activities or symbols.

The chronicle of churches in Aceh Singkil has been miserable. Since the first incident of religious violence in 1979, when churches were violently attacked and burned down, dozens of church buildings have been closed or even destroyed. Based on the peace agreement that followed a religious riot in 1979, the number of non-Muslim worship places allowed to operate in Aceh Singkil was limited to one church and four buildings of undung-undung. This consensus was reiterated with the same content in the 2001 agreement.[34]

The arrangement had something to do with efforts to establish the dominant culture along the border. As argued by Ansor, elites of the Aceh Singkil government were approached by the FPI to make a policy restricting the appearance of Christian symbols and influence in the region.[35] In the view of this group, Aceh, as *Serambi Mekkah* (Mecca's veranda), must have a prevalent Islamic identity in its borderlands, people with different identities who desire to remain in the region must comply with the dominant culture, and the symbols of religions other than Islam must be controlled. In 2012, the group was able to persuade the district government to form a team to oversee the development of churches of different denominations in Aceh Singkil. In the course of its evaluation, it was discovered that the number of illegal churches in the district had increased. The group insisted that the government take action against those church buildings that lacked a state permit. The result was that more than twenty church buildings were sealed or had their activities shut down.

The most recent attack, an act of arson, occurred in October 2015. Not only were a couple of buildings burned down, but one person died and others were severely injured. Muslim groups attacked Christian places of worship because they had lost patience with the slow response of the district government in closing down those illegal churches. The aftermath of this incident was a consensus that nine churches must be closed, while the remaining thirteen were to apply for a state permit as outlined in the 2007 regulation. Many Christian leaders were pessimistic that they would be able to afford the state permit or meet the complicated requirements to obtain it. Muslim communities in Aceh Singkil were advised by their leaders not to consent to the construction of church buildings.[36] Because the building of Christian worship places requires the consent of Muslim neighbors, the lack of such approval limits the spread of illegal churches in Aceh Singkil.

Conclusion

It is a significant challenge for peoples with different religions and a single prevailing ethnic culture to coexist in the same region. This becomes even more difficult along borders where contending identities are observed. Those with minority identities have to struggle endlessly to have their rights protected and fulfilled, unfortunately without guarantee of success. In the border region of Aceh–North Sumatra, Islamic identity has been strengthened. With the full support of the government, the official implementation of shari`a has consolidated a dominant culture that is Muslim and "Acehnese." In fact, in late 2007, Aceh's Department of Islamic Shari`a launched a program, the *program dai perbatasan* (border preacher program), to send young Muslim preachers to the borderlands to reinforce Aceh's Islamic identity (see discussion in chapter 6).

While it is much easier to discover the coexistence of different identities in borderlands than in other regions, the case of the Aceh–North Sumatra border suggests that difficulties remain. Thanks to the increasing implementation of shari`a in Aceh over the past twenty years, Aceh's Islamic identity has been strengthened throughout the entire province, including in the borderlands. The religious culture developed at the center of Aceh territory—Banda Aceh, Aceh Besar, Pidie, and down along east coast of the province—has gradually reached the periphery, as has the ways in which non-Muslim populations are treated by their conationals in the center. A sense of belonging to multiple or plural identities is absent or under siege. What remains is the process of homogenizing Aceh's Muslim identity, which purportedly prevails throughout Aceh, including in the border regions. The heterogeneity of cultural identity or the coexistence of subcultures in the borderlands is considered a threat to the dominant culture.

CHAPTER 2

Dormant Citizenship

There have been numerous discussions about citizenship along with an increasing concern about the growing presence of religion in the public sphere.[1] This is also the case in Southeast Asia,[2] including Indonesia in the postauthoritarian era following the collapse of Suharto's New Order in 1998.[3]

However, the issue of citizenship in Aceh in particular has been understudied, as if this matter was identical with that of the rest of Indonesia. There have also been many studies on the relationship between religion and political and cultural developments in Aceh in the last two decades,[4] but these studies did not raise the issue of citizenship. However, there were two exceptions: Arifah Rahmawati et al. discussed the social citizenship of women's GAM combatants[5] but paid little attention to religion, and Michael Merry and Jeffrey Milligan compared citizenship in the Netherlands and Aceh in relation to the Indonesian central government,[6] but they did not discuss citizenship and religious minorities within Aceh.

As part of Indonesia, Aceh undoubtedly follows the Indonesian political system. Although in general Indonesia embraces communitarianism,[7] it also adopts republican citizenship, which emphasizes the role of an active and informed citizenry.[8] Indonesia is a consensual nation-state in which different ethnicities, including the Acehnese, agreed to create a nation-state called Indonesia. It is the unitary state of the Republic of Indonesia, which is not an Islamic state but a state based on Pancasila. The first principle of Pancasila is "Belief in the one and only God." It is within this principle that the implementation of shari`a in Aceh is secured. As part of Indonesia, the Aceh people, like other Indonesian people, are equal and have equal rights. The non-Muslims of Aceh are equal as Indonesian citizens in accessing public services, such as health and education. As we will see, however, there are social inequalities in various issues.

This chapter aims to examine why the citizenship in Aceh has been (re)constructed in a different direction from the national citizenship. As a repercussion of the application of shari'a-derived bylaws or qanun, in Aceh, non-Muslims citizens have been excluded from the Acehnese legal system. They do not have the equal citizenship they deserve. Their citizenship rights are curbed and become dormant in most cases. They lost many of their civil and political rights, such as right to get elected, a right to obtain work in certain provincial government offices, a right to get religious education based on their respective religious affiliations, a right to build worship places, and so on as will be discussed in the following section. The fact that they still obtain certain rights (i.e., a right to vote and a right to work at national government offices) is partly because they are entitled to national citizenship rights. This is why the citizenship that belongs to non-Muslims has been dormant, or partially dormant, when they live in Aceh.

The Origin of Dormant Citizenship

The term "dormant citizenship" stems from, and is used in, the context of dual or multiple citizenship, meaning that citizens of two or more countries can activate their full citizenship only in the country in which they actually settle, while their full rights and duties in any other country or countries are suspended. They can activate their membership in another home country only when they officially return their residency to that country. This kind of citizenship is found, for example, in Spain, which has agreements with twelve Latin American countries.[9]

Dormant citizenship is applicable in a country with strong multilayered citizenship. Nira Yuval-Davis suggests that citizenship should be seen as a "multilayered construct."[10] In the context of Europe, such layers include local, ethnic, national, state, cross- or trans-state, and suprastate. Citizenship is affected and often at least partly constructed by the relationships and positioning of each layer in specific historical contexts.

Dormant citizenship is related to the communitarian concept of citizenship in which, for the sake of social harmony, certain members of society are prevented from enjoying full rights. Dormant citizenship is therefore related to the politics of exclusion rather than inclusion. However, exclusion here, like inclusion, does not represent an absolute dichotomy; rather, it reflects, as pointed out by Lister, a continuum.[11] This happens because there is in fact a hierarchy of rights rather than a dichotomy of rights. This hierarchy of rights brings about a hierarchy of citizenship or plurality of citizenship. The plurality of citizenship is reflected well in the allocation of host or guest status to citizens on the basis of, for instance, their religious affiliation.

Another Form of Dormant Citizenship

We propose in this study another form of dormant citizenship, which is different to the Latin American and European cases above. It is not interstate but internal to a state. The Aceh case represents "intra-nationally dormant citizenship." The term "dormant citizenship," as we argue throughout this chapter, derives from the concept of Aceh's religious ethnonationalism since religion and ethnicity are important defining factors of citizenship in Aceh. As Boland has acknowledged that "for an Atjehnese himself, being an Atjehnese is equivalent to being a Muslim; it is simply inconceivable that a real Atjehnese could adhere to a religion other than Islam."[12]

Religious ethnonationalism plays a key role in making such citizenship and it has influenced the way non-Muslim minorities are treated in Aceh. As Islam is an integral part of the construction of the Aceh regional identity and given that the Islamic-ness of Aceh is protected by religious ethnonationalism, citizens of Aceh are divided on the basis of religious affiliation, with Muslims considered as the "hosts" of the shari`a land with their full rights, whereas non-Muslims are "guests" with only partial rights provided by the "hosts." The terms "host" and "guest" reflect the ethnographic data we found in the field. This category (host-guest) has a long history in Aceh, as early as the incoming visitors who then resided in some parts of Aceh's territory. There was a term of *aneuk jamee* (children of the guests) to identify people who came from West Sumatra and live in Aceh's west coast (including neighbor areas of Aceh Singkil). In this case, the "aneuk jamee" are Muslim and more or less fully integrated into Acehnese society. Still at times they are considered "guests" and occasionally reminded of that.

The category "host-guest" remains applicable in the recent days. The term "hosts" is described as *asoe lhok* (local people), while the word "guests" is called *ureung tamong* (newcomers). The terms *asoe lhok* and *ureung tamong* are prominent in the years of post-tsunami recovery (2005 onward), where people outside of Aceh migrated to Aceh following the establishment of housing infrastructure in some tsunami-affected areas. These terms serve as a way to differentiate between the locals who resided in the area before the tsunami and those who came and migrated to the area afterward.

In light of religious ethnonationalism perspective, people in Aceh who are legally citizens according to national law are not always considered "citizens" in the local-provincial level. Despite being stipulated in national citizenship laws, anyone who was born from an Indonesian parent and lives in Indonesia's territory is a citizen of Indonesia. However, the fundamental local requirement for full citizenship in Aceh is to be Muslim.

From Hard to Soft Religious Ethnonationalism

Religious ethnonationalism in Aceh has manifested in both hard and soft ways. The former was reflected especially during colonial times and in the independence movement of Darul Islam (1953–63) and the GAM's struggle (1976–2005). Hard religious ethnonationalism here refers to ethnonationalism based on the comprehensive shari`a with the intention of establishing an independent Islamic state (under Darul Islam but not GAM). Meanwhile, soft religious ethnonationalism refers to ethnonationalism based on Islamic shari`a within a non-Islamic Indonesian state, as embodied in contemporary shari`a politics in Aceh.

Ethnonationalism in Aceh has been contingent from the conflict to the postconflict period. It evolved from the hard religious ethnonationalism that aimed to separate Aceh from Jakarta and establish an independent Islamic state, to the hard *non*religious ethnonationalism that aimed to establish no more than an independent state. Later, it shifted to soft religious ethnonationalism that advocated solely a special autonomy in implementing shari`a law in the region.

Given the fact above, it begs questions of whether ethnonationalism in Aceh reflects merely the implementation of shari`a or more. How do both ethnonationalism and shari`a come into play in this regard? In the view of McCarty and Aspinall, Aceh's ethnonationalism has a lot to do with the issue of conflict over resources, which led to the insurgence of the GAM separatist movement.[13] For Aspinall, the emphasis on Islam or shari`a to be linked with ethnonationalism was simply a marker of Aceh's ethnonationalism.[14] Other scholars, such as Feener, put a great emphasis in religious issues especially on the shari`a project as undertaken by Muslim technocrats and academics in Aceh.[15] However, Feener did not seek to link the shari`a project with ethnonationalism or religious ethnonationalism.

This study contends that despite the absence of shari`a and an Islamic state in its later agendas, ethnonationalism in Aceh would not be able to abandon Islam as the most important marker of citizenship.[16] This means that ethnonationalism is not merely concerned with the protection of an ethnic identity but, more important, with the protection of Aceh as *Serambi Mekkah* (Mecca's veranda) and Darussalam (abode of peace), hence Islamic identity. With this concept of religious ethnonationalism in mind, Aceh is *nanggroe syariah* (shari`a land) and Islam is the religion of the Acehnese and the only fundamental marker of citizenship. Reflecting on the current special governance of Aceh, it is often said that Aceh is "a province with the taste of a nation" (*provinsi rasa negara*).[17]

How Local History and Politics Matter

The history and politics of nation building in Aceh has been unique compared with other regions in Indonesia. Aceh sultanate was the last region defeated by the Dutch (in 1904), but the Aceh people did not automatically surrender; they continued their struggle against the Dutch until World War II and the Japanese occupation. Histories, as pointed out by Benedict Anderson, are important in forming communal and nation-state identities as well as in constructing, sustaining, and contesting them.[18] Ward Berenschot and Gerry van Klinken have underlined the importance of the history of nation building to understanding citizenship in Indonesia.[19]

Seven important historical and political features are important in the making of religious ethnonationalism (from hard to soft), and it is necessary to take them into account in turn to understand the current situation regarding citizenship in Aceh. As Graham Brown has rightly acknowledged,

A distinct Acehnese local history greatly at odds with the broader history of Indonesia, with a long and—from their perspective—glorious history of resistance to various imperialist powers, combined with a cultural identity more closely tied to Islamic orthodoxy than in much of the rest of the country had created in Aceh by independence a sense of identity that, whilst not necessarily anti-Indonesian, was at least distinctive and separate.[20]

First, the history of Aceh has been depicted as a history of Islamic kingdoms and societies. It began with the narrative of the establishment of the earliest Islamic kingdoms in the region (e.g., the Samudera Pasai in the thirteenth century and the Acehnese sultanate in the sixteenth century). These Islamic kingdoms survived for about six centuries until the last sultan surrendered to the Dutch colonial government in 1903.

Second, Aceh was a region in which the ideology of jihad or *prang sabi* (war in the path of God) against *kaphe* (Arabic *kāfir*, pl. *kuffār*; unbelievers) was used by the ulama to defend Aceh from the Dutch colonial invasion at the end of the nineteenth and the beginning of the twentieth centuries. The narrative of the undefeatable Aceh is supported by a local version that the Aceh people never surrendered to the Dutch (although, in fact, the latter did occupy the region) and therefore were able to maintain and sustain their Islamic identity.[21]

Third, Aceh's early relationship with Indonesia was led by the ulama and marked by a strong demand for the regional implementation of shari`a. The ulama led Aceh because there was no sultan and no "secular nationalist" leaders as there were in Java at that time.[22] When Sukarno asked Aceh for support in fighting against the returning colonial Dutch, the ulama leader, Teungku Daud Beureueh, agreed on condition that the fight be named "prang sabi" and that, after the war, Aceh would have more authority to implement shari`a. Sukarno accepted such demands though later they were not fulfilled.[23]

Fourth, Sukarno's unfulfilled promise led to a rebellion, which reflected hard religious ethnonationalism. Beginning in 1953 under the banner of the national Darul Islam movement, the rebellion sought to realize Sekarmaji Kartosuwiryo's vision for an Indonesian Islamic State or Negara Islam Indonesia.[24] Yet, all this failed. In 1957, Aceh was established as a separate province, and two years later (1959) given the status of a special administrative region (*daerah istimewa*), particularly in religious affairs, on the condition that it should not conflict with the constitution.

Fifth, a long conflict from 1976 to 2005 took place between Jakarta and GAM. Hasan Tiro declared Aceh independence in 1976, casting modern Aceh as the successor state to the historic Sultanate of Aceh Darussalam.[25] GAM initially claimed to be a continuation of Beureueh's Darul Islam movement but later dropped this Islamic mission to gain international support. Nonetheless, it continued to represent itself as an Islamic movement on the ground.[26] In response to the GAM rebellion, Suharto made Aceh an Area of Special Military Operations. Thousands of innocent people were killed and gross violations of human rights took place.[27]

Sixth, following the collapse of the Suharto regime in 1998, the demand for a referendum on whether Aceh should stay in the republic or become independent emerged. Jakarta was faced with two main demands: GAM's separatism and the referendum. Other options were offered, too, such as status as a federal state or special autonomy. Should a referendum be held, it was almost certain that people would choose independence from Indonesia, as had happened in East Timor.[28]

Seventh, Jakarta rejected the options of independence, a referendum, a federal state, and special autonomy and preferred instead to establish Aceh as a special region in the areas of religion, *adat* (custom), education, and the role of the ulama in local decision-making by promulgating Law No. 44/1999. Religion was understood to mean the implementation of shari`a. Later, special autonomy was granted with Law No. 18/2001 on the Special Autonomy of the Province of Aceh Special Region as the Province of Nanggroe Aceh Darussalam, through which shari`a was further strengthened.

Following this latest political development, a number of shari`a by-laws (qanuns) have been issued and shari`a institutions have been established.[29] This comprehensive implementation of shari`a was considered as both the fulfillment of Sukarno's promise and a way to win Acehnese hearts against GAM, which did not have a shari`a agenda.[30] After the Helsinki memorandum of understanding of 2005, the implementation of shari`a was strengthened by the promulgation of Law No. 11/2006 on Governing of Aceh, which states that the governor, mayors, and heads of districts are responsible for the implementation of Islamic shari`a in their respective regions.

All this is, in fact, a continuation of the earlier narratives in a unique way, as it is taking place not in an Islamic state but in the Pancasila state of Indonesia. Beureueh had demanded hard religious ethnonationalism, but the current approach to the implementation of shari`a in Aceh represents soft religious ethnonationalism—that is, the local implementation of Islamic shari`a without the establishment of an Islamic state. Without taking all these narratives into consideration, we cannot rightly understand the current citizenship in Aceh.

Dormant Citizenship in Aceh

The current state of citizenship in Aceh has been constructed under the influence of all seven historical and political factors described above. The term "Nanggroe Aceh Darussalam" signifies and justifies Aceh symbolically, legally, and politically as the Muslim land or the shari`a land and reflects religious ethnonationalism. The "nanggroe syariah" has gradually become a culturally and politically embedded concept underlying the whole claim to Muslim dominance and to priority being given to Islam in Aceh today. The enforcement of shari`a law by the authorities of Aceh province affects the state of citizenship in Indonesia more generally and the state of citizenship in Aceh in particular.

Citizenship in Aceh, unlike in other provinces in Indonesia, is characterized by the strong influence of shari`a and soft religious ethnonationalism. Nationally, it can no longer be said that Indonesia solely subscribes to a unitary citizenship. Because, locally, since 1999 there has been a remaking of citizenship based on shari`a, and this has taken place within the framework of the Indonesian nation-state. As shari`a has been implemented through the qanun, or local bylaws, religion has become an important marker of citizenship, apart from ethnicity, affecting the rights and duties of citizens of different religions in Aceh. The problem is that such citizenship prioritizes the religious majority and excludes the religious minority, an exclusion that has been justified by qanuns.

Even worse, qanuns take precedence over national laws regulating the same matters, based on the legal *maxim lex specialis derogat lex generalis* (special law repeals general law). If a specific rule stipulated in a qanun and a general national law govern the same factual case, the former overrides the latter.[31] In cases where the shari`a qanun is silent, national laws are followed. Soft religious ethnonationalism plays a role in the implementation of this legal maxim too, especially in strengthening the lex specialis—namely, shari`a qanuns. Thus, the lex specialis principle justifies the soft religious ethnonationalism of Aceh and the dormant citizenship of non-Muslim.

Historical Roots of Dormant Citizenship

Dormant citizenship is a synthesis between four political traditions: Islamic, ethnic, Indonesian, and Western. These four different traditions, synthetized creatively to serve soft religious ethnonationalism, have created the phenomenon of dormant citizenship for non-Muslims in the region. As discussed below, dormant citizenship can be traced back to Islamic as well as ethnic political traditions.

Islam has a long history of relations between the government and the people, from the Prophetic proto-state of Medina and the Rightly Guided Caliphs (*al-khulafā' al-rāshidūn*) to the Ottomans and beyond. In Islamic political theory, non-Muslims are divided into four groups: *ḥarbī* (those who live outside Islamic territories and are against Islam and Muslims), *dhimmī* (those who live within Islamic territories and under Muslim protection in exchange for paying taxes), *mu'āhad* (those who live outside Islamic territories but who have a truce or treaty with Muslims), and *musta'min* (ḥarbīs who are allowed temporary entry into Islamic territories). The first type of non-Muslims is subject to war if they threaten Islamic lands, while the rest should be protected and their lives should be guaranteed because they either pay taxes (dhimmī), are party to a treaty (mu'āhad), or have temporary entry permit (musta'min). This guarantee can be withdrawn should they betray Muslims or break the treaty. In this context, non-Muslims living in Islamic territory are either dhimmīs or musta'mins.[32] However, only dhimmīs are relevant for our discussion of citizenship. Dhimmīs are citizens, despite their secondary status, while musta'mins are only temporary guests.

Based on our interviews, some ulama and religious leaders consider non-Muslims in Aceh to be dhimmīs.[33] For example, in 2014, the Council of Young Indonesian Intellectuals and Ulama (Majelis Intelektual dan Ulama Muda Indonesia, MIUMI) of Aceh discussed the status of non-Muslims living in Aceh as *ahl al-dhimma*, people of protection. The head of the Aceh MIUMI, Mohammad Yusron Hadi, said that the Qanun Jinayat (Islamic Criminal Code) also applies to non-Muslim citizens living in Aceh (see chapter 4) because they have the same rights as Muslim citizens due to their status as *kāfir dhimmī* (protected unbelievers) or ahl al-dhimma—that is, people who enjoy protection under Islamic polity.[34] However, considering non-Muslims in Aceh as dhimmīs is problematic because non-Muslims pay taxes not because they are considered legally dhimmīs, but because they are citizens of Indonesia. All Indonesian citizens, regardless of their religious background, pay taxes. Muslims pay both taxes and zakat (religious alms giving), which did not happen in the pre-nation-state era. Nevertheless, the way non-Muslims are treated in fact indicates their status as non-full citizens.

Apart from Islam, Aceh also has its own political tradition—here considered as an ethnic political tradition—which is reflected in the proverb, "Adat bak po teumeureuhom, hukom bak syiah kuala, qanun bak putroe phang, reusam bak laksamana, hukom ngon adat, lagee zat ngon sifeuet"[35] (Adat [customary law] is in the hands the Respected [Po] who passed away [Teumeureuhom] [Sultan Iskandar Muda, 1583–1636]; hukom [shari`a law] is in the hands of Syiah Kuala—the pious and learned man of the estuary [ulama] [Syaikh 'Abd al-Ra'uf al-Sinkili, 1615–1693];[36] qanun [civil law] is in the hands of Putroe Phang—Princess of Pahang [Sultan Iskandar Muda's wife];[37] reusam [country custom] is in the hands of the admiral [Keumalahayati or Malahayati, 1550s–1906]);[38] shari`a and adat are like a substance and its attribute." This proverb reflects divisions of power as well as legal pluralism. There are four kinds of law (adat, *hukom*, qanun, and *reusam*) and each is handled by a different agency or institution. Shari`a (hukom) is only one of them. These are like the separation of powers in the West but in the context of an Islamic kingdom. This is considered an ethnic political system because it is different from the Islamic political structure referred to in books on Islamic politics, such as al-Mawardi's al-Aḥkām al-Sulṭāniyya, and from those found elsewhere in the Islamic world, such as in the Mogul and Ottoman Empires. However, Islam has an important place in the Acehnese kingdom as the official religion. The laws referred to above and the institutions that manage them should not contradict shari`a.

In Aceh, as part of the communitarian tradition, the common good of communities is prioritized over individual rights and freedoms. The Acehnese understanding of human rights is based on the paradigm of cultural relativism. Therefore, it is only natural that there have been conflicting views of human rights in Aceh. Human rights arguments would be accepted only if they support religious/Islamic shari`a and Muslim interests. Otherwise, they would be rejected. For instance, a human rights argument that wearing *jilbab* reflects freedom of religion and is therefore a human right is accepted when used to endorse the qanun regulating the jilbab covering for female police officers and members of the armed forces.[39] However, when human rights arguments are used to criticize certain shari`a punishments, including the punishment of non-Muslims, forced closure of some churches, and attacks on "deviant" sects, they are rejected.

Religious Minority Rights: Restriction and Erasure

Dormant citizenship causes not only the restriction but also the erasure of some rights of minority groups. Their freedom to enjoy certain rights is restricted when the latter clash with Muslim norms or interests. Below are a number of examples of the restriction or erasure of rights of non-Muslims—namely, (1) missionary activity, (2) establishing houses of worship, (3) pig breeding and pork consumption, (4) dress code, (5) employment in local government offices, and (6) religious education.

Missionary Activity

The right of religious minorities to proselytize in Aceh has been denied, while Muslims are encouraged to do so. As members of a missionary religion, Christians (both Protestants and Roman Catholics) have been suspected of trying to convert the Acehnese people to Christianity. Aceh's border areas (Singkil, Subulussalam, Kutacane, Tamiang, Langsa) are suspected of being areas of Christian mission. Therefore, programs and institutions were established to protect Aceh Muslims living in those areas adjacent to the province of North Sumatra from any possible *Kristenisasi* (Christian mission) or *pemurtadan* (apostasy). Among others are the *da'i perbatasan* (border preachers) program, *dayah perbatasan* (border Islamic boarding schools), and Islamic centers. Thus, non-Muslims are denied the right to carry out missionary work.

There have been several incidents related to Christian missionary activities. Soon after the tsunami of 2004, for example, there were reports of missionary activities, mostly involving non-Acehnese people and international actors or organizations. For instance, Bibles, crucifixes, books and comics about Jesus were clandestinely distributed with other items in aid boxes. A foreign missionary was held under citizen's arrest and brought to the police. He was not put in jail but was taken by the police to Medan (North Sumatra). No further news of him was reported. There was also a rumor that a number of Acehnese children were being taken abroad by a foreign missionary organization and many stories also circulated about missionary work among the people after the tsunami.[40]

In 2015, there was a rumor on social media that thirteen Acehnese people had converted to Christianity and that fifteen Acehnese people who had become Christian priests in various churches in Medan were ready to come back to Aceh to convert Acehnese to Christianity. The rumor was spread by Gusti Ilham Ramadan, who claimed to be a Christian convert to Islam. Protestant clergy in Aceh met Muslim leaders to convince them that there was no Christian missionary agenda in Aceh and that there were no Muslim converts to Christianity, as Ramadan claimed. They said that Ramadan was a liar because he said that he had been president of the missionaries and the highest priest in Asia, while in fact there was no such position. Muslim leaders and Protestant clergy jointly investigated the rumor and discovered that it was hoax.[41] In fact, Ramadan has eight aliases and has sometimes claimed to be a professor, although he only graduated from high school.

During our fieldwork in the border areas, we attempted to trace the validity of these reports, and we found they were nothing but rumors. On the issue of conversion to Christianity, no one could convincingly prove any conversions. Not only did Christian clergy and community leaders reject those rumors, but most Muslim leaders we interviewed did, too. The latter admitted that they had heard the rumors, but they had never encountered any actual converts to Christianity and said that it was quite the opposite: many Christians converted to Islam.

While rumors of mass conversions from Islam to Christianity in Aceh have circulated, these claims have been largely unsubstantiated. There have been a few documented cases, primarily involving individuals who have relocated outside of Aceh, such as to Medan or Jakarta. One of the most publicized instances was the conversion of Cut Fitri Handayani, a widow with children. Her family alleged that she was "kidnapped" and "brainwashed" by a Christian man whom she later married in a church. However, Handayani subsequently appeared in videos refuting these accusations, stating that her conversion was voluntary and her marriage was based on love.[42] Similar suspicions of religions that are considered nonmissionary religions, such as Buddhism, Hinduism, and Confucianism, have been minor. After the tsunami of 2004, Buddha Zuchi, a Buddhist philanthropic foundation, was welcomed and built a number of houses without being suspected of conducting missionary activities. There are Hindu and Confucian temples, but no suspicions of missionary activities are reported.

Establishing Houses of Worship

Restrictions have been placed on the right of non-Muslims to religious worship and especially to have places of worship. Establishing places of worship that belong to minority groups has been a sensitive issue in Indonesia in general and in Aceh in particular. The building of places of worship fulfills the right to freedom of religion and worship, as guaranteed by the 1945 Constitution. However, it is seen by some Muslims as a threat to their existence and identity.

At the national level, the Joint Decree between the Minister of Religious Affairs and the Minister of Home Affairs of 2006 regulates the building of places of worship. It stipulates that for a place of worship to be approved, it must get the support of ninety congregation members and sixty neighbors, verified by their ID cards. In addition, approval must be gained from the Forum for Harmony of Interreligious Communities (FKUB) and from the head of the local Office of Religious Affairs. These complex requirements make it almost impossible for the minority in Aceh to build places of worship.

Moreover, instead of implementing the above-mentioned Joint Decree, the Aceh government issued a Gubernatorial Decree (No. 25/2007) on Places of Worship, which made the rules even stricter, requiring support from 150 congregation members and 120 neighbors, so that building a place of worship in Aceh is twice as difficult as at the national level. It is virtually impossible for minority groups to meet these requirements.

There are also cases of churches being forcibly closed on the grounds that they were considered illegal because they did not have permission from local authorities.[43] In 2015, Muslim residents of Singkil mobilized demonstrations against the growing number of churches in the area, which led to the burning of one church and the enforced closure of other churches by the local government, as demanded by Muslim protesters. To overcome this problem, the Aceh government did not proceed with the legalization of the churches, as the Christians had expected. Instead, they issued Qanun No. 4/2016 on the Guideline for the Protection of Harmonious Relations among Religious Communities and Places of Worship. Unlike the previous regulations, the qanun stated that a place of worship should provide a list of 140 names of congregation members who are permanent residents (not migrants) and the support of 110 people from the neighborhood who are not congregation members, all verified by their ID cards. In addition, they should have a recommendation from the village authority (*keuchik*), the subdistrict head (*camat*), the FKUB, and the head of the local Offices of Religious Affairs. While the number of congregation members and neighbors appears to have decreased, migrants are excluded, and the recommendation procedure has become more complicated.

According to local Muslims in Singkil, the right to religion should be separated from the right to worship, and the latter should be separated from the right to have a place of worship.[44] Having the right to worship and to a place of worship are not seen as part and parcel of the right to religion. In other words, people are guaranteed the right to follow a religion and to perform religious worship to a certain extent, but this does not mean that they are freely allowed a place of worship. This view could explain why the burning of a church in Singkil in 2015 and the official closing of other churches was seen by local Muslims not as representing interreligious conflict but rather as a conflict over a Christian place of worship.[45] In their daily life, Muslims and non-Muslims can live side by side in many situations because many of them are in the same families, and sometimes even have the same ancestors, but having a place of worship is perceived as another issue entirely.[46] Local Muslims view the issue from a religiopolitical perspective in which a place of worship is considered a center for religious dissemination and propagation rather than a site of internal religious solidarity. This view considers that non-Muslim places of worship threaten the existence of Muslims. In this context, a church building has been associated with the issue of Christian mission rather than with the protection of religious rights.

Nevertheless, although Gubernatorial Decree No. 25/2007 and Qanun No. 4/2016 mostly affected non-Muslim places of worship, a Muhammadiyah mosque was also burned and vandalized in Samalanga in 2016, and the foundation frames of another Muhammadiyah mosque that was in the process of being built (not the mosque itself, as rumor suggested) were burned in Bireuen in 2017. These problems reflected latent internal Muslim conflict between the "modernist" Muhammadiyah organization and the "traditionalist" *dayah* (Islamic boarding school) supporters. The mosques belonging to the former were perceived to be a threat to the existence of the latter.[47]

Pig Breeding and Pork Consumption

During the Dutch colonial era, pig breeding in Banda Aceh was normal, just like cow breeding. After independence, pig breeding was regulated strictly. It was allowed only in uninhabited areas in a village and was performed mainly by the Chinese and Batak.[48] After the implementation of shari`a, the regulation became even stricter. The biggest demand for pork is in Southeast Aceh, Singkil, and Subulussalam, all border areas adjacent to North Sumatra in which a significant number of Christians and Buddhists live.[49] Most pork was imported from this neighboring region, though some was obtained from local pig breeding houses. Table 2.1 shows the consumption of pork in three Acehnese areas from 2014 through 2016. There is no available official data for other areas.

In Aceh Tenggara (Kutacane) district in which more than a hundred churches exist, many non-Muslims breed pigs, especially in the subdistricts of Lawe Sigala-gala, Semadam, Babul Makmur, Deleng Pokhisen, Lawe Bulan, and Badar. It was said that before the implementation of shari`a their number was limited because local authorities supported the shooting of released pigs. Despite a recent decree of Southeast Aceh district regarding pig breeding (No. 7/2010),[50] the number of pig breeders has risen in the last decade, albeit unevenly. During our fieldwork in Kutacane, we found pork being sold in traditional markets. Problems emerged, however, when pigs were released and not controlled. Muslims who lived in the surrounding villages were worried about the purity of their yards, the environment, and the water of the river should these pigs get around. The practice of free-ranging pigs was protested by a number of Muslims in 2014.[51] The local authorities promised to raid the released pigs.

Two years later, however, another protest was organized by the Muslim Student Association in front of the local legislature building. The

Table 2.1. Pork Consumption in Three Areas in Aceh (in kilograms)

Municipality/District	2014	2015	2016
Aceh Singkil	16,016	5,834	5,949
Southeast Aceh	14,300	13,614	15,101
Subulussalam	6,292	5,606	5,720

Source: Dinas Peternakan Aceh, "Data Peternakan Provinsi Aceh" (2017).

association demanded that pig breeding be controlled and managed responsibly by local government lest it "disturb religious harmony."[52] One of our informants said that many Muslims suspected that breeders released pigs on purpose so that Muslims would be disturbed and move to other villages. Some suspected that this was part of a Christianization strategy,[53] a suspicion that was rejected by Christian leaders.[54]

Despite the high consumption of pork, Singkil issued a qanun in 2007 excluding pigs from the list of allowed livestock. It seems that pork was being imported to Singkil from the neighboring province of North Sumatra. In the Tamiang district, which is also a border area, pig breeding was forbidden based on the Qanun on Prohibition of Releasing Animals (No. 15/2008). Article 2:4 reads, "Especially for pigs, it is forbidden to breed in all areas of the Aceh Tamiang district." Finally, in 2016, the Aceh provincial government issued Qanun 8/2016 in which pigs are categorized as a forbidden animal to breed, sell, or consume. This does not mean that people cannot find pork to eat. Based on our interviews with non-Muslims living in Aceh, we learned that in some districts and municipalities, they import pork from Medan, North Sumatra. With the above qanuns in place, however, it became more difficult to find pork in Aceh outside of the three regions mentioned above.

Dress Code

Even before the official implementation of shari`a in 2001, the matter of Islamic clothing, especially for women, had become a hot issue in Aceh. The Qanun on Islamic Belief, Devotion, and Symbols stated that Muslim women and men must dress according to Islamic norms. There is no explanation in the qanun of what this means, but as far as Shafi'ite *mazhab* was concerned, women should wear jilbab, covering all of their bodies except their faces and palms. Although Shafi'ite required men to cover only what is between their navels and their knees, in practice men are expected to cover from their chests to their feet in Aceh. Many raids have been conducted, not only by Wilayatul Hisbah, the Shari`a Police, but also in some regions by vigilantes and other groups. Women wearing tight clothes—even if they veil their heads—and men wearing short trousers are arrested during the raids. There is no punishment, but their names are recorded, and they are advised to dress properly according to Islamic code. Sometimes the Wilayatul Hisbah have given sarong to the arrested women.

Non-Muslims are not obliged to follow the Islamic way of dressing, but they are advised to honor shari`a by dressing "properly," in the sense that women should cover their bodies, though not necessarily their heads. Many non-Muslim women wear jilbab for pragmatic reasons, such as to avoid the Muslim gaze and possible raids.[55] They also wear crucifixes behind their veils,[56] which they can show if they are ever raided, clarifying that they are Christians.[57]

Since 2005, the jilbab has been the official uniform for women police. This is based on the National Police Commander's Decree (Skep/702/IX/2005 on Police Uniform), which was issued due to the fact that jilbab was regulated by Qanun 11/2002. Therefore, women police, including non-Muslims, must wear jilbab. It is said that this is to respect the local implementation of shari`a and for women police to be accepted by society. Since 2015, jilbab has been also obligatory for women military forces in Aceh.[58]

Employment in Local Government Offices

The right to work is a universal human right, but since the implementation of shari`a, it has not been easy for non-Muslims to get jobs in local government offices. Most non-Muslims in Aceh work in national government posts, including in the armed forces, the police force, and the Office of Religious Affairs. Most of them are immigrants or residents of non-Acehnese ethnicity. Apart from working in centralized government offices, most Christians work in private enterprises, such as Christian schools, national companies, and trade. There are hardly any Christians working in local government offices, except those who were already there before the implementation of shari`a, but most of these have retired. This means that the right to work is restricted.

Most Aceh citizens of Chinese descent are Buddhist, some others are Christian and Confucian, and some have converted to Islam. Most of them work in local trade and private enterprises, not usually in government offices. They are unable to gain access to government employment as a result of Suharto's policy against Indonesian Chinese. During Abdurrahman Wahid's presidency (1999–2001), this policy was abrogated and Indonesian Chinese are now allowed to adopt Chinese names, to use the Chinese language and script in their communication, and to follow Chinese cultural practices. Confucianism has also been recognized by the state as the sixth official religion.[59] However, government jobs are still restricted for people of Chinese ethnicity. Many of them leave Aceh after finishing high school or junior high school, most heading to North Sumatra, Batam, or Jakarta to pursue further study or work.[60] This has become common practice because they have limited opportunities for employment in Aceh.

Religious Education

The Qanun on Education (No. 5/2008, article 9.1.a and its revision No.11/2014, article 8.1.a.) plainly states that "students have the right to have religious education according to their religious affiliation and to be taught by teachers of a similar faith." However, despite this regulation, religious education is generally not adequately included for non-Muslims in Aceh. Public schools only provide Islamic religious instruction for Muslims, without providing other religious instruction for students of other religions. During the Islamic instruction class, non-Muslims students are allowed to stay or to leave. Some schools cooperate with local churches or Buddhist viharas to provide Christian and Buddhist students, respectively, with their own religious instruction. These students would receive marks for their religious subjects from those churches and viharas. There are so far no non-Muslim teachers of religion in public schools.

In Singkil, for instance, only Islamic religious instruction is available in public schools, including in the subdistricts where a significant number of Christians (both Protestants and Roman Catholics) live: Simpang Kanan, Danau Paris, Gunung Meriah, Suro Makmur, and Pulau Banyak Barat (see table 2.2). In these subdistricts, no Christian religious instruction is available either.[61] Some schools allow Christian students to stay or to leave during Islamic religious instruction, but others oblige Christian

Table 2.2. Number of Protestants and Catholics in Aceh Singkil District in 2018

Subdistricts	Protestants and Catholics	Total Population	Percentage
Simpang Kanan	4,567	14,882	30.68%
Danau Paris	3,774	7,719	48.89%
Gunung Meriah	2,658	35,704	7.44%
Suro Makmur	1,984	8,811	22.51%
Pulau Banyak Barat	1,425	3,094	46.05%

Source: BPS Statistics of Aceh Singkil District (2018).

students to follow Islamic religious instruction and forbid them from leaving class. In the case of the former, Christian religious instruction grades are given by local clergy or by teachers of Islamic religious instruction by considering students' ethical attitudes (*akhlak*). In the case of the latter, students have to take exams in Islamic religious instruction. The problem is that despite the clear approval of diverse religious instruction in the qanun, the Singkil Education Office obliges public schools to give only Islamic religious instruction.[62]

There have been calls for the government to provide Christian teachers for Christian students, especially in the regions where a significant number of Christians live, such as Singkil and Kutacane. Boas Tumangger, the head of Forum Cinta Damai Aceh Singkil (Forcidas), a forum in Singkil established to voice Protestant interests, presented this request to the local government in 2016. A similar request had also been made long before,[63] at least since the promulgation of Law of National Education in 2003, which states that religious instruction must be taught by a teacher of the same faith. However, at the time of writing this request had not yet been met.

There are some Protestant private schools in Aceh, such as a Methodist school in Banda Aceh, and Catholic schools, such as Budi Dharma (kindergarten, elementary, and junior high) in Banda Aceh, and Panti Harapan (secondary and high schools) and Santo Yosep Desky (elementary school) in Southeast Aceh. Some teachers and students in these Protestant and Catholic schools are Muslims. In Budi Dharma in 2014, for instance, there were six Muslim teachers and some Muslim students, but the majority of the students were Protestants, not Catholics.[64] Muslim teachers and students are also found in Panti Harapan. However, no Protestant or Catholic teachers or students are found in Muslim schools. Thus, the right to religious education for non-Muslims is restricted.

Conclusion

Citizenship in Aceh is not only defined by religious symbols and issues, the visibility of religion and its importance in public debates, religious interpretations and practices, or the construction of religious discourse but also by religious ethnonationalism and political processes. These include oppression, violations of human rights, and rebellion during the conflict period, as well as negotiation, deliberation, accommodation, and consensus after the conflict. Acehnese citizenship implicitly treats non-Muslims as dhimmīs, although this term is not mentioned explicitly in official discourse (including laws, qanuns, regulations, and policies). In fact, non-Muslims can exercise their rights only insofar as they are within the boundaries set up by shari`a. Non-Muslim citizenship becomes dormant; it survives but hardly functions normally. The problem with this "dormant citizenship" is that it allows discrimination based on faith on the grounds that Islam is the official religion of Aceh, and followers of non-Islamic religions are treated as "guests" in the land of shari`a. This has become "normal" in Aceh, along with the process of continuing "conservatization."

Aceh exceptionalism has led non-Muslims to live in dormant citizenship as a result of the strong unity of religion and ethnonationalism, legitimated by national laws. Religion in this context means a strict, conservative understanding of Islam. Up to the present, it has been almost impossible to change this construct. Any attempt to question the dominance of religion in Aceh has resulted in strong reactions by both the society and local government and has been seen as an effort to violate the national laws. In this situation, questioning religion is unproductive and even counterproductive. Attempts should be made to work out how to live with it, while democratizing citizenship by strengthening the synthesis of communitarian and republican citizenship by empowering citizens' understanding of civil rights for all residents and multiculturalism, on the one hand, and endorsing active participation of non-Muslims in Aceh public life to encourage mutual understanding, on the other hand. Liberal citizenship would not be suitable for Aceh because it runs counter to the communitarian nature of Acehnese society. Non-Muslims' active participation in the public good could build positive social and cultural citizenship in the future.

PART II

The Shari`a State

CHAPTER 3

Religious Bureaucratic Authority

Shari`a, or mostly known as Islamic law, has now become part of Aceh's development planning agenda. Based on the policy of special autonomy, the province has the full authority to enforce shari`a in a comprehensive manner. Numerous discussions of this development have arisen that look especially at the dominance of jinayah law enforcement and whether it can bring about social change.[1] Many studies have explored the roots and effectiveness of its implementation.[2] Little is known, however, about the bureaucracy that has sustained the shari`a implementation agenda since its initiation and particularly about the development of organizations within the bureaucracy. How organizations function to implement shari`a in Aceh remains generally unexplored.

The growth of regional organizational structures initiated a new phase of Indonesia's post-1998 reform in which politics have become decentralized. In Aceh, the Department of Islamic Shari`a (Dinas Syariat Islam, DSI) is a part of the provincial government offices established to implement shari`a. There are also other provincial offices bestowed with greater authority, higher status, and independence in support of the implementation of shari`a in Aceh, such as Aceh's legislature, the governor's office, the public prosecutor, and the police force. Other collaborating institutions, directly or indirectly, responsible for implementing qanuns include the shari`a court, the ulama council and the shari`a police (Wilayatul Hisbah).

Divisions within the DSI cover multiple domains, including the development of Islamic law, which extends to Aceh's Islamic development vision. In this sense, the establishment of the DSI as a government office indicates that shari`a implementation is intended to involve more than merely enforcing Islamic law.[3] The government of Aceh does not review the shari`a implementation goals, though it believes its implementation must be *kaffah* (comprehensive). Shari`a enforcement is not limited to legal renewal; its spectrum is as wide as the definition of Islam itself.[4] The majority population of Acehnese people expect that in Aceh, because it is a "shari`a province," shari`a should be reflected not only in legal reforms but also in social and political development.

From the beginning, shari`a implementation in Aceh has relied on a technocratic approach of establishing offices, creating recruiting apparatus, and arranging regulations. The DSI is one of multiple offices established to strengthen socioreligious development as well as to be a distinctive indicator of shari`a implementation. The DSI shares some common tasks with other offices in Aceh, including the branch offices of the Ministry of Religious Affairs in different levels of Aceh government. Since the establishment of the DSI, maintaining a high-quality and effective bureaucracy has been a substantial challenge, impeding development.[5]

This chapter argues that the DSI has weaknesses that affect the implementation of shari`a in Aceh. It attempts to shed light on the quality of local bureaucracy in the post-reformation era, especially relating to shari`a implementation and how the DSI contributes to this failure. This chapter also analyzes the challenges facing the DSI, including the weakness of the DSI's legal authority. The quality of legal authority is one of the four components of "acceptance of authority," a concept coined by Conrado R. Santos.[6] Another aspect this chapter will investigate is the hierarchy of positions in the DSI office. Although all of the positions seem to be filled, they are not effective. It is therefore relevant to consider the level of competence or expertise of DSI personnel, particularly in terms of how the relationship between head office personnel and office staff influences the office's effectiveness.

The Background of DSI

The Strategic Plan of the Special Province of Aceh, 2001–5, served as the basis for the implementation of shari`a in the early stages of Aceh's special autonomy. During the five-year period of this development plan, the government of Aceh introduced a "development of religion" plan to bring to fruition its special powers over the religious life of Aceh. The development of a religion plan was then translated as the implementation of shari`a.[7] This strategic plan also spelled out the roles and authority of the DSI, which was established with divisions of religious support, justice, and Islamic teaching. Each of these divisions has its own subdivisions. In relation to its mission to strengthen Islamic faith, the DSI established a technical work unit to assign da'i (preachers) to work at the Aceh border as contract laborers (program da'i perbatasan or the border da'i program). The DSI also recruited personnel for the Wilayatul Hisbah, or Shari`a Police, a unit later incorporated into the office of the Satpol PP, or Municipal Police Service. The Wilayatul Hisbah, however, have no authority to formally charge or detain suspects. They have to work along with the regular police officers and public prosecutors to oversee and enforce a number of qanuns.

The formation of the DSI was relatively quick; it was established by the time the Aceh strategic plan of 2001–5 had been formulated. Once the central government passed Law 18/2001 establishing Aceh's special autonomy, the strategic plan was already formulated, and Qanun 33/2001 on the Organization of the DSI was passed. There was likely strong political support for DSI's formation under the assumption that the strengthening of shari`a offices would produce important political capital.[8] Executives in Aceh do not seem to have conducted a feasibility study regarding the legal grounds for the formation of the DSI. Legal guidance on the establishment of organizations in Indonesia, such as the Decree of the National Law Development Agency Director No. G-159.PR.09.10 of 1994 on Technical Guidance for the Preparation of Academic Paper Legislation, was not followed. This decree emphasized the importance of performing a feasibility study before establishing an office. It was reaffirmed through Presidential Regulation 68/2005 and Law 12/2011 on the Establishment of Legislation. The new shari`a offices in Aceh should have followed this legislation in decisions related to structures, duties, and functions. That they did not opens up for further investigation the concepts, goals, objectives, scope, and direction of the office.

The DSI is a permanent department assigned to plan and coordinate shari`a enforcement in Aceh. The academic script (*naskah akademik*) for this planning and coordinating function remains unavailable, however, which makes it difficult to anticipate its political influence or to evaluate how well the DSI meets its institutional goals. Although some consider an academic script to be facultative, another view sees it as compulsory.

An academic script would have ensured a sufficient literature review and considered various useful opinions in determining the structure of the organization before pursuing any policy goals.[9]

In the absence of a long-term vision laid down in the early stages of its establishment, the DSI became prone to making internal structural changes following every change of its provincial-level leaders. When the governor is replaced, the DSI director also changes, and changes to the DSI's organizational structure seem inevitably to follow. In 2007, the DSI suddenly reduced the work programs of Bina Peradilan (Strengthening the Shari`a Court) on the grounds that the court could fulfill that function. The fact that the court or Mahkamah Syar'iyah had just appointed new judges and that some judges and officials had been transplanted from other areas into Aceh was not factored into this decision. In another case in 2018, the DSI proposed a work program to form the Technical Service Implementation Unit for Baiturrahman Grand Mosque, Banda Aceh, a purpose previously unrelated to the DSI's mission of implementing shari`a.

The formulation of the DSI was part of the government's efforts to put the draft policy on the implementation of shari`a properly into effect. To date, shari`a implementation has been carried out through trial and error without incorporating any comprehensive planning. This situation is not unique to Aceh, as similar challenges are common to bureaucracy throughout Indonesia.[10] It is possible that this trial-and-error approach to reform will continue should the DSI fail to strengthen its authority and align its work with a strong vision and mission.

DSI's Limited Authority and Outreach

The main issue with DSI performance to date relates to its performance as the leading office for socioreligious development. Since its establishment, the function of the DSI has been understood by other offices, including the Bureau of Organization and Governance at the office of the governor of Aceh and the Office of the Inspectorate of Aceh, as providing oversight for the implementation of shari`a. In 2004, Alyasa Abubakar wrote, in the first book on shari`a to be produced by the DSI, about the formulation of paradigms, policies, and activities of shari`a, and he offered his interpretation of the function of the DSI based on Qanun 33/2001: "It appears that the main task of the DSI is to be a planner[,] and [the office] is responsible for the implementation of shari`a in the Province of Nanggroe Aceh Darussalam." He referred to article 3 of the qanun, which states that "the DSI has duties to perform the general and special tasks of Regional Government in charge of the implementation of shari`a."[11]

Technically, the regional regulation did not mention the scope of the DSI's authority, particularly in terms of planning for shari`a implementation, which should have been spelled out comprehensively. No technical guidelines were provided for the DSI to do so; hence, the label given to the DSI was "Dinas Daerah," or "Executive Office." In the provisions of Government Regulation No. 18/2016 on Regional Organization, article 13, paragraph (4) states that the DSI has a specific task to execute special work. Although in this regulation the service is said to be able to accept other "duties" from the governor, the DSI did not acquire the typology of being a "service." Rather, it was ascribed a "special status" along with nine other offices based on regulations regarding "The Structure of Organization and Management" in Aceh province.

In 2006, many in Aceh were looking forward to the enactment of Law 11/2006 on the Governance of Aceh, or the UUPA, to accelerate Aceh's development and its implementation of shari`a. The UUPA introduced no new regulations regarding the authority of the DSI, but it clearly imposed the tasks and authority for implementing and coordinating shari`a implementation on the regional government heads, including the governors, regents, and mayors (article 42). The UUPA emphasized that the government should formulate regulations on the distribution of government responsibilities related to shari`a. The draft of this qanun was made available in 2013 and was approved by Governor Zaini Abdullah in 2015 as Qanun 7/2015. Unfortunately, this qanun did not succeed in regulating the authority of the DSI.

A Grand Design for Shari`a Islam

In 2014, the DSI, led by Syahrizal Abbas, attempted to implement shari`a with a wider dimension. The DSI began compiling its Grand Design for Shari`a Islam (GDSI), placing more attention on education, economics, governance, law, and custom. The DSI had discussions with local civil society organizations and the Civil Society Network for Shari`a Concerns; it also cooperated with many academics to jointly develop the GDSI.

Some parties involved perceived the GDSI to be DSI's effort to provide a clear road map for the implementation of shari`a in the province. At the same time, the DSI also constructed the Humanist Legal Analysis Framework in cooperation with the Civil Society Network for Shari`a Concerns, which was intended for legal use by law enforcement officers.

Some of the proposed drafts indicate that the DSI did not chart a new map concerning shari`a enforcement, however. Rather, it tried to escape a narrow interpretation of shari`a implementation that focused on jinayah enforcement. The DSI mentioned five sectors as a priority, although it remained unclear how these would be connected to other development sectors or how it could work with multiple stakeholders. To this day, the document has not been used as a reference for the implementation of shari`a. Nevertheless, the DSI did put a lot of effort into making the GDSI successful.

Within the GDSI design, the DSI did not propose any new work strategy for the implementation of shari`a. The proposed strategies include redefining the strategic position of DSI within the scope of shari`a implementation, remapping current needs for additional support to control the implementation of Islamic law, providing a critical review of the new strategic nomenclature for the DSI organization, and thinking more strategically about coordination and consolidation in implementing shari`a. Alyasa' Abubakar proposed a normative view that could have been made as the basis for a DSI academic script before the local regulations on the DSI were issued. Abubakar divided responsibility for implementing Islamic shari`a between three parties—namely, government, society, and the individual. He did not specify which government office he was referring to. Unfortunately, this manuscript was published after the DSI was established and after the regulations were issued.

Strengthening Coordination

The DSI also attempted to strengthen the implementation of shari`a within various provincial government offices (*dinas provinsi*). Coordination work was planned so that all these offices could synchronize their work. The DSI seeks to organize joint efforts on a regular basis to achieve common goals. The DSI also tried to negotiate its authority by encouraging other offices to engage in the implementation of shari`a. Munawar A. Djalil, DSI head in 2017, sent a cordial letter to a number of provincial offices, encouraging them to support the implementation of shari`a. These offices complained, however, that DSI did not specify programs and activities to be implemented. Munawar explains that it was therefore crucial for the DSI to develop the GDSI, which was to provide details of programs and indicators. The availability of the GDSI would help the DSI communicate its programs more effectively to other parties.

To help consolidate its efforts, the DSI also coordinated with other stakeholders, including police departments, the judiciary, shari`a court, municipal police service, Wilayatul Hisbah, and local DSI offices through its annual Technical Coordination Meeting (Rapat Koordinasi Teknis, or Rakornis). Rakornis is usually conducted for a couple of days to discuss the challenges of shari`a implementation from multiple perspectives. In 2017, Rakornis gathered more attendees than it had in the past, and the DSI invited more stakeholders to report their progress in developing GDSI. The DSI also invited the Aceh regional secretary (*sekretaris daerah*), Bappeda (Regional Development Planning Agency), and the head of the Aceh House of Representatives (DPRA). In addition to hearing comments and suggestions from attendees and learning from the Bappeda of Aceh about the Aceh Shari`a Development Index, the DSI sought support from the legislature to make the GDSI part of the Provincial Legislation Program in 2018.

As observed, some participants in the Rakornis were critical of the DSI. They argued that the DSI is not strong enough to coordinate programs beyond its authority. Some of the invited representatives were not from any of the Aceh regional apparatus; hence their recommendations could not be incorporated into operational aspects of the DSI. One of the recommendations was to strengthen "the cooperation of the enforcement of jinayah law," which is surely outside the DSI's authority.

Structural Problems within the DSI

The ability of any organization to exercise authority is determined in part by the level of structures that work together. For one, Santos's concept of "acceptance of authority" refers to Max Weber's theory on the existence of hierarchical office, while others entitled the position with authority of position or sanction, formal position, official authority, and authority of the job. In other words, the level of positions established in any particular organization determine the extent of its authority. Structure determines how an organization achieves its goals.[12] Local regulations and qanuns have established general guidance for the DSI regarding its basic structures. The key question is whether these predetermined positions are able to support the implementation of shari`a in Aceh. As a government organization, the DSI's organizational structure is instrumental in regulating and managing shari`a implementation policy in the region.

Cutbacks in the Research and Development Working Unit

A technocratic system strongly emphasizes the importance of an organization's working with available data in order to achieve optimal development outcomes. Government organizations in Indonesia are expected to develop research and development (R&D) units or offices, which the province of Aceh has yet to do. R&D crucial to strengthening the working principle of "evidence-based policymaking" established by Law No. 25/2004 on the National Development Planning System. Unfortunately, strengthening the R&D agenda was not a priority of the bureaucracy reform agenda in Indonesia, particularly in Aceh, where R&D remains a major challenge for most organizations. Twenty years after achieving autonomy, Aceh shows slow progress in terms of R&D due to the local government's low commitment to working with data.

In relation to shari`a implementation, R&D is instrumental for data-driven policymaking. In its early phase, the DSI had a unit for R&D under the Division of Program Planning. Over time, this subdivision got smaller, and now it has been completely removed from the structural nomenclature. Although the governor's Regulation 131/2016 on the Status, Organizational Structure, Duties, Functions and Working Procedures of the DSI Office mentions a duty of research, monitoring, and evaluation, the DSI's strategic planning (*renstra*) for programs and activities no longer mentions R&D, and DSI evaluation mapping does not discuss R&D as an internal strategic issue or as a challenge in implementing shari`a. Instead, the strategic planning document focuses on issues such as low societal awareness regarding the implementation of Islamic teaching.

The internal structure of the DSI reflects the way in which this organization sees R&D. For R&D to be allotted subdivision status indicates that it is not the DSI's priority. The DSI does not exhibit a commitment to studying, evaluating, or measuring the extent to which shari`a has been implemented in Aceh. The DSI cannot depend on external institutions, moreover, such as the Central Bureau of Statistics or the Regional

Development Planning Agency (Bappeda) to obtain data on shari`a implementation. In addition to the fact that doing so would indicate that DSI does not conduct research on its own territory and under its own authority, such cooperation is complicated due to the DSI's poor coordination record with other institutions.

This culture of working without data throws the DSI's authority into question. During a 2017 discussion about integrating the draft GDSI into the Medium-Term Development Plan of 2017–22, the DSI presented some dubious data. During the discussions that followed, the DSI was made aware of the importance of data; it cannot design effective policies without a complete picture of a given situation. Some data that it should be able to provide are unavailable: for instance, there are no data regarding Acehnese people's rate of Arabic literacy, even though a DSI program existed specifically to improve religious understanding and Qur'anic literacy among the people of Aceh. Apparently, the proposed program was executed without any data being recorded or analyzed. On another occasion, during a DSI budgeting consultation exercise in 2018, Bappeda questioned the DSI about the current condition of mosques and meunasah that were financially supported by the DSI. The DSI admitted that it never collected such data and did not know where to obtain it.

It is fair to say, then, that the DSI has not been strategic in designing its programs, nor has it collected data that would allow its progress to be measured or evaluated. The DSI does carry out numerous programs throughout the year, but these respond to community proposals or requests and are unrelated to a strategic plan. This work culture acts to thwart the DSI's authority. Should the DSI continue working in this manner, it will never accomplish its primary mission of enforcing comprehensive shari`a implementation in Aceh. Instead, shari`a implementation will be limited to ceremonial programs and less impactful activities.

The Ups and Downs of the Power of Supervision and Propagation

The DSI office has 108 staff at its headquarters and 200 contract personnel working as da'i (border preachers) at the Aceh borders. Between 2002 and 2007, before the transfer of Wilayatul Hisbah personnel to the Satpol PP department, the DSI also controlled this Shari`a Police unit. Today, Wilayatul Hisbah is designated for supervising and enforcing shari`a law, while the da'i are specially dispatched to teach and preach Islam in the six border districts of Aceh Tamiang, Southeast Aceh, Aceh

Singkil, Subulussalam, South Aceh, and Simeulue, where the government believes strengthening the Muslim faith is crucial.

The separation of the Wilayatul Hisbah from the DSI was widely opposed by Wilayatul Hisbah personnel, the DSI head, and members of the local community, all of whom believe this decision will weaken the Shari`a Police's authority to perform its responsibility of enforcing shari`a in society.[13] For the sake of the Wilayatul Hisbah's role and noble mission, DSI head Munawar A. Djalil once expressed the fundamental differences between Wilayatul Hisbah and Satpol PP: "Satpol PP is working to drive the cows that enter the market, while the [Wilayatul Hisbah] is working to drive people whose mentality is like [that of] cows" (Satpol PP nyan yang paroh leumo, WH yang paroh ureung lagee leumo).[14]

Satpol PP's tasks are unrelated to shari`a implementation. Therefore, its role is distinct from that of the Wilayatul Hisbah. In 2007, the governor of Aceh, through DSI head Ziauddin Ahmad, stated that the Shari`a Police has features that distinguish it from other law enforcement units; it provides better welfare and career trajectories for its personnel.[15] Do these special features of the DSI ensure shari`a enforcement in Aceh? There is no guarantee of that. Within a decade of shari`a implementation, a number of jinayah cases were instead being committed by Wilayatul Hisbah personnel, in addition to cases of physical clashes with citizens.[16]

Since the initiation of the border da'i program by the DSI, two major bureaucratic issues have emerged. The first relates to the monitoring mechanism for da'i performance. The border da'i are directly supervised by the DSI at the provincial level because this program is funded through the provincial special autonomy fund. This affects the nature of the program, which is quite similar to another provincial government program that provides incentives to local religious leaders. The direct chain of management causes problems in terms of monitoring in that performance assessment is conducted by the provincial DSI remotely through periodic coordination meetings and site visits. The DSI could have performed this assessment more effectively and less expensively, but bureaucratic procedure prevented this alternative approach from being taken.

In a report titled *Da'i Performance Assessment* released by the DSI in 2015, da'i teaching and preaching of Islam at the borders was found to be ineffective. Recruited da'is are mostly selected by the provincial government, and they are unfamiliar with the sociocultural contexts of the borders. Nasruddin, the manager of the border da'i program, has mentioned that there is no guarantee that the best da'is selected from the city are necessarily the best people to work in remote areas. The da'is' mission and approach often clash with local approaches to religious matters. Additionally, the metropolitan da'is often complain about the difficulty of transportation in the areas of their placement. Many da'is were reported to not have stayed in the border area during the period of their duty.

All of these dynamics of the border da'i were well captured and recorded by DSI offices at the district and regency levels. Unfortunately, these offices had no authority to address the issues, due to the overarching power attached to the provincial DSI. The absence of reports from local DSI offices, meanwhile, convinced the provincial DSI that the program was still feasible to run and did not require significant reform. The recommendation of the DSI assessment of the border da'i program focused primarily on fulfilling and increasing quotas for the number of da'is. In the past few years, this number has increased to up to two hundred personnel (twenty-five in Simeulue, nineteen in South Aceh, forty-seven in Aceh Singkil, thirty-nine in Aceh Tamiang, forty-six in Southeast Aceh, and twenty-four in Subulussalam). The report also mentioned a baseless claim from a district DSI that the ideal number of da'is per district was five hundred. The rationale for increasing da'i personnel at the borders was not given because no proper assessment had been conducted to provide one. It is an intricate challenge to decide how many da'is are needed per village; therefore, a strategic concept and preliminary assessment would be helpful prior to sending da'is to the borders.

Assessment of da'is' performance tends to focus on their experience and well-being rather than on whether their mission is being accomplished or how effective their presence is in achieving the program's goal. Due to weaknesses in monitoring and assessment, the effectiveness of this program cannot be comprehensively measured or analyzed. Every year, the border da'i program spends more than Rp7 billion, at least 20 percent of total DSI spending. This high cost does not produce any measurable indicators of effectiveness, such as the number of new Muslim converts or the level of religious compliance of the people at the borders. It is worthwhile to ask, is this huge cost worthwhile?

The second issue regarding the border da'i program is the adaptability of da'is into society. The DSI's working plan mentions that the program employs strategies to improve the people's religiosity and *aqidah*

Islamiyah (Islamic creed). To fulfill this goal, the DSI set only one indicator, that of "establishing and maintaining Qur'anic learning at the *gampong* [village] level" and "distributing incentives for *imeum meunasah* [local Islamic leaders]." In terms of this goal, it is worth noting that the mission of upholding aqidah Islamiyah carried out by border da'is, who are rewarded by a monthly salary, is significantly supported by the work of local Islamic leaders and Qur'an teachers who are rewarded only with incentives. That is, the da'is work less but are paid much more. Thus, society's support is indeed needed for the implementation of shari`a in Aceh, and a better system should be developed to distribute power between the government and society.

The border da'i program was understood as an effort to replace the role of local religious leaders, and questions arose whether to substitute community empowerment for preaching activities. The DSI staffs should have studied differences in the educational backgrounds of border community members and da'i, as well as differences in interpretations of Islam, before they deployed the da'is at the border. The local community needs programs that empower them, such as leadership training for village officers, ulamas, and adat leaders. The DSI at the provincial level could delegate these activities to the district DSI offices to minimize operational cost. Da'is in the area could serve as trainers for community members while also developing capacity building and performance assessment tools. The DSI could share the responsibility of strengthening the Islamic faith with the local community at the border.

Lack of Expertise and the Insufficient Managerial Capabilities

Every organization requires expertise to be successful. Expertise, or "technical knowledge," is an acquired competence in Max Weber's terms of rational organization.[17] Along with managerial competence and sociocultural competence, technical competence is needed to develop and manage organizational personnel in Indonesia. It can be assessed on the basis of academic capacity and professionalism, and it includes under its umbrella educational background, degree, coursework, and relevant training related to the duties and positions within the organization.

The DSI has displayed various levels of academic competence, which can be assessed in terms of normative competence (i.e., the ability to translate the Islamic development agenda into practice) and technocratic competence (i.e., the ability to perform organizational roles and functions).

DSI personnel seem to have an average level of technocratic competence. This can be seen in their relatively limited knowledge of the organization's legal authority and position, as described above. Although DSI leaders have high academic competence, they do not necessarily indicate that high-level competence in technocratic matters. Technocratic competence requires specific skills that are mostly nonacademic, including managerial skills. The DSI offers one case in which technocratic competence at the regional level is low. Since the agenda of bureaucracy reform began, many studies have attempted to measure the slow pace of development in the region, and they have found that the major cause of underdevelopment is political dynamics at the local level.[18] A similar study reported the low bureaucratic competence of Indonesian structural personnel and suggested an intervention to improve it.[19]

Based on our close observations of how the DSI plans, executes, and evaluates its annual programs as well as from our conversations in 2017 with a number of informants who have key positions in both the DSI and the Bureau of Organization and Governance (Biro Organisasi dan Tata Kelola) of the province of Aceh, it can be said that technical capacity of the DSI staffs at both provincial and municipal/district levels after more than fifteen years since its establishment remains unexceptional. Table 3.1 compares competence among the DSI apparatus in Aceh.

The issue of DSI staff competence has cropped up since their initial recruitment in 2003. The DSI office, which has the specific mission of managing shari`a implementation, should have been filled with qualified people whose academic backgrounds and experiences matched this mission. The DSI was clearly unprepared for bureaucratic reform. During the early reform period under the Abdurrahman Wahid regime, there was organizational downsizing and merging from the central to the regional levels. Staff of the Office of Information and Communication (Infokom), the Social Service, Youth, and Sports Office, inspectorate staffs, headmasters of madrassas, and others were assigned to be DSI staff. This

Table 3.1. Comparison of Competence among the DSI Apparatuses in Aceh

Competence	Office Head	Subhead	Staff
Technocratic	Middle	Middle	Middle
Normative	High	Low	Low

Source: Information derived from the authors' observations and conversations in 2017.

disorienting beginning to DSI staff recruitment indicated that the special autonomy did not count the implementation of shari`a as a major agenda item.

Under Alyasa Abubakar's leadership (2003–7), efforts were made to increase the DSI staff's normative competence by sending several staffs to pursue higher degrees in Islamic law at universities, including the Islamic universities of Ar-Raniry, Banda Aceh, and some universities in Malaysia. This endeavor was not sustained, however, and the staff members were never reassigned to their original posts. Some qualified staff were assigned to different offices, and the government failed to recruit new staffs who could support the DSI's tasks. To date, two decades after its inception, the DSI has not been able to resolve its originating lack of staff competence.

Due to these limitations, the DSI has relied heavily on cooperation with other parties in its activities of research, book publishing, and training. This type of cooperation is limited to certain circles, however. As a result, the DSI did not complete the drafting of GDSI, despite spending four years working on it. This failure pointed to the weak technical ability of the DSI apparatus, particularly in managing human resources toward strategic planning.

Another factor contributing to the low normative competence of DSI personnel is their personal interest in and understanding of how Islam ought to be enacted in Aceh's civic life. DSI personnel should have implemented an objective perspective and worked toward progressive religious and social development in the region, yet in some cases those staffs presented their personal views to the public. For example, a department head from the DSI spoke at an early 2018 discussion forum regarding the increasing violence against women in Aceh. He proposed the death penalty for those who commit murder, causing quite a public controversy. The uproar subsided soon after the DSI head clarified that the media had misquoted his original statement.

And there are other examples. A 2017 case related to former Jakarta governor Basuki Tjahaja Purnama, or Ahok: a DSI employee expressed his view that Ahok had offended against Islam.[20] A third case related to the decision of the Aceh Besar regent, through Regulation 451/65/2018, obligating airline stewardesses entering Aceh to wear hijab. The Aceh Besar regent, Mawardi Ali, appeared on CNN Indonesia on February 1, 2017 to give an exclusive interview about the policy. When the interview ended in deadlock, a DSI employee commented that CNN had attempted to embarrass the regent's implementation of shari`a in Aceh, and the employee referred to the news channel as an "inhibitor" of shari`a enforcement in Aceh, calling it a "TV kafirun" (TV infidel).

The media spotlight on the DSI has diminished since authority over the Wilayatul Hisbah was transferred to the Satpol PP department in 2007. The DSI's direct involvement in controlling the enforcement of shari`a in civic society was understood by many parties to violate the standards of human rights. There were some clashes between the Wilayatul Hisbah apparatus and citizens, as well as violations of jinayah law carried out by individual Wilayatul Hisbah personnel. Given these cases, had Wilayatul Hisbah remained a part of the DSI, it would surely have harmed the DSI's authority. Yet when the Shari`a Police functions optimally, it has the potential to strengthen the DSI's authority. In this sense, as an executive office, the DSI is overlapped by performing prosecution duties.

Office Leaders' Inadequate Experiences

As a government office, the DSI has been led by different figures with various levels of professional training. The DSI personnel nonetheless have to follow organizational rules and administrative procedures, just like personnel in other organizations. Likewise, the chain of communication and command between office leaders and subordinates must work well in its own dynamics. Santos notes that leaders such as directors or managers are significant figures for measuring organizational authority.[21] Changes of leadership have affected the internal atmosphere of the DSI. Subordinates who were used to being led by more senior directors felt awkward when their new leaders were younger than them. The appointment of Munawar A. Djalil as DSI director in 2017, for instance, shocked some DSI officers, though he had formerly been a section head at the DSI. Some DSI staffs said, "Young people can be emotional."[22] The staff's earlier experience under the leadership of Syahrizal Abbas' (2013–16) was better. They felt that he made every decision only after careful consideration. Under Abbas's leadership, the DSI conducted evaluative policy reviews, especially on the performance of the DSI itself. Munawar's leadership was seen as more assertive; his subordinates perceived that he did not practice bureaucratic leadership, which requires careful and deliberate consideration before making decisions.[23] Bureaucracy as well as authority is needed to reflect on organizational decision-making.[24]

Decisions prematurely arrived at or weakly considered are likely to fail to meet public needs.

Conclusion

The DSI is a government office with the mandate to develop shari`a. It has made some progress in terms of its legal status, structure, position, and efforts to better perform its responsibilities in support of the implementation of shari`a in the Aceh province. Some factors impede its authority, however. In the current state bureaucracy, the highest executive leader in Aceh is the governor. The governor can propose and determine changes in how shari`a is applied. Subordinates generally obey the governor's direction, nonetheless: one member of the governor's staff commented, "It is up to the governor's direction. If the governor wants [it,] we will follow."[25] The DSI is certainly a subordinate to the governor and would act accordingly if instructed.

The DSI's current authority is not strategic enough, and certainly, as things stand, the organization will not be able to bring about measurable changes. Thus, the DSI is not earning its large organizational budget. Regional budget support from the special autonomy is the primary provider of social-religious sector funds in Aceh, and these funds will cease to be available in 2027 when the central government will stop the payments. Should the DSI's authority fail to be properly evaluated and reformed prior to this time, the burden on the government of Aceh's operational spending will certainly be onerous in comparison to the return it receives in terms of the DSI's performance in shari`a implementation.

CHAPTER 4

Non-Muslims in Shari`a Courtrooms

The interactions and interrelations between adherents of different religious groups, such as Muslims and non-Muslims, remains a controversial topic, particularly in regard to non-Muslim minorities living under a Muslim-majority government. The contours of this relationship can be traced back to early Islam, when the Prophet Muhammad led various religious communities in Medina and later ruled the surrounding areas. Non-Muslims had a lower political status and were known as dhimmis. They were subject to the Muslim leadership and had to pay a yearly tax called *jizya*.[1] Imam Al-Mawardi, a Muslim political thinker, discussed this issue from the political-economic perspective of Islamic governance, wherein a jizya was imposed on a protected group of people (non-Muslims).[2] Al-Mawardi's work has inspired many similar works that approach the topic from a classical perspective or explore the experiences of Islamic Middle Eastern and North African countries, past and present. All these works prescribe that non-Muslims have different political status than Muslim residents.

The situation in Indonesia is different. Although Indonesia is the biggest Muslim-majority country in the world, its constitution grants equal rights to every individual, regardless of religious background. The rights of non-Muslims are equivalent to those of Muslim citizens. Located in the multiethnic and multicultural region of Southeast Asia and being the third largest democratic country in the world, Indonesia faces a serious challenge from the formal implementation of shari`a rule in one of its provinces, Aceh.

During the years of Indonesia's political transition following the end of Suharto's rule, from 1999 through 2001, Aceh was allowed to introduce shari`a law for Acehnese Muslims through regional legislation called qanun.[3] The new Indonesian political system also offered the province of Aceh the right to transform the existing Islamic religious court by rebranding it a Mahkamah Syar'iyah (Shari`a Court) and by including a new jurisdiction to examine jinaya, or shari`a criminal case.

While there are some works on the Islamic court of Aceh, existing studies of penal cases involving non-Muslim offenders at the shari`a court of Aceh are scarce.[4] Since the introduction of the 2014 Jinaya Qanun, non-Muslim citizens have been included into this new criminal jurisdiction. They may be prosecuted if they committed an offense together with Muslim offenders or opted for shari`a punishment. Additionally, they would be brought to the Shari`a Court if they committed a jinaya offense, which is not regulated under the National Criminal Code, such as khalwat (close proximity between unmarried couples), *ikhtilath* (openly intimate touch between unmarried couples), premarital sex, or homosexuality.

With such particular development, Aceh became a focus of both national and international attentions. The problem of establishing and enforcing equal rights between citizens who have different religious backgrounds and who coexist under shari`a enforcement in Muslim countries is one of great concern to scholars.[5] Punishing non-Muslim offenders in Aceh by Islamic penalty has been widely criticized. The criticisms stem not only from civil society organizations in Aceh but also from some human rights advocates outside Aceh nationally and globally. They fiercely condemned and questioned why such particular punishment is imposed on non-Muslims while they do not believe in Islamic faith.

This chapter focuses on how non-Muslim offenders deal with the complexities of legal procedures at Aceh's shari`a court. It reviews several criminal cases involving non-Muslim citizens who appeared at the shari`a court of Aceh, which is led by a council of judges comprised of one chair and two members. By delving into the details of the adjudication process applied to non-Muslims at the Aceh shari`a court, this chapter sought to answer the question, how have non-Muslims in Aceh been treated under the qanun or shari`a regulations? In addition, this chapter helps explain the recent dynamics of Indonesian citizenship in general, as well as to assess the extent to which the citizenship status of non-Muslims in Aceh has been lowered or otherwise. By examining legal options available to non-Muslim offenders in Aceh (despite the fact they expressed their willingness to get punished by caning), this chapter argues that the application of such stipulation is considered a fait accompli for them, if not a compulsion. Seen in a larger picture, this is one of many ways to deepen the politics of dominant culture in Aceh's legal sphere.

The Changing Islamic Court of Aceh

Mark E. Cammack and R. Michael Feener have discussed the development of an Islamic legal system in Indonesia, reviewing Indonesia's Islamic legal institutions from the colonial era to the present, including the establishment of the shari`a court in Aceh.[6] Under the series of laws regarding the special autonomy of Aceh granted in 1999 and 2001, not only was the Shari`a Court of Aceh, Mahkamah Syar`iyah, institutionally developed, but both the Ulama Consultative Assembly (Majelis Permusyawaratan Ulama) and the Shari`a Police (Wilayatul Hisbah) were founded as supporting institutions. To enhance the process of Islamic legal reform in Aceh, all these institutions play roles in the enforcement of shari`a at either the provincial or the district level.

There is no doubt that the Mahkamah Syar`iyah is a key institution of shari`a enforcement in Aceh. All shari`a regulations produced by collaboration between the executive and legislative institutions of Aceh require the Mahkamah Syar`iyah to apply them. The court was reestablished in 2002 by rebranding the existing religious court available in all Indonesian provinces, including Aceh. Unlike religious courts in other parts of Indonesia which adjudicate only Islamic marital, property, and financial cases, this new branded court in Aceh has wider jurisdictions including Islamic criminal justice. With the passage of a qanun and expanded in 2003, three qanuns on criminal justice that stipulated the banning of *khamr* (liquor), the prohibition of *maisir* (gambling), and the prosecution of khalwat had authorized the Mahkamah Syar`iyah to examine offenses by Muslims as well as by non-Muslim residents.

The three qanuns above were then revised and updated by the Department of Islamic Shari`a (Dinas Syariat Islam, DSI). In 2009, the DSI initiated the drafting of newly compiled jinaya rules that added seven new injunctions against Islamic crimes into the 2003 qanuns.[7] Additionally, to strengthen the legal competence of judges at the Mahkamah Syar`iyah, the shari`a office launched an Islamic justice development program (Bina

Peradilan Islam). Under this program, both existing judges and judges newly assigned to the region of Aceh received special training on how to address and adjudicate the Islamic criminal offenses included into the new qanun on jinaya. Of 132 judges at the Mahkamah Syar`iyah,[8] none have a legal background with this sort of crime.[9] Their knowledge of Islamic criminal justice is limited and is mostly based on workshops they have attended as well as literature read in their free time.[10]

The Mahkamah Syar`iyah was set up in Aceh as a modern court that welcomes every citizen regardless of their religious background. Although the Shari`a Court in Aceh was introduced in 2001 primarily to adjudicate Muslim litigants and offenders, the court has addressed both Muslim and non-Muslim individuals living in or visiting Aceh who violate the qanun stipulations. Initially, with the enactment of Law 11/2006 on the Governance of Aceh, non-Muslim offenders were given a choice to go either to civil court or to the Shari`a Court. Following the introduction of several new Islamic criminal stipulations in the revised qanun on jinaya in 2014, however, all Islamic penal cases that involve non-Muslim offenders began to be examined only by the Shari`a Court, and non-Muslim offenders lost the right to choose which court they preferred. This practical change of jurisdiction of Aceh's Shari`a Court means that the court's jurisdiction exceeds even the jurisdiction of the Malaysian shari`a court, which, as noted by Farid Sufian Shuaib and Helen Ting Mu Hung, only deals with cases submitted or committed by Muslim parties.[11] It is no wonder, then, that there has been fierce criticism, considering that the qanun on jinaya has unfairly affected non-Muslim residents in Aceh.[12]

Non-Muslims under the Qanuns

The 2015 National Demographic Census of Indonesia counted only 1.51 percent of the residents of Aceh as non-Muslims, a category that includes Christians, Catholics, Buddhists, and Hindus. After two decades of operation of the shari`a court in Aceh, some of these non-Muslim offenders have been punished based on the qanun on jinaya. These offenders are sentenced largely because they are found guilty of khalwat,[13] gambling, and all related to liquor. Table 4.1 shows the number of penal cases involving Muslim and non-Muslim offenders in which offenders were sentenced by reference to the qanun on jinaya.[14]

Table 4.1. Non-Muslim Offenders and Jinaya Cases in Aceh, 2016–2019

Mahkamah Syar`iyah (cities and districts)	Total of Jinaya Cases	Non-Muslim Cases: Single or All Non-Muslim Offenders	Non-Muslim Cases: Committed along with Muslim Offenders
Banda Aceh	134	–	3
Bener Meriah	16	–	–
Bireuen	9	–	–
Blangkajren	NA	NA	NA
Blangpidie	NA	NA	NA
Calang	3	–	–
Idi	33	–	–
Jantho	60	–	–
Kualasimpang	58	–	1
Kutacane	28	2	2
Langsa	7	–	–
Lhokseumawe	19	1	–
Lhoksukon	6	–	–
Mereudu	10	–	–
Meulaboh	NA	NA	NA
Sabang	28	–	–
Sigli	63	1	–
Sinabang	NA	NA	NA
Singkil	23	2	–
Subulussalam	NA	NA	NA
Takengon	25	1	–
Tapaktuan	6	–	–
Total	**528**	**7**	**6**

Source: Mahkamah Syar`iyah Verdict Directory, 2016–September 2019. NA = not available.

As the enforcement of shari`a in Aceh is within the framework of national laws and government administration, it has been assured that its implementation will not affect non-Muslim rights. Article 127(2) of Law 11/2006 stipulated that the government of Aceh, at the provincial and district levels, guaranteed the freedom of faith and worship of non-Muslim religious believers. Instead of emphasizing the intertwined identity of Islam and Acehnese culture, however, some proponents of shari`a in Aceh have ignored this principle of religious freedom, throwing the equality of non-Muslims before the law into question. In fact, it remains unclear how to put into practice the stipulation of Article 126(2) of Law 11/2006 that "everyone who lives or is present in Aceh has to respect the implementation of shari`a" while at the same time ensuring that non-Muslim minorities are not threatened or disadvantaged.

Adjudicating Non-Muslim Offenders

There are two recognized processes for settling penal cases in Indonesia—namely, court settlement and out-of-court settlement. Indrianto Seno Adji has called the latter a mediation process for the purpose of restorative justice.[15] It is also called "penal mediation," popularly known as "alternative dispute resolution." Although this particular settlement is widely known in Aceh villages, the implementation of shari`a penal law in Aceh that involves a non-Muslim offender only applies the court settlement method.

Three principles govern how the shari`a court deals with penal cases in Aceh. These are (i) the territory principle, (ii) the combination of territory and personality principles, and (iii) the subjugation principle.

The Territory Principle

The Indonesian criminal legal system applies the territory principle, as does the shari`a court in Aceh, since it is part of the Indonesian system. The territory principle specifies punishment for anyone (including non-Muslim) who has infringed the qanun on jinaya in any area of Aceh province. No exceptions are made for people who come from other provinces in Indonesia or from foreign countries. Enforcing this principle means that the locus of action becomes a primary ground in the decision to punish an offender. Under this principle, any offender in Aceh cannot escape being prosecuted except when they have committed an offense outside of Aceh territory (as stated by Article 129(3) of Law 11/2006). A resident from North Sumatra who visited Aceh and happened to breach the qanun in a way punishable with caning, for instance, would be executed in Aceh. Article 5 of the qanun on jinaya stipulates that an allegation is lawful even if an injunction of shari`a is not provisioned for in the National Book of Criminal Acts—that is, if the injunction that was violated in Aceh has no standing outside of Aceh. This stipulation is also supported by Article 129(2) of Law 11/2006.

The Personality Principle Combined with the Territory Principle

The personality principle requires that a religious adherence is the basis for applying shari`a rules. This principle applies to any Muslim (Acehnese or otherwise) who commits an Islamic offense as stipulated in the qanun of jinaya in any area of Aceh province. Under this principle, non-Muslims are excluded. The personality principle has been combined with the territory principle in implementing the qanun of jinaya. Whereas it is clear that the enforcement of shari`a law in Aceh is based on religious adherence, an Acehnese Muslim cannot be prosecuted in reference to the qanun when he or she commits an offense stipulated in the qanun *outside* of Aceh territory (Article 129(3) of Law 11/2006). Thus, the enforcement of shari`a penal law for Muslim offenders in Aceh adopts both the principle of territory and the principle of personality.

The Subjugation Principle

According to the qanun in Aceh, the subjugation principle can be applied when a non-Muslim offender willingly seeks and opts to be adjudicated by the shari`a law. In this case, the qanun gives non-Muslim offenders an option to subjugate themselves to shari`a rules. This principle can be traced back to the *Indische Staatsregeling* provision of the Dutch colonial era of Indonesia by which residents were divided into Indigenous, European, Chinese, and Far East people.[16] All these groups had their own courts and legal processes. In certain cases, a particular group was allowed to subjugate to the other group's court and legal processes.

There are two types of subjugation: voluntary (*Vrijwillige Onderwerping*) and tacit (*Verorderstelde Onderwerping*). The qanun in Aceh applies the former to provide non-Muslim offenders with the option to go to either the civil court or the shari`a court. It is important to note that the voluntary subjugation principle applies to *ta'zir* offenses (i.e., maisir, or gambling offenses) as well as to *hudud* offenses (i.e., *khamr*, or liquor-related offenses) whether an offense is individually committed by a non-Muslim offender or jointly committed with Muslim resident(s). This provision is arranged in the Qanun 6/2014 on jinaya law, Article 5(b).

However, non-Muslim offenders would be automatically prosecuted by the qanun without the prerequisite of their subjugation if they commit an offense included in the qanun (such as khalwat and ikhtilat), whereas this kind of offense is not regulated in the national laws. This is because Article 5(c) of the same qanun does not disqualify non-Muslims in Aceh who commit such particular kind of Islamic crimes. Article 5(c) stipulates that the qanun on jinaya shall apply to anyone in Aceh who commits an offense included in the qanun that is not regulated in the national laws regardless of the religious background of the offender.[17] In spite of the fact that the subjugation principle in the qanun may provide non-Muslim offenders with a legal choice to get a lighter punishment than imprisonment, this provision makes shari`a law in Aceh a subject of continued controversy and fierce debate.

The Arrest and Investigation Process

The Satuan Polisi Pamong Praja (Satpol PP)–Wilayatul Hisbah, popularly known as the Shari`a Police, are at the forefront of the implementation of shari`a in Aceh. They have direct responsibility for enforcing the qanun. In addition to conducting random patrols of the streets, the Shari`a Police commonly follow up on information received from villagers regarding the infringement of qanun. As far as legal procedure is concerned, the Shari`a Police have the authority to question and arrest offenders. When an offender is caught red-handed by villagers, the Shari`a Police will come to the site to investigate the case and transport the suspect to their office to prepare a report. This report records full information about the suspect, including residential address, age, occupation, marital status, and religion. The last two items are crucial in the report. Marital status is relevant to cases of accused khalwat, ikhtilat, or *zina* (adultery). Religious affiliation is relevant to determine whether an offense involves a non-Muslim. The Shari`a Police then informs the family or the spouse of the offender of what had happened and the legal process that will follow.

The accused are held in the detention room available at the police station until the next trial period.[18] The duration of detention depends on the length of the legal process, which involves preparing the offense report and prosecution documents as well trial at the court, decision on a verdict, and sentencing. For the initial step, the shari`a investigator explains to the suspect that she or he has the right to obtain a lawyer. This is to ensure that the investigation process runs fairly for the accused. According to one of our informants, however, no non-Muslim offender has ever requested a legal aid or hired a lawyer. Perhaps, there are two reasons why a non-Muslim offender does not need a lawyer. First, hiring a lawyer is costly and many of these offenders cannot afford to pay. Second, since a declaration[19] is already made at the beginning of the investigation process that there is no objection to being summoned by the Shari`a Court, a non-Muslim offender might think it would be irrelevant to have a lawyer.

The Prosecution Process

At the beginning of the prosecution process, a non-Muslim offender is asked whether she or he wants to sign a "no objection declaration" accepting that the Mahkamah Syar`iyah would examine the case. During our interview with the investigators, they showed us a sample of a signed declaration form. On this form, an offender provides relevant information such as name, date of birth, sex, religion, marital status, occupation, and address. This document of subjugation statement becomes a confirmation that non-Muslim offender voluntarily subjugates under the shari`a law without any coercion or threat. This confirmation is crucial to authorize the Mahkamah Syar`iyah to adjudicate the case and to determine the kind of law that would be applied for the whole trial process.

After the investigation report is finalized, it is then delivered to the state attorney (*kejaksaan negeri*) for the preparation of the prosecution document. At this stage, the process refers to the *Book of National Procedural Criminal Law* (*Kitab Undang-undang Hukum Acara Pidana*, KUHP), which describes the details of prosecution processes. That the implementing procedures of qanun in Aceh should refer to this book is quite ironic, given that the book was almost entirely adopted from the Dutch colonial legal system. Here, the implementation of shari`a penal law in Aceh has a kind of authoritative bias. This situation is unavoidable, given that Article 39 of Law 16/2004 specifies that the state attorney in Aceh has authority to deal with Islamic criminal affairs, but no further regulation is in place to guide the jinaya prosecution process in Aceh. Thus, it is no wonder if the National Procedural Criminal Law remains applicable in all kinds of prosecutions, including in Islamic penal cases. To obtain consistent application of the jinaya law in Aceh, it would be necessary to have specific regulations on jinaya procedures as well as a special jinaya prosecutor at the office of the state attorney.

At the conclusion of the prosecution process, an offender is customarily given additional detention days—perhaps one week or more, depending on when the prosecution document was completed. The prosecution officer works with the recent qanun on jinaya to determine the appropriate type of punishment, the amount of caning that will be charged to the prisoner if applicable, and whether exceptions are available for both hudud and ta`zir cases. Qanun 6/2014 accommodates ten actions as the outcome of a jinaya case. Hudud is action with punishment that is clearly described in the qanun, which effectively is caning, for liquor drinking, zina (adultery), sexual harassment, and *qadhaf* (accusing others of doing adultery). Ta'zir is action that is provisioned in qanun with a choice of punishment that takes character into account. The choices have upper and lower levels. These include caning, ransom, prison, and restitution for offenses including maisir (gambling), khalwat, ikhtilath, rape, *liwath* (sodomy), and *musahaqah* (lesbianism).

Although there are limits specifying minimum and maximum punishment, the prosecutor can decide how to charge an offender within the range of penalties. The final verdict then rests with the judge at the Shari`a Court. Before sending the prosecution document to the Shari`a Court, the prosecutor needs to check whether a non-Muslim offender has made the subjugation declaration. Once all the documentation is complete, it is submitted to the Shari`a Court. In the case where a non-Muslim offender does not sign the declaration and refuses to be adjudicated based on the qanun jinaya, the ensuing process of prosecution will go to the Civil Court and not to the Shari`a Court.

Trial Process and Verdict

Having received the prosecution document, the Shari`a Court prepares for trial. Regarding this trial process, it is worthwhile to identify some general observations from the shari`a courtroom. First, no provision exists regarding how to establish the required team of judges (Majelis Hakim), comprised of a chair and two members, to hear penal cases. Since judges at the Shari`a Court with a criminal law background are rare, available judges are assigned to examine cases by following a list. Only a few of them have experience dealing with penal cases that involve non-Muslim offenders. Thus, the adjudication of non-Muslim offenders is not considered to constitute a special case at the Shari`a Court.

For many decades, the judges at the Shari`a Court mostly deal with personal or family laws. Later, since the last two decades, they have an additional jurisdiction to examine disputes related to Islamic finance. Given the lack of relevant training background as well as less experience in adjudicating penal cases, these judges have to "learn by doing" the whole process of examining Islamic penal cases.

Second, the shari`a judge has no authority to go beyond what has been set in the qanun as the provisioned limits of punishment nor to make exceptions for non-Muslim offenders. It has been determined to treat non-Muslim offenders the same as their Muslim conationals since they have declared themselves willing to be adjudicated under the applied shari`a law in Aceh.

Third, the chief judge of the Shari`a Court has no interest in clarifying or verifying the motivation by which non-Muslim offenders have subjugated themselves to the court. For the judges at the Shari`a Court, the issue of subjugation is not principal. It is sufficient for them to know that the offender's declaration letter has been submitted to the court. The chief judge normally begins the trial by asking whether a non-Muslim offender has agreed to the enforcement of shari`a. Unlike in family cases, where the chief judge usually offers advice and mediation, in jinaya cases the chief judge has no obligation to provide non-Muslim offenders with advice or mediation. It is not the task of the judges of the Shari`a Court to ensure that non-Muslim offenders are satisfied with the court's legal procedures.

Fourth, the adjudication process of jinaya cases at the Shari`a Court is quite uncommon, a scenario that both investigators and prosecutors would rarely encounter at the Civil Court.[20] When examining an Islamic penal case, the Shari`a judges often appear relaxed and sometimes make "unexpected comments" when hearing the case. Perhaps this has much to do with their previous experiences in examining disputes between husbands and wives. This is unusual for criminal trials in Indonesia, which are normally rigorous and sometimes full of tension. From an observation at a trial, both the prosecutor and the investigator looked indifferent to the way the judges examine the case. Apparently, such kind of process is regarded tolerable to take place in the shari`a courtrooms of Aceh.

Fifth, the organization of Aceh Shari`a Court lacks required capacities to represent itself as an Islamic criminal court in its ideal sense.

There is still much to do to make the implementation of shari`a penal law effective in achieving its objective of preventing criminal cases from taking place in Aceh. The initiative of the Shari`a Court judge is important in ensuring whether non-Muslims are wholeheartedly willing to subjugate themselves to the Shari`a Court and to be examined under the qanun. Yet, in many cases, the judges at the Shari`a Court take a passive position rather than being active in producing innovative decisions or legal breakthrough opinions to improve the implementation of qanun in Aceh for non-Muslims.

Execution of Public Caning

Execution or carrying out a punishment is regulated in a number of parts of Qanun 5/2018. There are three types of punishment that may be imposed on Muslim or non-Muslim offenders: ransom, imprisonment, or caning. Whereas ransom and imprisonment are penalties derived from the National Criminal Law, caning is specific to Aceh's qanun, which is considered ta'zir. As a part of ta'zir, caning is incorrectly regarded as a genuine Islamic punishment. In fact, such penalty has been long and widely practiced in Southeast Asia including in a non-Muslim country such as Singapore.

As far as the type of punishment imposed on non-Muslim offenders is concerned, there is no consensus among people in Aceh as to which one is more severe than the others. For the investigators as well as the prosecutors, these three types constitute different hierarchical levels of punishment in which they start first by providing ransom, followed by caning as the next penalty before giving a sentence of imprisonment for repeating the same offense. It has been acknowledged that caning is a light punishment with an educational or reflective purpose (*tadabbur*). This corporal punishment is thus intended to wound the pride more than the flesh. If a non-Muslim offender repeats the crime, the investigator may ask the prosecutor to send the case to be examined by the Civil Court. In the investigator's view, imprisonment is a tougher punishment than caning. However, the proponents of shari`a consider caning to be much more pivotal in Islam than ransom or imprisonment. For them, caning is more relevant and necessary to demonstrate that the implementation of shari`a seriously takes place in Aceh.

The first public caning took place in June 2005. This was the case where more than twenty Muslim offenders were found guilty of committing the offence of gambling. They were sentenced by the Shari`a Court of Bireun to be caned in the mosque yard.[21] More than ten years later, public caning that involved non-Muslim offenders took place in 2016 for the first time. The Shari`a Court of Takengon sentenced a female Christian who was proven to have acted against the qanun jinaya (i.e., selling alcoholic drinks). She was lashed thirty times at the mosque yard as well. Despite criticism by human rights activists and differing opinions among Indonesian legal scholars about this case, such public caning has opened a door of punishing a resident or a visitor to Aceh who violates the rules of a faith she or he does not observe.

Since the very first idea of the caning penalty was introduced in early 2000s, the venue for caning has been disputed among relevant stakeholders as to whether it should take place at the mosque yard or elsewhere. The qanun on jinaya stipulated the caning should be held in public, usually at a mosque yard after the Friday prayer. After a few years of caning took place in Aceh, the front yard of the mosque as the caning location presented problems. The shari`a investigator notes that there was a report by religious authorities at the mosque who requested the relocation of canings to the prison because people were interfering, shouting, and taking photos of the canings with no respect for the process.

When the government of Aceh sought to revise the provision of caning location, a controversy arose. Governor Irwandi Yusuf, when returned to the governor's position for a second time in 2017, revised the regulations regarding public caning, usually conducted in front of the mosque, to be carried out at prisons instead. Many wondered whether he was pressured to enact this change by the international community, but he argued that he designed the regulation to hide the punishment process from children. He also wanted to ease the way for potential investors to come to Aceh. Irwandi received support from academics and politicians, though many people in Aceh were against him.

Despite the Governor's Regulation 5/2018 ordering the move of canings to prisons, people in Aceh resisted the idea of moving the caning process from a mosque yard to a prison. This shift in location was understood by many as undermining the prestige of shari`a and the idea of tadabbur (providing a lesson) in the public arena. For them, the relocation of caning to the closed areas in a prison would not achieve the ultimate objective of caning punishment in public, which is to wound the pride of an offender in particular and to provide a lesson for society in general.

Public Responses to Caning Non-Muslims

The public has reacted to the caning of non-Muslims since the first such caning was publicized by the media in April 2016. The issue is not only religion but also gender: the offender in the first case was an old woman who produced, sold, and distributed liquor in Takengon, the capital of Aceh Tengah, where the dominant population is ethnic Gayo Muslims. This district is known for multiracial residents, though they are a minority, including Batak and Chinese who share a single vihara and two churches for Catholic and Protestant adherents. The Protestants, including the woman who was caned, Mrs. Remita Sinaga, are usually migrants from North Sumatra, a neighbor of Aceh Tenggara district, to Aceh Tengah. Most of the Batak in Gayo highlands work as traders. There is a lot of vegetable, fruit, spice, coffee, and fashion trading among the Batak and other ethnic groups, including the Chinese, Minangnese, and Javanese.[22]

A year after the first caning of a non-Muslim offender, another caning took place in Jantho, Aceh Besar. This time, two male Buddhists were lashed on March 10, 2017 for committing a gambling offense. The prosecution was responded by a scholar from outside of Aceh, Wasisto Raharjo Jati, a researcher at the Indonesia Institute of Science. In an online interview, he explained that charging non-Muslims with caning penalty is a kind of substantial bias of shari`a law. According to him, caning only covers the humiliation aspect, but no one ensures the post-caning outcome will have a deterrent effect. For Jati, an ultimate goal of punishment would not be achieved by caning non-Muslim offenders, where they consider caning is merely a light punishment.[23]

The media actively inform the public responses about canings, particularly when women and non-Muslims are sentenced under the shari`a law. It can be understood from the language of media reports that media sympathy lies with vulnerable and minority groups. The media also focuses on why the government applies caning to non-Muslims. This is a crucial issue for human rights activists, and it raises questions about why the government is applying caning to non-Muslims when shari`a is supposed to be only for Muslims. The media do not provide information about the subjugation process, though subjugation is determined before any non-Muslim offender is being prosecuted.[24]

To obtain an official clarification, journalists requested an explanation from the head of Aceh's shari`a office, the prosecutor, and the investigator regarding why non-Muslims should be included in the enforcement of shari`a law. All of these officers explained that in jinaya cases, non-Muslim offenders would be prosecuted and sentenced by referring to jinaya qanun should two conditions be available: (i) when a committed jinaya offense is not regulated under national law, and (ii) when an offender voluntarily confirms to be whipped as stipulated by qanun rather than paying ransom or imprisonment.[25]

In response to these consequences, journalists share statements from human rights activists who want non-Muslims to be excluded from prosecution under shari`a law. Human rights activists (e.g., Lies Marcos and Otto Syamsuddin Ishak) contend for this provision by questioning the right of the central government to control the application of shari`a law in Aceh. They criticize shari`a lawmakers for offering no choices for non-Muslims besides those written in the qanun. They also question the government of Aceh for seemingly trying to expand the application of shari`a to non-Muslims.[26]

On a different occasion, the community leaders of Singkil considered the sentence in the case of Karnius Bancin, a non-Muslim prosecuted under shari`a law for violating the prohibition on liquor trading in August 2019, to have been incorrectly applied. The villagers in Singkil district protested this case, questioning why only Bancin (an offender in this case) was prosecuted while an officer of Wilayatul Hisbah who committed an Islamic crime in the other case had never been executed. The journalist sought clarification from the prosecutor until it was clear that the caning occurred based on the offender's request.[27]

National as well as Aceh lawmakers have not significantly taken up feedback regarding non-Muslim subjugation under shari'a law. At least, there has been no change in the treatment of non-Muslims under the qanun on jinaya since people began publicly voicing their criticism. It is clear, though, that subjugation remains a hardly discussed topic among law scholars.[28]

The Institute of Criminal Justice Reform, an active civil society organization that monitors developments in criminal law, discovers that shari`a law and its caning practice have been applied more excessively in Aceh.[29] In this case, the institute gives only a small amount of attention to the situation of the non-Muslim position. Instead, it focuses primarily on opposing the use of corporal punishment in Indonesian criminal law in general and advocates the elimination of caning penalty in Aceh in particular. The institute's division of advocacy matches the limited voice of Aceh's civil society organizations regarding the situation of non-Muslims. However, there has been no significant change in the application of shari`a law to the non-Muslim population in Aceh. As of August 2019, in fact, a young male Buddhist was lashed twenty-seven times in Banda Aceh for committing ikhtilat offense with his Muslim girlfriend.[30]

Conclusion

This chapter remarks on the increasing authority of the Islamic court, or Mahkamah Syar'iyah, in Aceh over all citizens regardless of their religious affiliation. From 2003 to 2014, the Shari`a Court was assigned only to penal cases involving Muslim individuals. It did not accept cases in which non-Muslim offenders were subjugated to the jurisdiction of the Islamic court.

Since 2015, the enforcement of shari`a, the caning penalty in particular, has been applied to any non-Muslim offender who happens to live in or visit Aceh. This condition is based on two different principles in the criminal law—namely, the territorial principle and the personality principle. Some lawmakers in Aceh may have thought that excluding non-Muslims from the implementation of Islamic penal law would be unjust to Muslim people. Therefore, given that certain offenses (*jarimah*) regulated in the qanun are not provisioned for in the national law, non-Muslims had to be included in this regional legal system.

All this confirms that the politics of dominant culture has been largely applied in contemporary Aceh. Thus, it obligates non-Muslims to respect the implementation of shari`a jinaya in Aceh by way of making in the qanun a vague provision for non-Muslim subjugation to shari`a law. The subjugation of non-Muslim offenders, in fact, has become a loophole or even a ploy for them to get a simple legal process and light punishment (i.e., caning). The enforcement of Islamic penal law for non-Muslim offenders seeks to meet these purposes. With this notion in mind, the citizenship in Aceh has been unequal between Muslim and non-Muslim residents. As a result, equal citizenship has been generally deficient and vague thanks to the politics of dominant culture applied in Aceh.

PART III

The Causes of Interreligious Exclusions

CHAPTER 5

Mutual Ignorance and Unreciprocated Relations

In our fieldwork, we were surprised to learn that many religious leaders, both Muslim and non-Muslim, as well as government officers and religious representatives in the state-created Forum for the Harmony of Interreligious Communities (FKUB), knew little about other religions. Muslim leaders and representatives in the FKUB, for instance, proposed that Christians should share the same church buildings like Muslims who, despite their sectarian differences, share the same mosque. When we explained that in Christianity, especially Protestantism, many denominations have different ways of worship that prevent them from sharing the same churches, they suspected this was only a strategy to expand Christianity.

Similarly, although they live in a province that officially implements shari`a law, many non-Muslim leaders know little about Islam. What they know of shari`a is that it only applies to Muslims and does not affect non-Muslims. They do not know, by and large, that non-Muslims can be the subjects of shari`a punishment if they violate shari`a qanuns, though they are given the choice as to whether to submit themselves either to Jinayat Qanun or to the national laws. Although the most recent Jinayat Qanun was enacted in 2014, replacing the earlier three passed in 2003, the knowledge of non-Muslims in Aceh about the shari`a qanun was not updated.[1] We found, too, that academics and university graduates are not so different, with the exception of those in the field of religious studies.

The "mutual ignorance" or "interreligious ignorance" between different religious communities of Aceh is widespread.

This chapter delves into the problem of mutual ignorance between Muslim and non-Muslim citizens in Aceh, seeking to discover the reasons behind it. We argue that being an absolute majority that has been granted special autonomy to implement shari`a has made Muslims ignorant of religious minorities and their religions because they are overconfident and feel that minorities cannot much affect their lives. Similarly, although they feel excluded from almost every field of life, minorities are ignorant of the ways of Islam, with the exception that they know shari`a is only for Muslims and affects their internal religious life. This mutual ignorance has been created by, and has also created, unreciprocated interreligious relations. We focus in this chapter on analyzing the absence of interfaith education and genuine societal interfaith institutions as two key factors that drive and deepen religious communities' ignorance of each other.

We focus on these issues because we assume that education and societal deliberative institutions are fundamental for building mutual understanding among citizens, including among religious communities. The state, indeed, has managed democratic intervention through civic education and the establishment of the FKUB. Due to the strong structural and cultural biases of the majority, however, these state interventions cannot bring about equal citizenship and have instead become means to perpetuate the mutual ignorance of religious communities in Aceh.

The Legal Status of Education in Aceh

Law No. 44/1999, which gave Aceh special status in the fields of religion, customs, education, and the role of ulama, was followed by the issuance of Qanun 6/2000 on the inclusion of Islamic subjects in public schools (*sekolah*). This qanun was strengthened by Law 18/2001 on Aceh special autonomy in which Aceh was given authority over its own education system.

Aceh's education system is based on the teachings of Islam and Islamic cultural values. In 2003, the central government issued the Law on the National Education System, which states, "Students have the right to have religious education according to their religious affiliation and to be taught by teachers of a similar faith." Later, this was strengthened by Law 11/2006 on the Governance of Aceh, some of whose chapters are devoted to Islamic education, strengthening aspects of education that are specific to Aceh within the framework of national education. Then 2008 saw the issuance of Qanun 5/2008 on Islamic education. Qanun 11/2014 on Education, article 8.1.a, uses similar language to the Law on the National Education System, but it also reads, "The national education system implemented in Aceh is based on Islamic values." In 2015, Aceh's parliament passed Qanun 9/2015, which revised Qanun 11/2014 on the organization of education. It contained an important point for our purpose—that is, it formulated the "Aceh Islamic curriculum" (*Kurikulum Aceh yang Islami*).

To implement the privilege of managing its own education, Aceh established its own Education Council (Majelis Pendidikan Aceh), which not only guarantees that all children and youth get a proper education but also ensures that education in Aceh does not deviate from Islamic shari`a and local wisdom.

The Madrasaization of Public School

Islamic education has become an important aspect of Acehnese society. Traditionally, Aceh's centers of Islamic learning have included *meunasah* (a local prayer venue) and *dayah* (Islamic boarding schools). These education institutions have existed since the early Islamization of Aceh, developing as centers of learning during the sultanate period.[2] In *meunasah*, children learn how to read the Qur'an and how to perform prayers, as well as the basic teachings of Islam. Those who want to learn further of Islam go to *dayah*, where they learn about the various branches of Islamic knowledge written in Arabic or Jawi (Malay or Acehnese in Arabic script) and in line with the teachings of Sunni doctrine (*Ahl al-Sunnah wa al-Jama`ah*). No instruction is offered that enables the students to understand other religions.[3] In dayah and villages, ulama have a central role in constructing students' and villagers' understanding of Islam and other religions.

In addition to these two traditional education systems, children and young people go to madrasa. In Arabic, *madrasa* means "school," but in Aceh (as in all of Indonesia) it refers to an Islamic religious school in which most of the curriculum is religious instruction. Some madrasas are attached to *dayah* or managed by (Islamic) foundations (*yayasan*) or Islamic organizations, while others are state owned. Knowledge of other religions is usually obtained through teachers' explanations of other subjects, but these explanations usually aim to show the superiority of Islam. In Aceh's border areas of Singkil, Subulussalam, Kutacane, Tamiang, and Langsa, moreover, there are some *dayah perbatasan* (border Islamic boarding schools) that aim to protect Aceh children from becoming targets of Kristenisasi (Christian missions) or *pemurtadan* (apostasy).[4]

In addition to madrasas being maintained, public (general) schools become madrasa-like through the insertion of Islamic religious instruction and information. There are no big differences between madrasa and public schools, except that the former are still called madrasa and the later sekolah. As far as the curriculum for religious subjects, sekolah have similar subjects to madrasa. Both types of school teach the Qur'an, Hadith, *'aqīdah* (Islamic theology), *fiqh* (Islamic jurisprudence), *akhlāq* (Islamic ethics), *Tārikh* (Islamic history), and Arabic. Some public schools also teach *kitab kuning* (the books of Islamic knowledge in Arabic), such as the *Kitāb Matn taqrīb*, the *Masāil al-muhtadī*, or the *Akhlāq li al-banīn*. These kitab are read in dayah but not in madrasas. Srimulyani called the phenomenon of the similarity of madrasa and sekolah a result of the "madrasaization of [public] school."[5]

Based on the Qanun Aceh 9/2015, the Aceh Education Council formulated an Aceh Islamic curriculum for kindergarten, elementary, junior high, and high schools as well as special education (Art. 19:1d). The Aceh Islamic curriculum, according to Syaridin, the head of the Aceh Office of Education, "is [the] national curriculum [with the addition of] Islamic and local wisdom content, meaning that the national curriculum is implemented fully by fulfilling its minimum standard but integrated with Islamic materials and values, [as well as] Aceh local content."[6] In practice, this amounts to the madrasaization of Aceh's public schools. In May 2019, about two hundred teachers of senior high school from twenty-three districts and municipalities participated in training on the Aceh Islamic curriculum in Banda Aceh. Whereas in the national curriculum there is only one class for Islamic religious instruction, in the Aceh Islamic curriculum, religious instruction is divided into instruction in the Qur'an and Hadith, 'aqīdah and akhlāq, fiqh, Islamic history, and Arabic language. Significantly more instructional time is required for this curriculum to be taught to students.

In addition to completing an Islamic curriculum, Muslim students must wear Islamic attire. Qanun 9/2015 specifies that the government of Aceh has the authority to facilitate the formulation of the curriculum of traditional dayah (*dayah salafiyah*).⁷ No point in the Qanun 9/2015, or its previous versions, demonstrates any concern for other religions, let alone for building bridges between different religious believers. On the contrary, the Aceh Islamic curriculum is formulated in part on Qanun 8/2015 on Cultivation and Protection of Belief (*Aqidah*). This means that education in Aceh must be based on Islamic shari`a and must forward the obligation to cultivate and protect Islamic belief. The government of Aceh has created a Module of Islamic Worldview (*Modul Wawasan Ke-Islaman*) for public school teachers. There is also training for trainers for public school teachers to disseminate the Islamic worldview during Academic Orientation Week (Masa Orientasi Siswa) for new students. This training for trainers was organized by the provincial Ministry of Religious Affairs and the DSI.⁸ Apart from that, teachers from public schools were trained on the Aceh Islamic curriculum.⁹

The problem is that public schools in Aceh, like other public schools in Indonesia, are supposed to be open to all children regardless of religion. Non-Muslim students are given a choice to be in class or to be outside the class during Islamic religious instruction.¹⁰ If there are teachers of their same faith, non-Muslim students can get religious instruction from those teachers. If not, the school offers cooperation with local religious institutions, such as a church for Christian students or vihara for Buddhist students, in order for the latter to give religious instructions and marks to the students. This is the case even in schools where the number of Christian students is significant. According to 2016 data, for example, in State Senior High School 1, Gunung Meriah, Singkil, there were 30 Christian students out of 742 students (the rest were mostly Muslims), but they had no teacher for Christian instruction. At Sikeras Elementary School in Suro Makmur subdistrict, Singkil, there were 120 Christian students out of 169 students, meaning they were the majority (70 percent), but they, too, had no teacher of their religion.¹¹

This situation holds not only for Islamic and public schools but also for Protestant and Catholic schools. These are found only in a handful of districts and municipalities, including Banda Aceh and Aceh Tenggara. They adopt most of the national curriculum but have their own Protestant or Catholic religious instruction. There is no instruction, however, that enables students to understand other religions, particularly Islam and shari`a. We underline Islam and shari`a here because the non-Muslim students live in a Muslim-majority province that implements Islamic law. Even though it is understandable that the schools should want to protect students' belief in Christianity, the absence of instruction about Islam might lead to ignorance of Islam and of shari`a in Aceh. This is what we have called "mutual ignorance": Muslims do not understand the religions of minorities, and non-Muslim minorities do not understand Islam, the religion of majority.

It would be possible for Aceh's education system to make space for non-Muslims based on the Qanun 11/2014 on Education, whose Article 13 reads, "The government of Aceh and district/municipality governments, in accordance with each authority, are obliged to: a. provide services and facilitate education in accordance with the National Education Standard; b. guarantee the organization of qualified, apportioned, just and Islamic education; c. provide teachers and administrative staff according to the need of education unit (including: c.1. to guarantee wider access for students to their rights)." Interpretations of this passage, however, depend on how the government of Aceh understands "Islamic" in this passage and whether it refers to prophetic values of blessing to the universe (*rahmah li l-'alamin*) and justice, or whether it refers to Muslim identity. The Aceh government seems to have adopted the latter notion of the meaning of "Islamic"—at least so far.

Shari`a Instruction in Higher Education

Indonesian higher education institutions are divided into Islamic and general schools, and both categories include private and state-owned institutions. The former are administered by the Ministry of Religious Affairs and the latter by the Ministry of Education.[12] State Islamic higher education institutions comprise State Islamic Universities (UINs), State Institutes of Islamic Studies (IAINs), and State Colleges of Islamic Studies (STAINs), as well as private Islamic institutes and colleges.

This is also the case for Aceh. In Aceh, there is one state-owned UIN, Ar-Raniry, three IAINs (Langsa, Lhokseumawe, and Takengon), and one STAIN (Teungku Dirundeng Meulaboh). Having transformed itself from an IAIN to a UIN in 2013, Ar-Raniry contains faculties that integrate Islamic studies with general sciences, such as the faculties of Ushuluddin (Islamic theology) and philosophy, shari`a and law, tarbiyah (education) and teaching, adab (literature) and humanities, Da'wah and communication, Islamic economics and business, science and technology, psychology, social science, and government science as well as a graduate school. IAIN and STAIN have faculties only of Islamic studies, such as ushuluddin, da'wah, tarbiyah, adab, and syari'ah.

Here, we will focus on UIN Ar-Raniry. As Ar-Raniry is an education institution under the aegis of the Ministry of Religious Affairs, Islamic religious instruction occupies a significant portion of its curriculum. Study of other religions is offered in the Faculty of Ushuluddin and Philosophy, where there are three relevant departments: comparative religions, sociology of religion, and philosophy of religion. The students of these departments are generally familiar with religions beyond Islam. It has special research institution, called Laboratory of the Study Program of the Sociology of Religion (Laboratorium Prodi Sosiologi Agama, LABPSA), whose programs include interfaith cooperation in organizing certain activities. It is perhaps the only university-based institution that facilitates such interfaith cooperation. In 2022, it transformed into an independent nongovernmental organization (NGO) with the name Laboratory of Socioreligious Development (Laboratorium Pengembangan Sosial Keagamaan), with similar abbreviation, LABPSA. However, the personnel and activists are similar—university lecturers and students. By becoming an NGO, it is more flexible for them to obtain external funding and to develop activities beyond campus.

Da'wah faculty is concerned with the issue of "trivialization of belief" (*pendangkalan akidah*) and Christian mission. It has issued an instruction letter that called on all civitas academia of the faculty to be careful to avoid any activity that could lead to this outcome.[13] It has also conducted research on protecting the border areas from Christian mission activities.[14] The lectures of the shari`a and law faculty play a vital role in the legal drafting of the shari`a qanun as well as training on Islamic shari`a for various government and education institutions. The lecturers of tarbiyah faculty contributed to the formulation of the Aceh Islamic curriculum.

Most legal drafters of shari`a qanuns are lecturers or graduates of UINs, especially from the shari`a and law faculty. Moreover, the DSI at both the provincial and district/municipal levels has been dominated by UINs alumni and the alumni of IAINs and STAINs.[15] Currently, some Islamic higher education in Aceh, UINs, IAINs, and STAINs share a course that introduces shari'a law to the students but with different names—such as *Studi Syariat Islam di Aceh* (the Study of Islamic Shari`a in Aceh) at UIN Ar Raniry and STAIN Meulaboh and *Syariah dan Adat* (Shari`a and Customary Law) at IAIN Langsa—which is taught across faculties and fields of study as a general subject. As a "new" subject and local, this course does not yet have a fixed syllabus or common teaching materials, at least until 2023. It seems that it is taught based on the instructors' experience and existing knowledge.

While UINs, IAINs, and STAINs are Islamic higher education institutions, the public (general) universities, such as Syiah Kuala and Malikussaleh, also have to implement the Aceh Islamic curriculum. It is less developed in these universities, however. In addition to the national curriculum of Religious Education (Pendidikan Agama), which is given about two hours a week early in the semester, there are local courses or programs. In Syiah Kuala University, for instance, students should pass the "Character Building I and II" course (0 credit point) containing such subjects as correct reading of the Qur'an, *fiqh 'ibadah* (particularly ablution and prayers), *aqidah*, *akhlaq*, Prophetic biography (*sirah*), and Islamic worldview. If they pass this course, they can proceed with the religious education course.[16] In Malikussaleh University, apart from religious education, there are courses called *aqidah* and ethics and Kemalikussalehan (Malikussaleh education). Whereas the former aims to educate students in correct Islamic belief and good ethical behavior, the latter aims to connect students with the history of the Samudera Pasai under Sultan Malikussaleh and building good characteristics of tolerance and passion, and having good conduct that are in line with the teachings of the Qur'an and the Prophetic traditions (Sunna).[17]

Aceh has no higher education institutions owned by religious minorities. Non-Muslims usually study in public universities, but there is no specific religious instruction for them, nor are there lecturers who teach non-Islamic religious subjects.

Pancasila and Civic Education

In madrasa, public schools, and Islamic and public higher education institutions, civic education (*pendidikan kewarganegaraan*) is part of the national curriculum. Through this instruction, students learn about being good citizens of Indonesia, including how to live in harmony with other citizens of different religious backgrounds. Religion is considered among many other aspects in this instruction, such as ethnic, linguistic, cultural, and political differences.

Civic education is not new to the national curriculum. It was implemented long before the "Aceh Islamic curriculum." In the 1962 curriculum, it was called "Civics," in 1968 "Pendidikan Kewargaan Negara" (National Citizenship Education), in 1975 "Pendidikan Moral Pancasila," in 1994 "Pendidikan Pencasila dan Kewarganegaraan," and in 2003 "Pendidikan Kewarganegaraan." At the university level, there was Pancasila dan Kewiraan Nasional (Pancasila and National Patriotism) in the 1960s, Pendidikan Pancasila dan Pendidikan Kewiraan (Pancasila and Patriotism Education) in 1985, and Civic Education in 2003.[18]

At Syiah Kuala University (Unsyiah), a state-owned university, and Abulyatama University, a private university, there are specific Pancasila and Civic Education programs of study for undergraduate students. At Abulyatama, such a program was established in 1985, while the one in Unsyiah seems to have been established since the first decade of the New Order period as an ideological counter to the remnants of the Darul Islam ideology and the Free Aceh Movement. In 2019, Unsyiah's Pancasila and Civic Education study program organized the Second Annual Civic Education Conference. Although the conference was about civic education, the rector said in his opening address that Indonesia has been undergoing moral and character degradation marked by violence, pornography, sexual deviance, and drug abuse.[19] Such a statement is more about education and religious ethics than it is about citizenship.

Civic education is actually a strategic form of instruction that can be used to develop students' awareness of their fellow citizens as equals regardless of religion, gender, ethnicity, and ideology. Civic education can also be used to endorse interreligious tolerance and coexistence. In Law 20/2003 on the National Education System, the aim of civic education stated as creating students who have a sense of nationalism and love of the country (Art. 37: 1). In practice, however, this instruction cannot compete with religious instruction in the framework of the Aceh Islamic curriculum, as students receive only about two hours of civic education once a week. Moreover, teachers of this subject are also trained in the Aceh Islamic curriculum and are asked to ensure that civic education does not contradict shari'a.

There is a significant gap between the principles taught in civic education and the Islamic Aceh curriculum and the realities experienced by citizens. While civic education emphasizes the equality of all citizens regardless of religion, in practice, there is a clear divide based on religious affiliation. This has led many to believe that Muslims in Aceh enjoy a privileged status akin to first-class citizens, while non-Muslims are treated as second-class citizens.

A Controversial Case

The case of Rosnida Sari offers insight into how higher education in Aceh comes to tolerate or even perpetuate interreligious ignorance. A lecturer on gender in Islam in the Faculty of Da'wa and Communication at UIN Ar-Raniry, Banda Aceh, Rosnida took her undergraduate students to the city's Protestant church in December 2014 to learn about Christian teachings and gender relations directly from the Christian priest Domidoyo Ratupenu. Her aim was for students to learn not only about gender in the Christian tradition but also about understanding others' religions and tolerance. Nothing happened after that until Sari's essay about her experience with her students appeared in *Australia Plus* a year later.[20] Her article went viral when it was circulated on social media and quoted in local mainstream media with comments from ulama, Muslim activists, and leaders of Islamic organizations.

Controversy arose. Some people charged Sari with "supporting Christian missionary activity in the hearth of Islamic ummah" and promoting trivialization of belief (*aqidah*) among her students. They considered her behavior to be dangerous. Some said she was against local culture and local wisdom, while others charged her with being against shari`a and being an apostate (*murtad*). They demanded the IAIN where she taught give her severe sanctions.

In an interview with senior journalist and human rights activist Andreas Harsono, Rosnida said that she received many messages threatening her and her family.[21] On the second day after the appearance of her article, her friends helped her and her family to leave their house after they were informed a group of people was heading to her house to attack them. Although the police succeeded in stopping the mob, Rosnida decided to leave Aceh for Medan and then for Jakarta.[22] She received support from NGOs concerned with human rights, women's rights, and interfaith relations. At the national level, she also received support from the minister of religious affairs, who commented on his Twitter account, "This lecturer should be protected." He invited Rosnida to meet with him at his office in Jakarta. Activists such as Arabiyani Abubakar and

Fuad Mardhatillah, director of the Aceh Institute, also backed Rosnida's position. Arabiyani posted on her social media about the absence of the state from the case.[23] Fuad Mardatillah encouraged people to view the case wisely, without prejudice or special interests.[24]

The Faculty of Da'wa and Communication imposed sanctions on Rosnida. First, she had to apologize openly for what she did (bringing students to the church) to the leaders and civitas academica of the Faculty of Da'wa and Communication, the rector, the parents of her students, societal leaders, and all the people of Aceh through mass media. Second, the faculty provided her with religious consultation to restore her belief (*aqidah*). Third, she was prevented from teaching and supervising student theses for two semesters. In fact, this sanction lasted beyond the specified two semesters. When we invited Rosnida to our focus group discussion in 2016, we learned she had been shifted to serving as a lecturer in the Islamic studies master's program instead of teaching in her own subject area.

Interestingly, the Islamic university Ar-Raniry has departments of comparative religion (*perbandingan agama*) in the past, and in such departments, events like Rosnida's church visit or a lecture to students by a visiting Christian priest would not be unusual. Such practices continued among a few lecturers in the Faculty of Theology and Philosophy (Fakultas Ushuluddin dan Filsafat) and have not prompted serious resistance from the public. And indeed, efforts on behalf of Islamic university lecturers to bridge mutual ignorance and promote tolerance are ongoing, though of minor impact. The program of Labpsa (Laboratorium of Penelitian Sosial Kegamaan), the Department of Sociology of Religion's social media and YouTube channel promoting tolerance and religious harmony advocacy, is one example.

Unreciprocated Relations between Religious Organizations

Each religious community has its own organization to deal with its internal needs and interests. Within Muslim circles, there are a number of countrywide organizations, such as Muhammadiyah, Nahdlatul Ulama, Dewan Dakwah, Al-Washliyah, Perti, and Islamic Defense Front (Front Pembela Islam); local or provincial organizations, such as Inshafuddin, Himpunan Ulama Dayah Aceh (Association of Dayah Ulama of Aceh), Majelis Ulama Nanggroe Aceh (Ulama Council of Aceh), and Rabitah

Thaliban Aceh; not to mention the government institution Majelis Permusyawaratan Ulama. There are even transnational movements, including Salafism, Hizbut Tahrir, and Jama'ah Tabligh (Tablighi Jama'at).

Catholic national organizations include Wanita Katolik Republik Indonesia (Catholic Women of the Republic of Indonesia), Mahasiswa Katolik Republik Indonesia (Catholic Students of the Republic of Indonesia), and Pemuda Katolik Republik Indonesia (Catholic Youth of the Republic of Indonesia). These are nonchurch organizations dedicated to supporting the mission of the Catholic Church.

Apart from individual denominations, the Protestant community in Aceh has also some organizations, such as Huria Kristen Batak Protestan and Forum Cinta Damai Aceh Singkil (The Peace and Love Forum of Aceh Singkil, Forcidas). The former is a Batak-based Protestant religious organization that is considered the third biggest religious organization in Indonesia after Nahdlatul Ulama and Muhammadiyah. Forcidas is a local organization in Singkil that aims to voice Protestant interests, especially regarding the problem of the building of churches in the region.

The organizations of the Buddhist community, whose adherents are mostly Chinese,[25] include Majelis Buddhayana Indonesia, Persatuan Umat Buddha Indonesia (the Indonesian Association of Buddhist Community), and Perkumpulan Majelis Pandita Buddha Maitreya Indonesia. Buddhayana Buddhism is organized additionally at the national level into Keluarga Buddhayana Indonesia (Indonesian Buddhayana Family), Persaudaraan Muda-Mudi Vihara-Vihara Buddhayana Indonesia (Buddhayana Viharas' Youth Brotherhood, shortened as Pemuda Buddhayana or Buddhayana Youth), and Ikatan Pembina Gelanggang Anak-anak Buddhis Indonesia (Indonesian Association of Coaches of Buddhist Children). There is also a transnational organization, Buddha Tzu Chi, a Buddhist philanthropy foundation. Unlike the first two Buddhist organizations, Buddha Tzu Chi was able to bridge religious differences by playing a role in the postdisaster recovery program by building a housing complex and sports building for the victims of the tsunami of 2004. In 2018, Buddha Tzu Chi rebuilt the Akademi Komunitas Negeri in Pidie Jaya, which had been affected by earthquake a year before. When the ceremony to mark the beginning of construction was conducted according to allegedly Buddhist ways, however, two Islamist movements, the Mujahidin Aceh and the Islamic Defense Front, protested.[26] Mujahidin Aceh charged Buddha Tzu Chi with being a communist organization that was attempting to establish its influence in Aceh. They said that they were ready for "jihad" to destroy the building.[27] Islamic Defense Front protested the use of Buddha Tzu Chi identity and called on Pidie Jaya's government not to allow a *kafir* (infidel) organization to build the building.[28] The problem was later solved, however, when the chairperson of the Deliberative Council of Ulama of Pidie Jaya, Tgk Said Abdullah, clarified that the building had nothing to do with religion.[29]

Because of their very small number of Indonesian adherents, Hinduism and Confucianism have no organizations but the foundations attached to their houses of worship.

There are a number of civil society organizations in Aceh that deal with issues including human rights, women's rights, the environment, corruption, and democracy, but there is no single interreligious or ecumenical institution established by different religious communities. Issues of human rights that include religion, especially Islam, have usually been addressed by NGOs including Aceh Institute, Koalisi NGO HAM Aceh, and Pos Bantuan Hukum dan Hak Asasi Manusia. Issues of religion in relation to women's rights are usually addressed by women's rights NGOs such as Balai Syura Ureung Inong Aceh, Flower Aceh, Solidaritas Perempuan, and Jaringan Pemantau 231, a network of sixteen women's organizations. KONTRAS, a national NGO, to date usually deals with human rights issues during the GAM-Jakarta conflict period. In the Muslim community, there are some NGOs that deal with issues of human rights and religious tolerance, such as Jaringan Masyarakat Sipil Peduli Syariat and Forum Islam Rahmatan Lil 'Alamin.

The lack of an NGO focused on interreligious relations seems to be a problem of highly homogeneous societies in general. Minorities' needs are not understood by the majority to be the real needs of society. Interreligious institutions are considered by the majority as unimportant, if not as a threat. And because of the strength of the majority, the minority prefers to remain silent; the gap between the majority and the minority is too wide, and the wall built by the majority is too strong to risk breaching it.[30] The segregation of Aceh society is backed up by the national Law on Special Status of Aceh (1999), the Law on Special Autonomy of Aceh (2001), and the Law on Governing Aceh (2006). The only institution shared by representatives of Muslim and non-Muslim communities is the state-created FKUB.

Aceh FKUB's Reactions to Religious Harmony and City of Tolerance Indexes

There are two important indexes of interreligious relations in Indonesia: the City of Tolerance Index, managed by Setara Institute, and a second Religious Harmony Index managed by the Ministry of Religious Affairs. These indexes are created nationally, but we will focus on Aceh. Setara Institute is an NGO that endorses democratic society and an open political system based on respect for diversity, defense of human rights, and elimination of intolerance and xenophobic attitudes. It also conducts research and advocacy on democracy, political freedom, and human rights. This research includes an index survey of tolerance conducted in a number of cities in Indonesia.

In 2018, Setara conducted an indexing survey in ninety-four cities. Some systemic variables affect the social behavior of cities' citizens, including government policies, the behavior of government officers, behaviors among citizens and between citizens and government, and other relations in the demographic heterogeneity of the city's people. A "city of tolerance" has the following characteristics: (1) the city government has regulations conducive to practices and promotion of tolerance, both in plans and in reality; (2) the statements and behaviors of city government officers are conducive to practices and promotion of tolerance; (3) the city has low or no violent events or actions; and (4) the city makes adequate efforts to govern the religious diversity of citizens.[31]

In its 2018 City of Tolerance Index, Setara Institute placed Banda Aceh, the capital of Aceh, in the second lowest position, with a score of 2.830; the lowest-scoring city was Tanjung Balai, with 2.817. Responding to this survey, the mayor of Banda Aceh, Aminullah, protested and said that the city planned to sue Setara Institute. In his view, the index was unfair because it did not reflect reality. There was no conflict (*kericuhan*) in Banda Aceh based on religion. He was afraid that the index would affect development programs in Banda Aceh. He also said that every year, the FKUB reported that interreligious relations in Banda Aceh were harmonious.[32]

In recent years, the Ministry of Religious Affairs has conducted an annual survey on interreligious harmony, as a result of which it launched the Interreligious Harmony Index.[33] In 2019, this survey was conducted in 136 districts and municipalities in 34 provinces. Surveyors interviewed 13,600 respondents (about 400 in each province) on May 16–19 and June 18–24,

Table 5.1. Top Five Lowest Scores of National Interreligious Harmony Index (2017–2019)

Province	2017	2018	2019
Aceh	60.03	64.12	60.24
West Sumatra	66.98	62.49	64.36
West Java	68.52	65.69	68.51
Banten	60.66	65.86	68.87
Riau	67.35	68.41	69.26

Source: Agency of Research, Development, Training, and Education, Ministry of Religious Affairs (2019).

2019. The survey looked at measures of tolerance, equality, and cooperation between different religious communities. Based on this survey, the ministry set the national Interreligious Harmony Index at 73.83.[34] Of the thirty-four provinces surveyed, Aceh received the lowest score of 60.2.

Perhaps unsurprisingly, the results of the index survey drew protests, both from the government and from society. The acting governor of Aceh, Nova Iriansyah, drew attention to problems in the methodology used in the survey and the way it was conducted. He said that it was simply unfair to judge the government of Aceh with numbers. The FKUB's chairperson for Aceh Province, Nasir Zalba, also complained about the research methodology; he, as the person responsible for interreligious harmony in the province, was never consulted or interviewed. He said that the researchers should have asked non-Muslim people how they felt about being non-Muslim in Aceh. He believed there was no intolerance in Aceh. Interreligious relations had been no problem, he said, and there had never been conflict between the religious communities of Aceh. He also said that he had never heard of non-Muslims being prevented from conducting their devotion. He charged the survey with aiming to blame Aceh and destroy its peace.[35]

At least two interreligious meetings were organized in response to the survey. The first was an internal meeting of the FKUB on December 16, 2019. At this meeting, Reverend Idaman Sembiring, a representative of Protestantism, said, "Islamic shari`a is not for non-Muslims. We feel more Christian in Aceh." He suggested, however, that FKUB conduct its own research in order to have its own data on the real condition of interreligious life in Aceh.[36]

A second meeting was held by the FKUB at Hotel Grand Arabia, Banda Aceh, on December 23. Representatives of government bodies and religious leaders were invited. Participants in this meeting rejected the survey altogether and charged that it had "violated the noble values of Acehnese people, who are civilized, egalitarian, harmonious, and religious in the framework of the unitary state of the Republic of Indonesia." The participants also declared that interreligious relations in Aceh during 2019 had been "dynamic, harmonious, and peaceful." Paradoxically, the participants acknowledged interreligious problems in Aceh but argued that these were not caused by religious teachings. Instead, they were driven by "religious attitudes" and a "lack of communication and interaction among religious communities." They also acknowledged that there was problem with churches in Singkil, which the FKUB viewed as a result of the weak role of the provincial and local government.[37] The chairperson of the provincial FKUB said that the organization stood ready to become "the mediator and catalyst for solving the religious problems in Singkil."[38] This statement implies, however, that the provincial FKUB intended to wait passively for the conflicting parties of Singkil to come and ask it to become their "mediator and catalyst," *not* that FKUB was in fact the institution with the legal authority to seek a solution. Until 2022, no new Christian churches had been legalized in Singkil.

The above reactions to the tolerance indices suggest that tolerance is understood in Aceh merely as the ability of various religious communities to perform prayer peacefully in their respective places of worship without being disturbed and without physical conflict or violence between religious communities (although there was in fact such conflict in Aceh). This paradox reflects ignorance of what is meant by "religious tolerance." The religious and government leaders of Aceh seem to understand tolerance in the sense of "negative tolerance"[39]—that is, as the absence of manifest conflict, mostly due to ignorance. They do not think of "positive tolerance" in the sense of tolerance constructed through conscious understanding of each other toward the integration of society.

Conclusion

The mutual ignorance of Muslim and non-Muslim citizens of each other's religion, and therefore their unreciprocated interreligious relations, is almost a normal phenomenon in Aceh. The knowledge of most non-Muslim lay people about Islam and shari`a, and of Muslim lay people about non-Muslims and their teachings, is similarly limited; coming mostly from social media and from fellow religionists, it is mixed with biases and prejudices. On the surface, the interreligious situation in Aceh appears peaceful (with the exception of Singkil). That is why most Muslim leaders consider Muslims to be tolerant of other religions and also why they protested when Setara's and the Ministry of Religious Affairs' indices put Banda Aceh at the lowest level of tolerance and harmony. As we have seen, majority-minority relations in Aceh show the impact of this mutual ignorance.

We consider that education and societal deliberative institutions are key factors in building democratic citizenship. Indeed, the state has set up a national curriculum of Pancasila and civic education from elementary school to university in order to cultivate nationalism and equal citizenship. Since the issuance of the Law on the Aceh's Special Status (1999), however, and especially of the Law of Aceh's Special Autonomy (2001), which gave Aceh special authority in managing shari`a and education, it has been the case in Aceh that Pancasila and civic education are not permitted to contradict shari`a. This means that Pancasila and civic education are interpreted in Aceh according to the Aceh Islamic curriculum in accordance with the 2015 Qanun on Education.

We have also seen how the absence of genuine societal interreligious institutions reinforces mutual ignorance. Each community lives with its own perceptions and prejudices about other religions, without any space to communicate. Indeed, even though the state has established the FKUB at the provincial and district/municipal levels, it cannot facilitate fairness within that organization or comprehensive discussion of the various problems of interreligious relations. Furthermore, minorities' problems are not always understood as such by the Muslim majority in the FKUB. What is valid at the national level, moreover, is not always operable in Aceh due to the legal principle of *lex specialis derogat legi generali*.

Education and the state-created FKUB have not been able to enhance mutual understanding among religious communities but instead perpetuate mutual ignorance and the segregation of the citizenry along religious lines. Therefore, shari`a in Aceh thus far, as reflected in qanuns and policies, reflects a conservative understanding of Islamic norms that does not forward interreligious understanding and tolerance, let alone coexistence, as *shar`i*, or in line with Islamic values. This interpretation is actually not the only way to understand shari`a; interreligious understanding, tolerance, and coexistence are completely in line with the Islamic values taught by the Prophet Muhammad. Education that synthesizes Islamic values, state ideology, and civic education on the one hand and the establishment of a genuine societal interreligious deliberative institution on the other hand could perhaps drive Aceh to adopt more democratic citizenship and to live in a state of positive tolerance among religious communities.

CHAPTER 6

Officializing Confessional Exclusion

As mentioned in previous chapters, the legal recognition of shari`a implementation has enabled the Acehnese people to officially "reclaim" Aceh as an "Islamic region." Through reclaiming Aceh as an Islamic land, the government of Aceh has obliged itself not only to ensure the implementation of shari`a but also to protect the Muslim faith—as protective action is part and parcel of the implementation of shari`a intended by the laws.

There has long been a generalized belief that non-Islamic missionary activities, especially Christianization, were taking place in Aceh, especially in the eastern border areas adjacent to North Sumatra. This belief has been justified in at least two ways. First, the neighboring areas in North Sumatra have a significant number of Christians, and many of them have migrated to Aceh's border areas for work or for other reasons. Second, the number of churches in the border areas has grown from time to time. Belief in the threat of Christianization at the eastern border has been transformed into government policies in the form of institutions, regulations, and programs designed to directly or indirectly prevent it.

This chapter discusses the involvement of the government of Aceh in protecting the Muslim faith—but not other religious faiths— in the eastern border areas and the hinterlands, which the government calls "areas prone to trivialization of belief" (*daerah rawan pendangkalan akidah*), through legal, proselytizational, educational, and financial protections. "Trivialization of belief" includes not only assumed non-Islamic missionary activities (especially Christian ones) but also the possibility of Muslims adopting "defiant beliefs and practices"—meaning non-Sunnism and including Shi'ism, Ahmadiyyah, Millata Abraham, Gafatar, and heterodox Sufi teachings and groups. These non-Sunni Muslim minorities are beyond the scope of this chapter, which will argue that government efforts on the eastern border and in the hinterlands reflect the dominance of religiously inspired ruling political and civil societies in the government and their success in canalizing and transforming their confessional identity and interests into official policies by which they legally exclude other religious minority communities. This chapter will also argue that these policies, along with the politics of dominant culture, are actually aimed at protecting majority (Muslim) belief against assumed minority (especially Christian) missionary activities in Aceh, especially in the eastern border areas and hinterlands. Although this aim is not mentioned explicitly in government documents, it is clearly expressed in mass media and interviews. In the conclusion to this chapter, we will show how religiously inspired governance has disregarded the beliefs of religious minorities and made Muslim belief the official religion of the local state.

Threatening Borders and Hinterlands: Assumed Targets of Christian Mission

The "areas prone to the trivialization of belief," defined by the Governor's Decree 54/2014 on a Technical Guide for Da'is of Border Areas and Hinterlands, are as follows:[1] (1) border areas, referring to districts and municipalities that abut North Sumatra province, including Tamiang, Aceh Tenggara (Kutacane), Subulussalam, and Singkil;[2] and (2) hinterlands (*daerah terpencil*), referring to areas that are far from settlements and have no access to public transportation, and that include Aceh Selatan and Simeuleu.[3] "Hinterlands" does not refer to whole districts; rather, there are hinterlands in these two districts.

The above eastern border areas of Aceh are important in terms of religious and ethnic minorities because they are more heterogeneous and pluralistic than other parts of Aceh. Migration of mostly Batak Christians from North Sumatra to the border areas of Aceh has been common practice, usually for work in palm oil factories. Due to this migration, the number of Batak Christians living in Aceh's border areas has been increasing. Unlike many other parts of Aceh, then, the eastern border areas are religiously and ethnically plural. In some cases, religion has

Table 6.1. Religious Populations of Border Areas, 2018

District/Municipality	Muslim	Protestant	Catholic	Hindu	Buddhist	Other
Aceh Singkil	111,194	14,118	1,188	7	2	259
Subulussalam	83,273	2,026	430	–	2	–
Aceh Tenggara	182,220	40,898	2,020	–	1	–
Aceh Tamiang	292,621	574	77	5	1,073	–

Source: *Aceh's Statistics 2019.*

become ethnic identity. Becoming Acehnese, Alas, Tamiang Malay, and Boang means becoming Muslim. Likewise, becoming Toba Batakese and Karo Batakese means becoming Christian. There are also ethnic groups with plural identities, such as the Pakpak, whose members may embrace Protestantism, Catholicism, Islam, or a local religion called Pambi. Finally, there are migrant ethnic groups that identify themselves as Muslim (Minang) or pluralist (Javanese).[4]

Although Islam is embraced by the majority of people in the eastern borderlands, the presence of non-Muslims, especially Christians, is significant, as reflected in table 6.1. Protestantism has been present in the border areas since the Dutch colonial period. Its presence cannot be separated from the Dutch colonial policy of Christianizing the neighboring areas of the Bataks as a way of separating the two strongly Islamized regions of Aceh and West Sumatra. These two regions were understood by the Dutch to be potentially subversive and dangerous to the maintenance of Dutch authority in the northern part of Sumatra.[5] Batak people were increasingly Christianized, mostly by becoming Protestants, although some converted to Catholicism.

The gradual migration from Batak lands to the Acehnese regions has resulted in a gradual increase in the presence of Batakese Christians in the Aceh border areas of Singkil, Subulussalam, Aceh Tengara (Kutacane), and Tamiang. Most of the Protestants in these areas are Batakese or non-Acehnese migrants. It is natural, therefore, that due to the presence of Christian migrants, the number of churches in the border areas of Aceh has increased. Some were established during the Dutch colonial period, but most came into being in the postcolonial period. The Statistics Bureau of Aceh presents confusing data regarding churches. The data from 1975 give the numbers of Protestant and Roman Catholic churches in the whole of Aceh as 87 and 17, respectively, while the data from 2002 are 145 and 19. In 2015, these figures were 36 and 6.[6] In 2016, only data on the number of religious adherents, and no data on places of worship, was collected. In 2017 and 2018, no data on either religious adherents or places of worship was collected. The problem with the yearly reports of statistics of Aceh is that they do not always include data on the number of religious affiliation and houses of worship, or they include the former but not the latter. It is assumed that this is the case because mentioning the number of the places of worship is problematic, as there has been a discrepancy between official and unofficial (usually called "illegal") places of worship. The other problem is that data of Protestant and Catholic churches are not always separated. For these reasons, we use only the data that separate Protestant from Catholic churches. This reflects the sensitivity of the issue of number of non-Islamic religions in Aceh.

Like Protestantism, Roman Catholicism benefited from Dutch colonial policy in Aceh's border areas. Some Catholic churches have been present in these areas since colonial times, and others were established in the postindependence era. Their development has not been as rapid as that of Protestant churches. The structure of Catholic churches does not follow the structure of the state. Aceh has no independent archbishopric (*Keuskupan Agung*). All of Aceh's six Catholic churches, including those in the border areas, are administered under the archbishopric of Medan.[7]

Consequently, these border areas, and especially Singkil and Aceh Tenggara, have a large number of churches compared to other regions in Aceh. Singkil has 24 churches (though only 2 churches and 2 *undung-undung* [chapels] are recognized), and Aceh Tenggara has the highest number of churches in Aceh with 124 (38 of them recognized). The difference between these two regions is that Muslim-Christian relations have frequently been tense in Singkil, while they have been peaceful in Aceh Tenggara. Subulussalam has four churches,[8] whereas Tamiang had only one church, which was closed by the government. Recognition of a church means that it has official permission to exist and has been recognized by the government. Most of the churches in the eastern border regions belong to Batak and Pakpak people.

The eastern border also hosts Buddhists and Confucianists, who are primarily ethnic Chinese. Buddhism has been present in some regions of Aceh for a long time, dating to even before the Islamic presence in the region. The Buddhists who live in Aceh today, however, migrated during the Dutch colonial period, as did the Confucian Chinese. Most Buddhists and Confucians of the eastern border live in Tamiang, which has three Buddhist temples (vihara).[9]

There is also a local religion in Singkil called Pambi (as well as Parmalim). It is a Batak Toba local religion, influenced by both Christianity and Islam. It is said that this religion was established by Sisingamangaraja and is an exclusive religion in the sense that membership is limited to Batak people. It is not clear when Pambi entered Singkil, but it exists today mostly in the border areas near Pakpak Dairi—namely, Pakpak Barat, Dairi, and Central Tapanuli.[10] Pambi is not considered a religion by the government but merely a "belief stream" (*aliran kepercayaan*). Like other belief streams, it is not administered by the Ministry of Religious Affairs but rather by the Ministry of Education and Culture.

A number of villages or subdistricts are considered "hinterlands," but both districts of Aceh Selatan and Simeulue are particularly important for the presence of non-Muslims, especially Protestants, Catholics, and Buddhists. In 2019, there were 234,431 Muslims in Aceh Selatan versus 184 Protestants, 33 Catholics, and 133 Buddhists. Similarly, there were 92,740 Muslims in Simeulue versus 213 Protestants, 10 Catholics, and 13 Buddhists (see table 6.2). Protestants and Roman Catholics are suspected of spreading their influence through missionary activity, either openly or in a hidden way, while Buddhists are not suspected of proselytizing. In Aceh Selatan, Christians have spread into fourteen out of eighteen subdistricts, whereas in Simeulue they have spread into five out of ten subdistricts. Although their numbers are small, it seems that they have been viewed by Acehnese people as a threat to the Islamic character of Aceh.

Along with the shari`aization of the political process since 2001, the heterogeneous and pluralistic nature of the border areas and the isolation of the hinterlands have been understood to threaten the Muslim

Table 6.2. Religious Populations of Aceh Selatan and Simeulue in 2018

Districts	Muslim	Protestant	Catholic	Hindu	Buddhist	Other
Aceh Selatan	234,431	184	33	–	113	–
Simeulue	92,740	213	10	–	13	1

Source: *Aceh's Statistics 2019.*

faith and Aceh's identity as the "land of shari`a" (*nanggroe syariah*). These regions, especially those with a significant non-Muslim presence, are considered to be "prone to trivialization of belief" (*daerah rawan pendangkalan akidah*). One of the most important issues in the eastern border areas has been assumed Christian missionary activities. The growing number of churches and the rumors of Kristianisasi (Christian missionary activities) have become a concern among the Acehnese Muslim community as well as to local authorities, which are obliged by law to ensure the implementation of shari`a. In the shari`a land, the existence of non-Islamic places of worship is understood as "abnormal" and threatening to Islamic existence in the region.

Like Islam, Protestantism and Roman Catholicism are missionary religions, while Buddhism, Confucianism, and the rest of the minorities religions of Aceh are not. That is why, despite being in the overwhelming majority, Acehnese Muslims are afraid of Christianity in the borderlands. During the post-tsunami reconstruction period, the Indonesian government and its people welcomed all forms of aid, whether or not they had religious affiliations. Yet those who came to help were warned they should not use the opportunity as a means of forwarding their religious mission. While Buddha Tzu Chi's aid helped build houses in an area that was later known as the Kompleks Perumahan Cinta Kasih Tzu Chi (Tzu Chi Housing Complex of Compassion), Christian relief NGOs were suspected of coming to the country not only to help people but also to spread Christianity. A number of Christian religious books, including Bibles and comics, were found amid donated goods. There was also a rumor that Acehnese orphans were being shipped abroad by a certain international Christian missionary organization. The Indonesian Council of Ulama asked the Indonesian Church Council to help bring them back to Aceh. The Protestant's Indonesian Council Churches (Persekutuan Gereja-gereja Indonesia) and Roman Catholic Bishops' Conference (Konferensi Waligereja) rejected any abuse of humanitarian mission for Christianization.[11]

Christian missionary activity has been viewed by Aceh Muslims as a threat because it could lead Muslims to convert to Christianity, which is considered as one of the greatest sins. Sociologically, it would also reduce the number of Muslims in the region and in the long run could erase the special status of Aceh as the "veranda of Mecca"—that is, the Islamic land.

Officially Confessional Protection of Faith

In the secular world, faith is private: it belongs to the individual. Faithful individuals are allowed to form a community but not to interfere in the faith of other members. It is the individual who is supposed to protect his or her own personal faith, and it is the community, not the state, that is supposed to protect the faith as a whole. The state has nothing to do with the internal affairs of the religious community, let alone with protecting any particular faith against any other faith. The state is supposed to adopt equal distance between itself and all religions.

In a religiously communal society like Aceh, by contrast, faith is not only private but also public, and not only personal but also communal. The state, as a site of both ruling political society and religious civil society, is supposed to protect the majority's faith. As a consequence of the implementation of the laws guaranteeing special status and shari`a enforcement, shari`a institutions were established at the provincial level (1), the municipal level (5), and the district level (18). Policies and programs are also created, and budgets allocated, to ensure the implementation of shari`a. One aspect of the implementation of shari`a involves strengthening and protecting the Muslim faith from any efforts of "trivialization of belief" (*pendangkalan akidah*)—a term found in some Aceh regulations as well as government discourse. It is not clear from whom Islam is under threat of trivialization. Yet the regulations passed to prevent *pendangkalan akidah* suggest trivialization is a threat from both Muslims (who might introduce "deviant belief") and non-Muslims (due to their missionary activities). The Muslim faith is protected officially in various ways: legal, proselytizational, educational, and financial.

Legal Protection

As mentioned in part I, the strongest protection of Muslim faith is the official implementation of shari`a itself. The Law No. 11/1999 on Aceh's status as a special region, Law No. 18/2001 on Special Autonomy for the Province of Aceh as the Province of Nangroe Aceh Darussalam (or the Law on Special Autonomy of Aceh), and Law No. 6/2006 on the Governing of Aceh justify shari`a implementation, which means also taking sides with the majority's religious affiliation. Thus, protecting the Muslim faith is not only justified but a responsibility of the legal system to enforce. In other words, non-Islamic missionary activity that targets Muslims is illegal.

There is also legal restriction for building places of non-Muslim worship. At the national level, there was the Joint Decree between the Minister of Religious Affairs and Minister of Home Affairs Nos. 9 and 8/2006, which regulates the building of places of worship and created the Forum for the Harmony of Interreligious Communities (FKUB). This joint decree states that a place of worship, in order to be established officially, must have the support of ninety congregation members and sixty neighboring people, as proved with copies of their ID cards. In addition, they have to gain a recommendation from the FKUB and the head of the local office of the Ministry of Religious Affairs.

As mentioned in chapter 2, in Aceh, the requirements for establishing a new place of worship are even more difficult. The Aceh government issued Gubernatorial Decree No. 25/2007 on Guidance for the Establishment of Houses of Worship. Unlike the Joint Decree, this gubernatorial decree demands that a place of worship have support from 150 congregation members and 120 neighboring people, proved by copies of their ID cards. It requires not only the permit from the FKUB and the head of the local office of Ministry of Religious Affairs but also a separate permit from the head of the local village. This decree has made it almost impossible for the religious minority in Aceh to build officially recognized places of worship.

Soon after the Singkil incident in 2015 (on the incident, see chapter 2), the government of Aceh issued Qanun No. 4/2016 on the Guideline for the Protection of Harmonious Relations among Religious Communities and Places of Worship. Complicating previous regulations, this qanun states that a place of worship must provide a list of names of 140 congregation members who are the permanent residents (not migrants) and demonstrate the support of 110 surrounding people who are not congregation members, all supported by copies of their ID cards. In addition, the congregation must get a recommendation from the village authority (*keuchik*), the subdistrict leader (*camat*), FKUB, and the head of the local office of the Ministry of Religious Affairs. While the number of required congregation members and neighborhood supporters decreased, the recommendation procedure became more complicated.

This qanun reflects how the government of Aceh perceives "harmonious relations among religious communities." The qanun is aimed at responding to the practice of illegal establishment of churches and of foreign humanitarian donations to religious minorities. It seems that "harmony" in this qanun refers to the restriction of the religious minority's activities in order to prevent them from causing "social problems" in the eyes of the majority.[12] The minority is seen here as the source of disharmony, and to stabilize harmony, it is required to restrict its activities, including the establishment of churches. Such regulations are formulated to restrict the religious minority rather than to protect the right to practice religion. For the minority, the requirements of the regulation are almost impossible to fulfill. It seems that this impossibility is the aim of the regulation. Indeed, such regulations are quite effective at preventing the number of officially sanctioned churches from growing not only in the eastern border areas but in Aceh in general. This means, however, that legislation is being used to protect the interests of the majority and powerful against those of the minority and the weak.

It is worth noting here how the concept of "tolerance" is understood and applied in light of the above context. The way the Muslim majority perceives tolerance and works for it with different non-Muslim groups has been tremendously influenced by the politics of dominant culture (see chapter 1). Many of our Muslim informants (e.g., government officials, religious leaders, and ordinary people) argued that according to the local view, "there is no intolerance in Aceh." They said that on the contrary, they have shown "quite high tolerance" of non-Muslims, a statement that in itself implies inequality. As the majority (both as the host and the ruling group), they see themselves as "quite tolerant" to non-Muslims as their guests by allowing them to live in Aceh to work, to form organizations, to establish places of worship (although limited), and so forth. These all represent what they call "tolerance."

In return for such "tolerance," the guests should respect the host's customs, traditions, and religion, including the implementation of shari`a and the regulation of worship places. As guests to the land of Aceh, non-Muslims are not allowed to make demands beyond the boundaries set up by the host. This kind of (in)tolerance may also be called "asymmetric tolerance"[13] or, as Chabry and Chabry put it, "tolerance of religious pluralism based on inequality."[14] That is why the surveys conducted by the Setara Institute and the Ministry of Religious Affairs in the last few years put Banda Aceh, the capital of Aceh province, among the cities with the least religious tolerance.[15]

Official Proselytization

As mentioned earlier, the government set up official proselytization programs in the border areas and in the hinterlands to protect the faith of Muslims against alleged Christian missionary activities as well as against heterodox non-Sunni teachings in those areas. These preachers are supposed to deepen Muslims' understanding of Islam and protect the faith from trivialization. Their tasks include delivering a Friday sermon (khutbah) and religious speech (*pengajian*), mobilizing devotional practices, guiding youth, and organizing social activities.[16] On the ground, their work is variable depending on the context; they also deal with drugs, daily conflicts, and *khalwat*.[17] The preachers of this program get a monthly salary, health care, housing rent, motorcycle maintenance, insurance expenses, as well as a motorcycle.[18]

Government-Funded Islamic Boarding School

Dayah are Aceh's traditional Islamic boarding schools, which date back to the early Islamization of the region. These schools are nationally called *pesantren* or *pondok pesantren*.[19] Dayah are where Muslim children and youth learn about Islam and are trained to become ulama.[20] Following the emergence of madrasas in the modern era, some dayah establish their own madrasas, too, while others maintain their traditional form. Ideologically, dayah belong to both the "traditionalist" group, which study primarily Shafi'ite *madhhab* (Islamic fiqh, or the legal school), Ash'arite theology, and orthodox Sufism (sometimes heterodox Sufism, too),[21] and to the "reformist" group, which are more puritanical, non-madhhab, and usually critical of Sufi practices. Dayah in Aceh mostly belong to the former type. Some modern dayah have also been established. The existence of dayah has been strengthened by local bylaws and qanun.[22]

The government of Aceh has established some dayah in the eastern border areas, called dayah perbatasan (Islamic boarding schools in the border areas). Like the official proselytization program, the dayah perbatasan is aimed to protect the faith of the ummah and to develop religious Islamic knowledge. The planning for the establishment of the dayah perbatasan was made in 2008, and the survey for deciding proper locations for the dayah was conducted in 2009.[23] Four official dayah perbatasan were established: Dayah Manarul Islam, located in Seumadam village, Tamiang, on June 18, 2010; Dayah Minhajus Salam, located in

Kampung Baru village, Kota Subulussalam, established in May 2010; Dayah Safinatussalamah, located in Bingkang vilage, Danau Paris, Singkil, established on July 12, 2010; and Dayah Darul Amin, located in Tanoh Alas, Aceh Tenggara. However, unlike other three dayah, Dayah Darul Amin was established on November 8, 1998, long before the existence of the dayah perbatasan program.

There actually were already some dayah in these areas, but with the exception of Darul Amin they were mostly traditional dayah. There were also many Islamic schools (madrasas). The government established new dayah for their project, again except for Darul Amin, because the traditional dayah had their own curriculum, and it was difficult to make them adopt current interests. All of the government-supported dayah perbatasan adopted a modern curriculum and offered both informal education in dormitories and a formal school. The government established dayah instead of other types of Islamic schools because it wanted to nurture the ulama (religious scholars) and Muslim intellectuals toward mastering religious Islamic knowledge; this effort, they hoped, would develop the border areas into Islamic strongholds in the future. Moreover, those in power believed education would be an effective way not only to teach Muslims about the faith but also to challenge the trivialization of belief, including Christianization.

Financial Support

The government allocates budgets for shari`a implementation but are not supposed to fund non-Islamic religions. The government pays, for instance, the salaries of borderland preachers and village imam (*imeum*) along with those of members of the Deliberative Council of Ulama, but does not pay the leaders of other religions. The government pays for the rehabilitation of Islamic boarding schools and helps to build mosques and Islamic centers but does not support non-Islamic places of worship or religious centers.

The government of Aceh officially grants funds to Islamic affairs in their various aspects. The *Short-Term Development Plan, 2012–17* shows that the government of the province funded various programs related to shari`a, Islamic education in general and dayah in particular, ulama, Qur'anic learning, the Shari`a Court, and *da'wah* (Islamic propagation).[24] There are also programs that seem on the surface to be general (for all religions), such as enhancement of *religious* life, *religious* services, *religious* education, and *religious* tolerance, that refer to Islamic affairs rather than to interreligious affairs. The governmental fund for non-Islamic institutions and places of worship is not provided by the Aceh government but by the Ministry of Religious Affairs.[25] In 2016, this ministry donated Rp1 billion for churches in Aceh—a donation that triggered controversy when the ministry was accused of funding Christianization.[26] The fund actually went not only to Acehnese churches but to places of worship and religious organizations of all types all over Indonesia.

Official Forum for Interreligious Harmony

The only state-supported religious institution shared by Muslims and non-Muslims is the FKUB, which exists at the provincial and district/municipal levels. This is a forum in which representatives of different religious communities meet to discuss and deal with issues of interreligious relations and problems. The FKUB is also in charge of giving permits for building houses of religion.

In most cases, Muslim biases dominate the forum because the number of Muslim representatives is larger than those of other religions. In Singkil, for instance, the chairperson, two vice chairs, and the secretary are Muslims, whereas Protestants have just three representatives and Roman Catholics have one.[27] Forum members are religious leaders, and in this regard, they represent and articulate the interests and voices of their own communities rather than acting as interfaith activists to promote genuine peaceful relations among religious communities.

The dynamics of the FKUB differ from region to region. The most troublesome region in the border areas is Singkil, which has twenty-four churches—twenty of which are considered illegal. On October 13, 2015, a Protestant church in Singkil was burned down by a Muslim crowd organized by Pemuda Peduli Islam (Youth for Islamic Concern, PPI) in cooperation with Front Pembela Islam (Islamic Defenders Front, FPI).[28] The PPI had conducted a demonstration on October 8, 2015 in front of the government building of Singkil. They did not protest against Christians for building churches but against the government for being silent about the unprecedented spread of church building beyond the number agreed on in 1979 of two churches and two chapels. The FKUB had advance warning of the action and the protesters' demands but could not do much. The burning of the church, according to Suriadi, head of PPI, was not in their plan. They just wanted to conduct a protest march, but he could not prevent it when a number of people deviated from the plan and attacked the church.[29] Soon afterward, based on a meeting between representatives of the government, FKUB, and local ulama, ten other churches were closed by the government.

After the attack, the FKUB mediated between two communities and promised to manage the permits of existing churches. The FKUB of neighboring districts Aceh Tenggara and Tamiang soon held their own meetings, anticipating that the conflict might spread to their regions. Representatives of the provincial FKUB also came to Singkil to observe the situation and coordinate with the local FKUB. About a year after the conflict, the Qanun on Harmonious Relations among Religious Communities and the Building of Places of Worship was issued. As discussed, no permits have been issued under this qanun. Christians in Singkil and in the other regions of Aceh need additional churches to accommodate their growing congregations. Many of these Christian communities have fulfilled the requirements outlined in the qanun, but obtaining building permits remains a significant challenge. It is nearly impossible for Christians in Singkil to gather the necessary 110 support documents (identity cards and family cards) from non-Christian residents. Even eight years after the enactment of the 2016 Qanun, the FKUB in Singkil has failed to draw the attention of provincial government to address this issue. The strong Islamic bias within the FKUB and the government of Aceh appears to be a major obstacle. The FKUB is an elitist institution. Its members are religious leaders who represent and articulate the interests of their own communities rather than acting as interfaith activists to promote genuine peaceful relations among religions. In 2019, the provincial FKUB supported the fatwa of the Deliberative Council of Ulama prohibiting interreligious greetings and prayers and the use of interreligious symbols.[30] Such support reflects the dominance of Islamic interests in the FKUB, which follows the logic of the special autonomy of Aceh as well as the politics of dominant culture in the region.

Conclusion

The religiously inspired governance of Aceh has made the confessional affairs of the ruling established religion into the official affairs of the province. "Problems" are defined in terms of whether they negatively affect the faith of the majority—or even have the potential to do so. The eastern border areas are understood to be prone to the "trivialization of Islamic belief." For this reason, the government considers those regions to house a serious problem that it must address because it sees the Muslim faith to be in danger and in need of state protection.

This chapter has demonstrated a number of ways the government has approached its duty to protect the Muslim faith. New laws have been launched, dozens of Islamic preachers have been sent out, a string of *dayah perbatasan* have been established, financial support has been allocated—all to protect the Muslim faith against the so-called trivialization of belief, including the possibility of Muslim conversion to Christianity and to prevent or restrict the development of religious minorities. In taking these steps, the government of Aceh has made the internal confessional affairs of Islam into the affairs of the local state. The consequence of this position—perhaps unintended or perhaps intentional—is the exclusion of religious minorities from the business of the state.

PART IV

Lived Experiences of Minorities in Aceh

CHAPTER 7

The Negotiated "Space" of the Chinese Community

The remarkable sociopolitical changes that arrived in Aceh after the signing of the peace agreement between the Indonesian central government and the Aceh Independence Movement (Gerakan Aceh Merdeka, GAM) in 2005 made a variety of events possible. These changes were triggered by the armed conflict that preceded the Helsinki peace agreement, the 2004 tsunami disaster, and the aftermath of both. The phases of rehabilitation and reconstruction in the wake of both disasters occurred almost at the same time, particularly over the period of 2005–9, and were coordinated by the Executing Agency for Rehabilitation and Reconstruction (Badan Rehabilitasi dan Rekonstruksi) Aceh-Nias. The reintegration of ex-combatants was tackled by the Aceh Reintegration Body (Badan Reintegrasi Aceh).[1] Consequently, post-tsunami and postconflict humanitarian programs in Aceh catered to both physical infrastructure reconstruction and nonphysical rehabilitation through empowerment projects, training, capacity-building programs, and more. Several sociopolitical issues, including self-governance and special autonomy, became familiar subjects of public discourse that were inevitably related to notions of "identity." In Aceh, notions of identity are very important and cannot be separated from religion and culture. Indeed, identity, religion, and culture are interrelated, intertwined, and to some extent, indistinguishable.

The issue of identity was understood to be a rationale behind the aspiration of people in some districts of Aceh province, such as the west and south coasts and the highland communities of Gayonese, as well as a few other minority ethnic groups, to struggle (*berjuang*) to establish a new province separate from Aceh province. Interestingly, this aspiration intersects with ethnicity and cultural identity. Both regional and national politics had created ethnic-based tension, apart from issues of social injustice and human rights abuses, especially during the period when Aceh was classified as a military operations area (Daerah Operasi Militer). As part of the effort to resolve armed conflict in Aceh, the central government in Jakarta granted special autonomy to Aceh to apply shari`a law.[2] Yet three decades of armed conflict in Aceh enhanced the tendency of the province's dominant culture to consider its nondominant cultures socially and politically inferior.

Given the above context, this chapter focuses on observing the sociocultural identity of the diasporic Chinese community in Banda Aceh[3] in a "socio-spatial dialectics" of "space, time and social being."[4] Through understanding the personal and social narratives of this community, we observe and establish a pattern of how sociocultural identity has been constructed and reconstructed over time within a negotiated social space.

Existing studies of Chinese Indonesians focus mostly on the Chinese in Java, as in the works of Tan, Suryadinata, Godley, Lloyd, Giblin, Hoon, Coppel, Dawis, Dieleman, Koning, Post, Lindsey, and Pausacker.[5] While studies of diasporic Chinese outside Java exist, such as those of Ananta, Arifin, and Bakhtiar on the Chinese in Riau,[6] Tsai and Kammen on the Chinese in Medan,[7] and Hui on the Chinese of West Kalimantan,[8] as well as the latest overarching work from Arifin, Hasbullah, and Pramono on the Chinese in Indonesia[9] and who and where they are, these works offer limited insight into the Chinese in Aceh.

There are some studies on the Chinese in Aceh, including those of Ahok, Irchamni Sulaiman, Rusdi, Ananta, and Usman,[10] but no work has yet looked specifically at the intersection of religion and cultural identity in relation to the interactions of diasporic Chinese subjects with the Muslim majority in postconflict Aceh. Considering the Chinese in Aceh is important because they have existed in the region since the sultanate of Aceh in about the seventeenth century, and they live in a region strongly influenced by Islam since the New Order period (1996–98). And now, there have been some changes in the societal dynamic since Aceh entered the special autonomy era and officially implemented Islamic law (shari`a). Few scholars adhere to the idea that shari`a law has led Aceh to enter an Islamic fundamental era, becoming a more fanatic society and less accommodating to diversity.[11] Known as a non-Muslim and different ethnic group, this chapter examines the effort of Chinese in Banda Aceh in negotiating their minority identity, nondominant religious[12] and cultural group in the current politics of dominant culture in Aceh, especially during post-Aceh conflict and after the enforcement of shari`a law.

The Chinese in Banda Aceh: A Glimpse

In 2010, the population of Banda Aceh consisted of 216,914 Muslims, 1,571 Christians, 431 Catholics, 50 Hindus, 2,535 Buddhists, and 3 Confucianists.[13] The diasporic Chinese organization Hakka Banda Aceh estimates that there were approximately four thousand ethnic Chinese residents in Banda Aceh following the 2004 tsunami disaster. The religion of the Chinese discussed in this chapter are Buddhism, Protestant, and Catholic.

Geospatial Distribution over Time

There are limited data available on the history of early Chinese in Banda Aceh. Historically, we know there were at least a few Chinese groups in the sultanate of Aceh during the seventeenth century, but their precise number is not known. The presence of the Dutch in Aceh at the beginning of the twentieth century provided an opportunity for the Chinese to migrate to the province and maintain their identity under the umbrella of the apartheid policy of the Dutch East Indies government.[14] That is why some scholars believe the biggest wave of Chinese immigrants arrived on the coast of Aceh during the Dutch colonial period.[15] Leo Suryadinata also states many new immigrants left China at the end of the nineteenth and early twentieth centuries during the colonial period.[16] And according to some Chinese in Banda Aceh, these immigrants left their home country for safety and to avoid war. Some of the diasporic Chinese in the archipelago were also brought to Aceh or recruited by Dutch colonial agents to work on major construction projects.[17]

The current neighborhood of diasporic Chinese in Banda Aceh has been maintained since their ancestors' arrival in the area. The descendants of those who arrived from Ulee Lheu harbor live in Seutui area, and the descendants of those who arrived from Lampulo harbor are today in Peunayong. This strongly suggests that historically there were several waves and groups of Chinese diasporic arrival in Banda Aceh. It also implies the diversity of the places of their origin in mainland China. Seutui area is dominated by Hokkien Chinese, whereas Peunayong is dominated by the Khek group, as well as Canton, Hainan, Thio Chu, and Hinwha. The name Seutui itself is believed to derive from the Chinese "Go Sun Tui," the younger brother of Go Heng, who was among the migrants' leaders. Seutui and Go Heng are now two quite well-known and central neighborhood areas in Banda Aceh. Seutui used to be a popular business area in the city, similar in some ways to Peunayong. Administratively, both Seutui and Go Heng are part of Gampong (village) Lam Teumen Barat. Apart from Seutui and Go Heng, three other areas in Banda Aceh host a concentration of ethnic Chinese—namely, Gampong Peunayong, Gampong Laksana, and Gampong Mulia. According to a local historian, the name "Peunayong" derived from the word "Peumayong," which originated from *payong* (umbrella), because there were some traders who were also quite skillful in repairing broken umbrellas.[18]

Peunayong is a "Chinatown" of Banda Aceh municipality and located in the central business district of Banda Aceh city. The social composition of the ethnic groups living in Peunayong is relatively multicultural, including Chinese, Acehnese, and ethnic groups from North Sumatra province, such as Batak. Most residents engage in trade in what is the largest traditional market in Banda Aceh. The community leader in Peunayong has promoted this area as *kampung keragaman budaya* (village of cultural diversity). During the Imlek 2018, a banner reading "Peunayong Kampung Keberagaman Budaya" was erected near one of the entrances of Peunayong popular market. Peunayong has long been well known as a popular market in Banda Aceh, while the surrounding villages of Gampong Laksana and Gampong Mulia were known for farming and plantations as well as for livestock. Today, both Gampong Laksana and Gampong Mulia are residential areas, where some Chinese families who work in Peunayong live.[19] Until now, Peunayong remains the largest Chinese neighborhood in the city of Banda Aceh. The houses and shops in Peunayong are the personal property of Chinese residents, who purchased them from Acehnese in the past.[20]

Since its establishment, the Chinese diasporic community of Aceh has been known for their skill in trading. Shoes, leather making, and repair are distinct skills among the Khek subethnic group, whose business centers on Kampung Baru. With the growth of the shoes industry, however, only one shop remains. The Hinwha subethnic group has several bicycle-related businesses in Banda Aceh. The Thio Chu and Hokkien ethnic groups are generally skillful in automotive, pharmacy, optical, and stationery-related businesses. Hotel businesses have been developed by those from the Hainan subethnic group, including Hotel Parapat and Hotel Medan, which are located in front of the well-known Peunayong culinary center of "Rex area." Business has also influenced Chinese residents' decision to reside in specific areas. After the tsunami, some moved out to other areas in the city, including Lamlagang, Keutapang, Jambo Tape, Darussalam, and Simpang Surabaya along the new Mr. Muhammad Hasan Street of Batoh. Some live in their shops for reasons of efficiency and security; these shops are places of business and residences at once.

The tsunami hit Banda Aceh and Aceh Besar coastal areas badly; it also affected the social and spatial settlement of the Banda Aceh community, including Chinese neighborhoods. A few Chinese have established new settlements in Gampong Pante Riek, located in Banda Aceh, and Gampong Neuheun in Aceh Besar district. Most of those who moved to Gampong Pantee Riek and Gampong Neuheun came from Seutui and Goheng. They received the aid of houses from the yayasan (foundation) of Buddha Tzu Chi. The Chinese settlement in Neuheun area began in the 1970s, when the municipal government of Banda Aceh rearranged the community settlement and some Chinese families in Go Heng shifted to Neuheun in the meantime; most of these people returned to Go Heng or at least continued to do their business in Banda Aceh.

Negotiated Space and Social Capital

Especially within the current sociopolitical situation of strong ethnonationalism, the diasporic Chinese community in Banda Aceh has for the most part tried to build good rapport in its social interactions with the Acehnese. This rapport begins with relatively harmonious social coexistence and ranges to include humanitarian acts and acts of volunteerism.[21] For the ethnic Chinese, to live harmoniously in a "negotiated" space with locals is part of their effort to accumulate social capital. As Field has mentioned, the core of social capital is indeed a "relationship matter," as with social capital, people are able to achieve objectives they could not achieve without good relationships and connections.[22]

Sociocultural Identity: Changes, Challenges, and Commitment

Over generations and decades, the Chinese of Aceh have gone through a continuous assimilation and adjustment process because they inhabit the same area with other ethnic groups, especially the local Acehnese Muslims. Amid this assimilation, however, a few scholars have noted the persistence of exclusivity among certain groups of the diasporic Chinese community in Banda Aceh. Rani Usman, an expert from the State Islamic University of Banda Aceh who conducted fieldwork on the Chinese in Aceh, notes four social adaptations his subjects have gone through—namely, language communication, education, religion, and marriage.[23] Our data suggest another important strategy of social adaptation is engagement in unofficial "politics" and organizations that negotiate, socially and politically, the Chinese presence as a minority among the majority.

For the Chinese of Aceh, their ethnic language is also among the most prevalent markers of social identity they have preserved, although most of them also speak and read the national language, Bahasa Indonesia, and some also speak the Aceh language. The usage of their own subethnic language is preserved especially within microlevel social interactions and communications within their households as well as within their in-group daily social interactions. Their commitment to utilizing their own language is supported by their tradition of preserving and mainstreaming the usage of Chinese names, which, from a practical perspective, also makes it easier to trace their families' places of origin.[24]

In addition, diasporic Chinese in Banda Aceh place strong emphasis on religion as a foundation of social and cultural identity, especially because religion is a legacy of their predecessors. Nonetheless, the history of the diasporic Chinese in Aceh is marked by significant conversions from Buddhism to Christianity. The Methodist church was established in Banda Aceh in 1958, while most of Buddhist temples were established earlier as evidence of this conversion. The Buddhist community in Banda Aceh has four temples in the areas of Gampong Peunayong, Gampong Mulia, and Gampong Laksana. Dewi Samudera temple, established in 1936 and managed by the Hainan subethnic group, is also used for teaching Buddhism. Dharma Bakti temple was established during Japanese colonization (1942–45). Its first location was in Ulee Lheu, and then it moved to the current location on the main road of Teungku Panglima Polem in Peunayong. This temple is managed by Hokkien. Similar to

Dharma Bakti, the Maitri temple is also open and available to all; it was established in 1913 and is managed by a central office in Medan. The fourth temple is the Sakyamurni temple. It was established in 1969 and is used to teach Buddhism and is managed by the Khek ethnic group.[25] There is no serious conflict between the different temples in terms of management or activities. They even have a common funeral home, Rumah Duka Umat Tionghoa, located in Gampong Mulia.

The perspective of ethnic Chinese in Aceh on mixed marriages with Acehnese Muslims has become more flexible over time. Marriage was previously restricted to only Chinese partners but has shifted to include people with different cultural identities and religions. Those who marry Muslims convert to Islam, becoming muallaf. Deciding to convert is a complex decision for Chinese women, however, as mixed marriage and conversion frequently has serious social penalties. Family members and relatives—especially parents and immediate family—may offer social resistance. Chinese women in Aceh who marry Muslim men are perceived as not only changing religion but also changing their "culture." An Acehnese interviewee explained, "For [the Chinese], it is much more difficult, because . . . if they marry our people [Acehnese], they have to change not only their religion but also their culture."[26]

The Chinese community in Banda Aceh has found a space for cultural and social engagement in the field of education, particularly for those who study in regular public schools. Their children's interactions with children outside the ethnic Chinese community, including with children and people from other religions (especially Islam), have also caused some conversions among diasporic Chinese children in Banda Aceh. Only a limited amount of Chinese in Banda Aceh prefer to send their children to regular public school, however; most of them continue their studies beyond junior high school and university levels outside Aceh in places like Medan and Jakarta. This is quite common especially for wealthy families. Alternatively, their children may choose to help with the family businesses.

Although the Chinese in Aceh include Buddhists, Confucians, Christians, and even Muslims, their shared social and cultural identity means that they have common activities and cultural events, including the celebration of the Chinese New Year, widely known in Indonesia as "Imlek." For 2018 Imlek, residents and visitors in Peunayong could watch a Barongsai performance by both Chinese and local Acehnese people and children.[27] They performed the Barongsai dance on the main road of

Peunayong, and some of the dancers with dragons entered the shops and interacted with the shop owners.

Our study found that one of the strategies, which diasporic Chinese in Banda Aceh employ to adjust to living with the Muslim majority, operates through ethnic-based organizations that engage in humanitarian activities. One of these organizations is Hakka, which the Khek ethnic group founded for social and humanitarian missions. Hakka later became a social organization that represents not only Khek but all Chinese ethnic groups. At the national level, an organization called Indonesia Tionghoa similarly focuses on social missions. This organization has assisted people in post-tsunami Aceh through its humanitarian programs. These groups and their work have helped to give Banda Aceh municipality a higher degree of social coexistence and plurality compared with other districts in Aceh.

An article in a well-known local newspaper from Ramadan 2017 is titled "Komunitas Tionghoa Hakka Bagikan 1.950 Paket Sembako" (Hakka Chinese community distributes 1,950 food packages). In it, the leader of Hakka Aceh foundation, Kho Khie Siong, mentioned that distributing food had been a regular Ramadan activity of the Hakka foundation for the past five years. It was a token of empathy of the Chinese community for the poor people of Aceh. "During Ramadan, there are some increasing needs," Khie Siong explained. "Therefore, we tried to help.... We hope this activity can sustain the friendship between Chinese and Muslim [people]."[28] This activity can be understood as part of a strategy for nurturing social capital through building and strengthening relations with local Muslims during the special religious moment of Ramadan. Khie Siong emphasizes the Chinese/ethnic identity of participants in Hakka (*warga etnis Tionghoa*), not their religion (Buddhist or Christian); religion is mentioned only in reference to the local community as *warga Muslim* (Muslim citizens). Organizations such as Hakka, through their humanitarian activity, attempt to bridge Aceh Chinese relations with the local Muslim majority.

Social Dialectics in the Neighborhood

For diasporic Chinese in Banda Aceh, peaceful social coexistence with Aceh Muslims is of significant concern. The intention to build good relationships with local Muslims is relatively strong[29] since this will also help the diasporic Chinese to survive socially and even politically. This effort is apparent in their choice of neighborhood, near to the Acehnese majority, as well as in their daily social interactions.

Through the years of peaceful coexistence of these two communities, a few ethnic Chinese in Gampong Mulia have been elected to the village youth committee. Another ethnic Chinese person was elected as village council member in Gampong Peunayong. Notably, though, next to no Chinese in Aceh have successfully pursued higher political office, such as becoming a member of parliament.

There have been some changes for the worse, however, for instance in the engagement of Chinese in mosque-based activities. The Chinese used to be asked to contribute to certain Muslim activities or charities, but they are no longer asked to do so. Their participation in nonreligious activities, such as the celebration of Indonesian national independence on August 17, continues. As a result, some Chinese feel they are socially "segregated." This may indicate that social interactions between the non-Muslim Chinese and Muslims in Aceh are not stable. One informant said that as small a trigger as a social media post, for instance, has the potential to harm the peaceful coexistence of the two communities. As a minority group within a Muslim majority neighborhood, it seems, the Chinese are careful not to cause problems, as they had a difficult experience of anti-China sentiment in 1983: "They tried to be very careful; they would not cause [the] anger of the local[s], as they could be still traumatized with the anti-China sentiment of the 1980s."[30]

At first glance, the characteristics of housing for the Chinese residents of Banda Aceh differs from that of Muslims. Most Chinese shops and houses are surrounded by a high wall of metal fencing. The Chinese are perceived as people who earn more money than other locals, according the Keuchik[31] of Gampong Laksana: "If our local people sell the[ir] inherited land, it is Chinese who can purchase it. Although it costs three million rupiah per meter, they will take it."[32] Shifts in economic development and local government structure, especially since the tsunami, however, have given more access to business opportunities for the Muslim majority in areas such as contracting,[33] which has made some Muslim businessmen overshadow Chinese businessmen. The shift has also affected spatial arrangements: some informants said that a handful of shops in Peunayong that have belonged to ethnic Chinese for generations have now been purchased by Muslim businessmen. Still, the diasporic Chinese have not expanded their activities beyond business and trading. Politics, for example, largely does not interest them. At the village level, they are for the most part uninvolved in governance. They are represented in the Forum for the Harmony of Interreligious Communities (Forum Kerukunan antar Umat Beragama, FKUB) and National Integration Forum (Forum Pembauran Kebangsaan, FPK)[34] in Aceh, but their roles in this forum are limited to the point of near insignificance.

As a religious minority group, the diasporic Chinese of Banda Aceh have shown their intention for peaceful coexistence side by side with the local Muslim majority under the current policy of shari`a law. The local government claims that it does not discriminate against the religious minority in Aceh. On paper, as non-Muslims, ethnic Chinese are basically exempt from shari`a law implementation. But in practice, certain policies have limited the ability of Chinese in Aceh to attain sociopolitical positions, such as district governor or head, as well as to engage with and offer input on public policies.

Relations with the Muslim Majority

The current sociopolitical situation of diasporic Chinese in Aceh, and particularly in Banda Aceh, is affected by ongoing sociohistorical dialectics established long ago. These dialectics incentivize diasporic ethnic Chinese to negotiate their identity as part of the Acehnese society. We will consider these separate and influential contexts one by one.

Before Armed Conflict

Prior to the Aceh armed conflict period in 1976, the Chinese were affected mostly by national policy, such as the anti-China policy that arose alongside the anti-communist political party. They were accused of supporting the September 30th Movement (Gerakan 30 September).[35] Many of them were still citizens of the People's Republic of China (Republic Rakyat Cina) and at the same time members of the Indonesian Citizenship Consultative Body (Badan Permusyawaratan Kewarganegaraan Indonesia, or Baperki), an organization composed primarily of Chinese Indonesians. Prior latent conflict then changed to an open one, followed by mass action. Action organized by the Indonesian Student Action Corp (Kesatuan Aksi Mahasiswa Indonesia) occurred from April to August 17, 1966. Soon, they were deported back to China by the government of Indonesia during August 9–17, 1966, from Banda Aceh and Aceh Besar.[36]

Mevlin saw this event as a violent expulsion where Aceh's military commander Ishak Djuarsa took the unprecedented measure of issuing an expulsion order demanding "all alien Chinese" leave the province.[37]

In the 1970s, when the conflict situation was stabilizing, some Chinese returned to Banda Aceh and regained control over their resources. The political dynamics of the intervening years had affected their identity, however: Chinese people were encouraged, for example, not to use their ethnic language in public spaces. Some Chinese in Banda Aceh thought that it was in 1970 when quite a significant number of Chinese people proposed themselves as candidates or applied for Indonesian citizenship. But for Leo Suryadinata, after the Suharto government issued a presidential decision simplifying the procedure to become Indonesian citizens, many alien Chinese applied for Indonesian citizenship by the end of the 1980s.[38] Many Chinese in Banda Aceh were also successful in obtaining Indonesian citizenship, and therefore the next generation of Chinese born in Banda Aceh automatically gained Indonesian citizenship.

Under the New Order regime, the Chinese community in Aceh was made to concentrate in urban areas. Some previous Chinese residential areas can still be identified by what has been left behind there, such as a complex of Chinese tombs in Peukan Bada, though very few Chinese now live nearby. Some of those who worried about the future of their business and employment decided to leave Aceh. Others were successful in generating income and gaining assets.

The Armed Conflict Period, 1998–2005

The armed conflict between the Aceh independence movement and the Indonesian central government occurred over three decades (1976–2005), during which large numbers of civilians, GAM members, and Indonesian security forces were killed.[39] Here, we focus on the later years of the conflict, which affected the Chinese community most especially after the "reformation era" that began in 1998. Two prominent aspects of the conflict affected the Chinese in Banda Aceh: the armed fighting, which caused terror and trauma, and the policy of President Abdurrahman Wahid to recognize Chinese culture and traditions.

During the period of armed fighting, those of minority ethnicity, culture, and religion were threatened, including not only the Chinese but also the Javanese. Sutrisno sees the ethnicity conflict that engaged the Javanese in Aceh as a biggest horizontal conflict during this period.[40] Quite a significant number of Javanese who had migrated to Aceh under government program of *transmigrasi* (transmigration) were forced to leave Aceh for their own security.[41] Although Banda Aceh was regarded as among the safest zones, some Chinese did leave the city—a decision that was also started since the anti–New Order regime riot of May 1998 that affected Chinese in Indonesia badly,[42] by fury of looting, burning, and rape.[43] Despite the lack of specific reports on Chinese ethnic issues during the armed conflict, some Chinese in Banda Aceh recall that this period of armed fighting forced some of them to leave, even if only for a short time.[44]

After the Armed Conflict (and the Application of Shari`a Law)

The peace agreement that ended the prolonged three decades of conflict in Aceh was signed in August 2005. The official implementation of shari`a law in Aceh was declared before the 2005 peace agreement, and to some extent this policy was considered the key to resolving Aceh's armed conflict even many questioning the logic.[45] Yet in any society, much less one that has recently experienced armed conflict, religious- and culturally based tensions are inclined to cause serious horizontal conflict between groups. Therefore, the notion of tolerance became important in Aceh, especially in social relations between Muslims and non-Muslims, including Buddhists. In Qanun 8/2014 on the Principles of Shari`a Law Implementation, Article 24 deals with the issue of jinaya punishment for non-Muslim people.

The Chinese understood the limited support that the government could provide to Chinese (Buddhists) regarding religious education and religious activities, but they still felt there were some activities the government could support, such as the arts and sports, including Barongsai performance. Although there is a specific Barongsai organization across Indonesia, including in Aceh (as Barongsai is also considered a sport), in general the responsibility of preserving this art has been left in the hands of the Chinese themselves.

Under the presidency of Abdurrahman Wahid (1999–2001), the Barongsai and certain other aspects of Chinese cultural identity and tradition were given more public space in Indonesia. The Barongsai is a dance that dates to the fourth century of Chinese history on the mainland. It is considered an important Chinese Buddhist tradition. In addition to cultural performances such as the Barongsai, Indonesian national policy also permitted the usage of Chinese names in public spaces or out of necessity, a right that had been restricted during the New Order regime.

In Banda Aceh, Barongsai have even been performed at a big public event, the Festival Peunayong, in 2011. Prior to the 2011, the Banda Aceh authority banned the Barongsai performance to avoid protest from other citizens. Again, in 2012, the Barongsai performance was restricted by the Banda Aceh authority.[46] And after the introduction of bans and restrictions, the Barongsai began to be performed again in 2014. To avoid controversy and rejection, the Barongsai dance troupe has incorporated local cultural elements, such as the Aceh Seudati dance, according to a Chinese leader of the Aceh Barongsai.[47] The adaptation was likely a response to accusations that Barongsai performances were associated with mysticism. Today, the performances engage Muslim children, and the magical elements have been removed, focusing on the dance as a purely athletic and artistic activity.

Efforts toward Meaningful Plurality

Challenges

For a few diasporic Chinese, the feeling of being an "Acehnese" (*orang Aceh*) is quite apparent. One interviewee said, "I am a local product, originally from Aceh. If someone asks where my hometown is, it is Aceh, and I am Indonesian, because my ID card is an Indonesian identity card."[48] "Aceh" in this regard refers not only to Aceh as a governmental territory, a province, but also to a cultural and ethnic identity. The question here might be to what extent the issue of citizenship relates to the sociocultural aspects of society since cultural and religious identity is tightly held and preserved by the Chinese diasporic community in Banda Aceh. The diasporic Chinese in Banda Aceh are quite aware they cannot live separately from other social groups, especially from the Acehnese Muslim majority.

They have acknowledged some changes in child-rearing and education, however, in recent years. Their children are free to choose if they would like to pursue higher education, which was not encouraged in the past when their children were generally prepared only for participation in family business. Most Aceh Chinese are known as businesspeople, locally addressed as *toke*. Within the past two decades, however, a number of diasporic Chinese children have completed their university degrees, and some have even decided to work outside Aceh due to available employment opportunities. A Chinese businessman whom we interviewed acknowledged the increasing competition: "Acehnese people now are also experts in doing business, so [the business] competition is becoming tough. Secondly, the businessmen in Medan are no longer picky, they would lend to anyone (including businessmen in Aceh) if they do not have money."

Humanitarian Works/Activities

The diasporic Chinese of Aceh have tried to gain social capital through organizations, in this case mainly Hakka. Approximately half of the Chinese in Banda Aceh support Hakka and its activities. The organization embraces all Chinese (Buddhists, Christians, and Muslims). Although it is still young, Hakka is developing a network both within and outside its membership, integrating with other ethnic groups and with the dominant social group of Aceh. Before Hakka, the diasporic Chinese never thought of initiating network and cooperation with Muslim organizations. One respondent explained: "If we do not do anything, the gap becomes bigger. Before, we never thought of having a network with the Nahdlatul Ulama and friends from Muhammadiyah. Before, Chinese never cared about stuff like that."[49]

Hakka exists in several countries to forward a common concern and objective, as well as to meet challenges faced by Chinese communities across many nations. It holds international conferences, the most recent of which were in China and Jakarta.[50] The committee of the Hakka organization in Aceh says that the organization is relatively well managed, which might contribute to its sustainability. Hakka also aims to promote Chinese heritage, history, and culture. In areas of Aceh that do not have Hakka, diasporic Chinese cultural- and humanitarian-related activities are much more limited.

Regarding its organizational outreach strategy, Hakka develops networks among students from different major campuses in Aceh. It also cooperates with other organizations, such as Muhammadiyah, Nahdlatul Ulama, the Nahdlatul Ulama women's wing organization of Fatayat Nahdlatul Ulama, and others. With its external activities, Hakka

The Negotiated "Space" of the Chinese Community   145

attempts to nourish tolerance in a multicultural and multireligious society and is actively involved in forums to promote harmony. In cooperation with the Young Generation for Change (Kader Damai/Generasi Muda untuk Perubahan), Hakka supports the concept of the "Kampung Inklusif" (inclusive village) in three villages with larger Chinese populations. One of their [Acehnese] supporters was elected village head in Gampong Mulia.

Convert (Muallaf) Chinese

Hakka aims to produce a community that embraces social tolerance. It places great hope in those Chinese who convert to Islam—specifically through the convert organizations Aceh Converts Forum (Forum Muallaf Aceh, FORMULA) and Association of Aceh Converts for Prosperity (Persatuan Muallaf Aceh Sejahtera, PMAS)—to bridge the relational gap between the Chinese of Aceh, as a minority, and the Muslim majority. Although these two convert organizations are not solely Chinese, both are coincidentally led by Chinese people who converted to Islam. FORMULA was founded in 2009 and is led by a Chinese person from the Khek ethnic group. PMAS was founded in 2012 and is led by a Hokkien Chinese woman. Both organizations are hubs for converts in Aceh, especially in Banda Aceh, and they include under their umbrella ethnic Indonesians such as Batak, Nias, or Toraja who have converted to Islam.

By placing hope in both convert organizations, the Chinese of Banda Aceh show how social organization might be promoted to strengthen social cohesion and bridge the gap between the Chinese and the majority Muslim population. One Hakka member said of his conversation with a convert Chinese, "From a religious point of view, you are Muslim, and from an ethnicity point of view, you are Chinese."[51] Once, in a public carnival to celebrate state independence in Banda Aceh, the Chinese carnival group included Muslim converts in their Chinese traditional dress in order to demonstrate their inclusiveness. By the time this research was conducted organizationally, converts in Banda Aceh, and Aceh in general, belong to either FORMULA or PMAS. Among the Muslim converts, the ethnic identity is still applied, so there is a term of Chinese (Muslim) convert or Batak (Muslim) convert; although they adhered to the Muslim and Islamic identity after their conversion, their ethnic identity background is not "absorbed" automatically into the local dominant culture.

Nevertheless, as religious identity has been shared with the dominant culture group, their acceptance and interaction are becoming smooth with less resistance and conflict.

Conclusion

The history of diasporic Chinese and their social relations with the ethnic majority of Acehnese has been dynamic, continuously constructed, reconstructed, and changing within a negotiated space of sociospatial dialectics between minority and majority groups. This suggests an inconsistent relationship that has changed in some ways and continued in others because of negotiation, assimilation, and accommodation with the host culture and its society. Narratives of "who is local" and "who is nonlocal" have become more fraught in contemporary Aceh, especially during the period of armed conflict and since.

Whether they are aware of it or not, it is an intention of the diasporic Chinese in Aceh to identify themselves with the narrative of the dominant culture. This intention does not always succeed. Our study has also found that in addition to education, religion, and marriage, ethnic-based organizations such as Hakka are among an important means of social adaptation and facilitating relation of minority and majority Acehnese Muslim, including through humanitarian and philanthropic programs. Conversion to Islam has been a special case in which the forming and deforming of "identity" occurred. The case of Chinese ethnic groups with majority Buddhists and Christians also shows the challenges and the intersection of citizenship and the politics of recognition that ideally imply equal participation, rights, as well as entitlements.

CHAPTER 8

The Uprooted Identity of New Muslim Converts

Conversion has some complexities, as the process of conversion not only relates to the shifting of religion per se, but it also, in some cases, is a shifting from one particular social and cultural identity to others. Especially, within the earlier years of conversion, it significantly alters converts' relationships with others, with the social groups they belonged to (before the conversion). Meanwhile, the conversion also has some economic, social, and political challenges. Being a new Muslim convert left particular implications and challenges to their life that require personal struggle, psychological endurance, social adaptation, and integration. It has been commonly known as a muallaf, they might be expelled from their family and social or cultural groups including religious and ethnic groups. Meanwhile, they also have to devote specific efforts to be accepted and rerooted in their adopted community.

Within the Islamic discourse, the new convert is known as *muallaf*, and particularly within Islamic jurisprudence, there has been specific attention granted to the muallaf group in which (in the Islamic jurisprudence) muallaf is a group that deserves to receive a specific portion of zakat (almsgiving). A well-known Muslim scholar, Yusuf Qardhawy, even provides a specific sociological perspective on the types of muallaf. He explains that muallaf include not only people who have converted to Islam but also those non-Muslims who are expected to become (obedient) Muslims who live in heteroreligious faith families.[1] However, in this research, the term *muallaf* refers to the common understanding among the mainstream of Muslim society as those who converted to the new religion, Islam.

A number of studies on muallaf have revealed the complexities of problems they faced and the needs to handle those issues carefully, particularly by the state.[2] Their problems are not only related to economic issues as commonly understood but also to the nonmaterial ones. Those who decided to convert are considered as those who "exited" from their previous group and detached from their previous identity, at least religious identity. A thesis written by a student in the Department of Psychology at the Islamic University of Ar-Raniry Banda Aceh identified several stages that a new convert would proceed after their conversion until they could have the meaning of life (*kebermaknaan hidup*).[3] The earliest phases were the most difficult ones, and this has something to do with the problem of identity and its uprooting process. This chapter focuses on the Muslim converts in Aceh, those who are Muslim but come from different ethnic backgrounds from the majority. The discussion will examine the challenges of uprooting identity and the state's intervention tied to the politics of recognition matters as it is also the focus of this book.

Guleng and Muhamat quote the popular saying when referring to conversion to Islam, "Becoming Muslim is becoming Malay," which encompasses this perspective. The above well-known citation in the study of religion (conversion) in Southeast Asia means that those Chinese or Indian people who convert from their religion of Buddhism or Hinduism, respectively, to Islam are not only perceived as Muslim but as "Malay" culturally.[4] If this is the case, it means the convert has a new "identity," and the question is, what happened to their earlier social as well as cultural identities? In this study, such a stage and process are identified as the "identity uprooting" situation. The rejection from their previous groups, including their family after the conversion, and the fact that they are not integrated yet into the new adopted community or groups has left those converts with a dilemma and struggle for recognition. As part of the effort to examine this identity uprooted phase, this chapter will also pay attention to the government and other relevant organizations or institutions that handle or provide support to muallaf.

Since its inauguration in the early 2000s, the government of Aceh has made some effort toward the enforcement of shari`a law, starting with the drafting of Islamic local bylaws (qanun) and approving and publicly enacting them. Although quite limited, there has also been a few programs and interventions from the provincial or municipal/district government for new converts, especially in the form of grants, such as cash, financial support for purchasing homes or livestock, and even scholarships for the children of muallaf. In addition, Islamic organizations and the Muslim community often provide limited assistance to muallaf. Based on Act 44/1999 on Keistimewaan Aceh (Aceh's special privilege), the government of Aceh has the flexibility to handle issues related to those converts. However, in practice, these are not adequate yet and still limited in solving problems, especially those of nonmaterial matters.

In Aceh, the notion of ethnic identity is also closely associated with religion so that it is common to hear people refer to the "Cina muallaf" (Chinese converts), "Batak Islam," "Pak Pak Muslims," and so forth. In light of this, the chapter also explores how the politics of shari`a rhetoric in Aceh responds to these problems and to the challenges faced by new converts. Their life stories suggest an uneasy spiritual journey that includes family and their social groups' resistance as mentioned earlier in the form of uprooted identity.[5] Due to this uprooted identity, in some cases, muallaf can be identified as a socially and politically vulnerable group despite belonging to the religious majority of Islam.

Being a *Muallaf* in Aceh

Historically, in his book on Aceh, James T. Siegel recorded the story of the first Aceh sultan, Juhan Shah, who converted the people of Aceh to Islam on Friday, the first day of Ramadan.[6] There are also stories of when non-Muslims came to Aceh or came to live together with Muslims; these stories refer particularly to the Chinese migrants who arrived during the Dutch occupation. There are also those who live at the border of North Sumatra and Aceh in the 1940s. Nevertheless, the term *muallaf* was not known widely, or at least referred to in the case of the above historical record. However, in recent times, the term *muallaf* became more well known and has been a specific social group identified easily and mostly as those with different ethnic group background from the majority.

Nowadays, Muslim converts in Aceh come from Protestant, Catholic, and Buddhist backgrounds. One notable factor behind their conversion to Islam is usually their marriage to Muslim spouses, who are mostly Muslim men. For this reason, the number of female muallaf is relatively higher. For some converts, their conversion to Islam is also the result of their personal interest or willingness after learning about Islam from their peers, teachers, or speeches or sermons. In our research, we discovered that most conversions were voluntary and had not been forced by any particular party or agency. We did not find any political motivations for the cases of conversion so far, nor did we learn of any forced conversions to Islam. However, a scholar, Wei Weng, in his research mentions an economic factor behind a few conversion cases in which muallaf wished to receive the portion of almsgiving (zakat) provided for the muallaf group (based on the injunction in Islamic jurisprudence)[7] as discussed earlier in this chapter. In practice, however, few muallaf utilized their conversion certificates as proof to ask for donations from the Muslim community or request financial support from Muslim social institutions.[8] One officer we spoke with from the Aceh government expressed his concern about the possibility of the fact that the conversion certificate could be abused for this public donation collection purpose.[9]

On the other hand, close observation of the life of those converts reveals that the consequences of conversion are not always easy to deal with personally. A convert needs support and assistance in various forms from their social circle. One of the muallaf leaders interviewed said that consequences faced by muallaf were the reason why he established a muallaf organization to provide help and assistance for new converts in a more organized way. Aceh Muallaf Forum (Forum Muallaf Aceh, FORMULA) was established in 1999. The leader of this organization, Muhammad Rasyid, noticed problems faced by new converts after their conversion. He provided testimony of his personal experience in facing his family's resistance to his conversion and his ongoing attempts to maintain a relationship with his large family even though he now has a different religion.[10]

In response to similar problems, another muallaf organization in Aceh, the Association of Aceh Converts for Prosperity (Persatuan Muallaf Aceh Sejahtera, PMAS) was founded in 2012 and led by a woman, Fatimah Azzahra. As the leader of PMAS, she acknowledged difficulties experienced by many newly converted Muslims in Aceh. She said that she sometimes arranges temporary shelter for new converts whose families have expelled them from their home. She also helps new converts to find work, especially converts who plan to marry but are jobless and lack family support.

The problems of young converts can be more serious since they are not yet economically and socially independent. A Buddhist leader in Banda Aceh suggested that teenagers who want to convert to Islam should approach their parents properly to avoid family conflict that might ruin their education and their future. This approach, he hoped, would at least prevent them from missing their study after conversion due to internal family conflict as well as a lack of educational support from their parents.[11] A head of Gampong Laksana village told us a story of a male muallaf who took several years to reconcile with his parents. Some converts do manage to reconcile with their families, but their rights as children of their Buddhist or Catholic families remain "revoked" due to their conversion.[12]

With all situations mentioned above, a new convert is not only prone to but also could be perceived as a person of double "minority" although religiously, they belong to the religion of the majority. Still, they are perceived as "different" or "other." Again, identity, whose (ethnic) group someone belongs to, is a "problematic" matter. Although on the other hand just like other minorities, there is always intention and effort from the minority to submit to the dominant culture.

Beyond the Conversion

A community or villagers always enthusiastically respond for a moment when someone officially converts to Islam. The conversion ritual is usually facilitated by a religious or local community leader. Often, the event takes place in a mosque and is observed by many people, especially the mosque's congregation. This conversion brings good news and happiness to the congregation and others. Yet soon afterward, only a few cared how the convert would continue their life after their uneasy and challenging conversion. They have already exited from their previous community but are not yet fully integrated into their new adopted community.

A Chinese leader in Banda Aceh, Ko Khie Siong, chief of Hakka, said that he said to the chief of FORMULA, "No need to be fractious when being muallaf." This was his response to a claim made by the head of a muallaf organization—who is also Chinese—that no one cares about muallaf issues in Aceh. Ko Khie Siong informed us that he talked to the person twice, asking him to keep calm and take on all of his own risks after the conversion. He insisted that new converts should live in harmony and support one another and reconcile well after their organizational conflict. He really regrets the 2012 muallaf's organization disunity, and another muallaf organization was then founded known as PMAS. Ko

Khie Siong said, "It is shameful when people look at us. We have conflict among us."[13] For him, keeping the peace among muallaf organizations should be a priority among the converts. According to Ko Khie Siong, the muallaf at the end of the day are also expected to be "ambassadors" to bridge their connection to a larger Muslim majority.

Nevertheless, for the converts, it is not always easy to adapt to their new situation. When someone converts to another religion, leaving behind their former religion, it means that they have left their earlier social and cultural identity, affiliations, and circles. On the other hand, most converts apparently fail to follow their new religion faithfully, as there is no well-organized system to support them in this regard. Then, in a few cases, this failure can affect their integration into their newly adopted community and can become a barrier in their socioreligious interactions and communications. Their conversion is not considered *murni* (sincere) but as having hidden or private selfish agendas behind it. However, in reality, those new converts do not have good access to learn their new religion from authoritative sources or parties.

A female muallaf in Banda Aceh who converted to Islam more than twenty years ago, for example, said she only waited for the class organized by a muallaf organization to learn about her new religion. Unfortunately, the class also has to struggle to maintain regular meetings due to a lack of support and resources. She cannot rely on her (Muslim) husband or just on an individual Muslim to teach her about Islam. It is quite common that some muallaf's husbands are not able to teach their convert wife about Islam properly.[14] If the organization discontinues the class on learning about Islam, they would not be able to find a suitable class, except for a children's course on Qur'an recitation, which is not optimum. To join the regular adult Muslim class means that they are not left further behind.[15] This was among the reasons why PMAS was founded.[16]

FORMULA and PMAS work to help converts to overcome this problem, but to some extent, their efforts have met with only limited success. PMAS's learning Islam course seems to be participated by women converts predominantly or limited to a certain group. It actually offers teachings at two places: a private *musholla* (small mosque) donated by a political leader of Banda Aceh Municipal Parliament and at the two other places, the Banda Aceh Municipal musholla building (as the mayoral administrations' commitment) and sometimes at the Banda Aceh Shari`a Office musholla. An older woman mentors the students using the *tadarrus* method (reading the Qur'an collectively). The students' recitation sounds unclear, not simultaneous, and reveals a number of mistakes. Yet these muallaf come to the religious congregation regularly, and they interact socially well after their lessons—for instance, teaching peers on how to knit a bag.[17] Women converts seem to be more active in participating in their new religious congregations than are men; women are pushed by their desire to improve their knowledge and their practice of Islamic teachings.

Classes for converts are not available in most of Aceh's districts or subdistricts. There is also a limited number of suitable instructors who understand muallaf situation and can adapt their teaching method and content to the muallaf's current state of knowledge on Islam as well as their needs. To have an appropriate mentor for their class, PMAS established connections with several Muslim organizations, including Muhammadiyah, Hizbut Tahrir Indonesia, and Front Pembela Islam. By relying on these organizations' support, the muallaf was able to obtain teachers from various backgrounds such as activists, lecturers, and teachers from Islamic traditional schools or dayah. Consequently, there is no single teaching method to the course provided and there is no structured curriculum with a basic curriculum that meets the needs of those muallaf. For instance, a teacher from an activist or university lecturer background use the *halaqah* (a traditional preaching method where all students sit in front of the teacher), while a teacher from a dayah background uses the traditional model of Islamic learning through *kitab* (Arabic textbook). The muallaf congregation is requested to read the text and repeat the instructor's reading as the way of teaching in the Islamic traditional boarding school (dayah). The situation is among the challenges faced by muallaf to gain knowledge qualification, which also affect not only their religious observance as a new Muslim believer but also their possible integration into the Muslim community.

There is no standard as to who is eligible to teach in this case; anyone can be the instructor so long as they can preach. As the general effort, according to the leader of PMAS, the organization has not yet put conditions on what kind of instructor they need to teach muallaf, especially since the teachers help teach them on a voluntary basis. As a result, sometimes muallaf could not follow the class effectively. For instance, one afternoon, the members of the class became confused when they had to read the Malay Arabic book *Kitab Jawi* used by the instructor as the textbook, even though most of them still struggle to recite the Qur'an fluently. After half an hour was spent on listening to the instructor, they finally proposed to change the method of instruction when both men and women students confessed that they could not read the Arabic or even read the Qur'an properly yet.[18]

Muallaf as a Community as Well as a Minority

As mentioned earlier, conversion is not always or only a religious matter; it also has social and cultural dimensions. This work sees the importance of an integration process to be among the problem-solving options. Some converts in Aceh come from a diasporic Chinese background, and most new converts come from minority ethnic groups who have lived in Aceh for short amount of time. As in other places, muallaf in Aceh thus also have a double-minority identity—of ethnicity and religion—of the type described by Hew Wei Weng in Indonesia.[19]

Weng's work articulates four categories of Chinese Muslim. One of the most relevant to this study is the category of those who are observant Muslims and have culturally assimilated into the local ethnic majority. Those few Chinese women in Banda Aceh who convert to Islam, for instance, tend to stop wearing traditional Chinese dress and adopt the dress of local Muslim women, concealing their cultural identity in public. They also change their names to names more familiar to the majority of local Acehnese, usually Arabic-derived names. They stop participating in celebrations for Imlek, as they consider such celebrations are not part of Muslim culture.[20] Such comprehensive change is not easy, as efforts to root in the new culture could also take many years, and for some, it sometimes results in a feeling of having gotten nowhere, with only an ambiguous sociocultural identity.

In Malaysia, the term "new brother" (*saudara baru*) is used to describe recent Muslim converts. It is used to indicate and state that someone has embraced Islam. Referring to Muhamat and Puteh, this term is a way to enhance Islamic brotherhood care for and love of converts.[21] However, this is also the case with converts, and it causes them to become separated from the mainstream of the Muslim *ummah*, as the converts may feel that they are not included among those born Muslim. This terminology can divide Muslims into born Muslims and converts. This is not quite suitable for integration process—that is, to encourage them to socialize and mix freely as Muslim brothers. The term *muallaf* seems to indicate that there is a gap between them, and it is certainly considered a racism issue. All this makes integration between Malays as a majority and the muallaf as "newcomers" to Islam deteriorate.[22]

The term *saudara baru* can be considered an effort toward the social integration of converts as "brother" or "sibling." The term blurs the dichotomy of born versus convert Muslim. But the Acehnese Muslim community has no specific term for converts except the term derived from Arabic, muallaf, which is understood to describe someone who has newly converted to Islam, and term *muallaf* conceptually has nothing to do with identity matters. Seemingly, a social appreciation system needs to be set up to assist muallaf with integration and complete acceptance in their new culture. For some in Aceh, it has been an issue that certain Chinese muallaf continue to commemorate Imlek. The presence of muallaf shows a cultural challenge that will remain a challenge if it is not adequately addressed.

Socioreligious Life and Governance of New Converts in Aceh

Following conversion, muallaf have to deal with certain issues they cannot resolve by themselves, and they require serious help, especially from the government. The leader of PMAS advocates for Aceh Muslim converts to receive government support through the establishment of muallaf centers. She has learned that the government of Malaysia not only provides muallaf with temporary settlement during the period of their coursework on Islamic faith but also the life skills lessons and small business grants to help them achieve a better standard of living as converts in a country like Malaysia.

Almost two decades after creating new Islamic religious offices, the government in Aceh has not yet applied a better muallaf empowerment. In a discussion on muallaf issues, leaders of the two respective muallaf organizations had hardly discussed the muallaf database.[23] Alyasa' Abubakar,[24] a former leader of the Provincial Shari`a agency, stated that the government of Aceh is not yet working on muallaf issues properly, including the fact that there is no reliable muallaf database available,[25] which makes any arrangement for muallaf program support more difficult and challenging.

It is obvious that muallaf need both government and community support. However, such support is often missing rather than provided. Although the community usually welcomes the Muslim "newcomer," after the "euphoria" of the conversion ceremony, new converts are abandoned to struggle by themselves. The situation becomes more unfortunate if the muallaf cannot communicate effectively or articulate their unfortunate situation to relevant parties to gain support and assistance. As mentioned earlier, this problem also relates to the problematized identity they carry after the conversion as the "uprooted" identity process or phase.

Conversion and Religious Social Life in the Community

The primary responsibility for the Islamic education in Aceh has traditionally fallen on the family and village levels.[26] Acehnese families have historically placed a strong emphasis on instilling religious values in their children. However, this dynamic has shifted somewhat in recent decades, as modernization has increasingly drawn educational resources away from the home and village toward school and even media. As observed by Christian Snouck Hugronje in the 1890s, Islam plays a central role in regulating domestic life in Aceh.[27] Faith is not merely a private matter but also a community concern. This principle applies not only to the majority Acehnese ethnic group but also to other Muslim ethnic groups in the region. Religion is a significant aspect of social life, and conversions must be publicly acknowledged making them a matter of community interest. Individuals who convert from the village's dominant religion may encounter difficulties, potentially including being forced to leave the village as a penalty or a consequence of their religious choices.

Few villages in Aceh develop Islamic education programs. There are activities such as the Qur'anic early teaching program and Islamic teaching groups called Majelis Taklim, as well as private Qur'anic teaching by individual religious leaders in *balee seumeubuet* (a traditional building for religious teaching). An *imeum* (Muslim community village leader) will organize not only a solemn conversion ceremony but also provide muallaf with instruction on how to read the Qur'an proficiently and perform the quintuple daily prayer. Reinforcing the faith of new converts, the village leader offers religious guidance through courses for children as well as adults who need to start their Islamic knowledge from ground zero.

Of course, with special autonomy status, Aceh has a special right to handle the issues of religious governance, which would also include program and support for new converts. The support for muallaf known widely by the majority of the community in Aceh is normally an economic support from a specific portion of almsgiving.[28] Generally, there is no knowledge in how to support muallaf except from the almsgiving portion or economic support. Before the establishment of a shari`a office, it was only Badan Amil Zakat, Infak, and Shadaqah (BAZIS), which allocates financial support to the muallaf group. Soon after special autonomy status was granted, the governor of Aceh released the Decree 18/2003 for a new office establishment, including the Baitul Mal.[29] The establishment of several new offices that govern religious life has indeed created more opportunities for specific programs to support muallaf. These programs can now extend beyond the economic support provided in earlier practices to include other forms of assistance as well. Officially, there are the Department of Shari`a Offices (Dinas Syariat Islam, DSI), the Aceh Privilege Bureau (Biro/Bidang Keistimewaan Aceh) at governor and municipality/district offices across Aceh that could consolidate to carry out the same support. The functions of those agencies could ease the issues and complexity among muallaf as a vulnerable group as well as "minority" within the society. While there has been increasing support, particularly in recent times, it primarily focuses on economic well-being (such as cash assistance, scholarship programs, housing for new convert families, and business development assistance). However, it does not adequately address the deeper issues of integration, including the challenge of identity loss, conversion experiences, and other related difficulties.

Religious Life and the Conversion in the Border Areas

The government of Aceh considers people living in the border areas as living in areas of religious pluralism. So, with this fact, the government pays special attentions to the area, including conversion issues. The border areas consist of villages either with majority Muslim or non-Muslim residents. According to the local government regulation, the program of da`i perbatasan (Muslim border preacher) was set up to focus on Muslims only and emphasize the approach of *mauidzah hasanah* (wisdom).[30] The Islamic mission (*dakwah*) to the border areas is understood to mean not interfering with non-Muslims' faith but rather strengthening the capacity of people who have converted to Islam. Although Muslim preachers assigned to the border areas are not asked to carry out their dakwah mission to non-Muslims, they do assist non-Muslims who express an intent to convert to Islam.

Conversion is a specific issue found in the border areas. Apparently, the threat of Muslims' conversion to other religions has been a serious issue in the border areas like Aceh Tenggara and Singkil, even though demographic data show an increase in the Muslim population in the five border areas. In Aceh Tenggara from 2010 to 2014, there was a notable decrease in the number of Protestants from 21,230 to 10,537. In Singkil, while the Protestant population rose significantly from 5,080 to 8,282 in those years, the number of Muslims also dramatically increased from 94,550 to 98,833.

Programs and Efforts for Assistance

In 2017, an officer at the Aceh Shari'a Office from one of the districts in Aceh posted on his Facebook account a photo of muallaf training in a small room without any chairs or tables. Mostly female muallaf sit on the floor. A four-meter-long green banner hangs on the pale-yellow wall. The post explains that the office conducted a training for muallaf, those who are considered as *masyarakat dangkal akidah* (people with little knowledge of Islamic theology). The post simply explained how muallaf are perceived by some people. Their limited knowledge of their new religion is highlighted, but nevertheless, relevant training and support were not provided accordingly.

Since there is no fixed database on muallaf, data collection is mostly voluntary. This has been the start of several problems in handling the muallaf problem in Aceh. Thus, the office of civil registry cannot count the exact number of muallaf in Aceh; even village databases at the lowest level of current government administration do not track this information. The problem occurs when people and relevant agencies are surprised by the higher data of muallaf, which limit relevant agencies' ability to provide support or assistance to muallaf.

In general, muallaf sometimes have poor economic status due to the situation as mentioned earlier in this chapter (e.g., severance from their family and family's resources). They actually need cash and skills to support their livelihood activity, including better education for the children in muallaf families. Some converts divorce after conversion, which sometimes make the situation even worse. There are, for instance, female muallaf as a single parent in need of legal assistance regarding her status. For other women with the support of their family, being a single parent would not be as difficult as muallaf women who get divorced after their conversion and become a single parent. The PMAS leader told us that a woman convert in Aceh Besar was abandoned by her husband after she converted to Islam and migrated to Aceh from West Java. As the leader of PMAS, she took the initiative to approach the village government to provide this convert and her three children with a new identity and family register to access government social aid or support.

On the other hand, there have been difficulties in assisting new converts since no database about this kind of household is available. The existence of two muallaf organizations (FORMULA and PMAS) in Aceh, led by muallaf themselves, cannot resolve the data issue. The leaders of both muallaf organizations seek to advocate on behalf of converts by utilizing social capital and social networks. The leader of FORMULA, for instance, has used a connection with a politician who happens to be a member of the local legislature. Through this connection, FORMULA can gain support and resources to help the organization's activities. PMAS, on the other hand, works in a different style. The leader of PMAS has devoted some of her efforts to data gathering, sending a pedicab driver from one village to another in the municipality of Banda Aceh to count converts (data from the rest of Aceh province remains unrecorded). Both leaders, even though their advocacy style differs, have been outspoken about the need to provide assistance to muallaf in Aceh.

Muallaf's and muallaf organizations' relation to the government is not always stable. There have been a few instances that show this unstable relationship and disagreement. One of the muallaf leaders, for instance, was banned by the municipal government because of the transparency issue related to government assistance received by the organization. The problem with the province of Baitul Mal emerged when the muallaf organization leaders talk to media to express their criticisms on related government agency in dealing with muallaf support programs. They disagreed on how the support for muallaf should be handled. In their view, there was no effective communication taking place between the government and the organization to identify the amount of demand and supply. Later, in a focus group discussion on muallaf attended by stakeholders, government agencies (including Baitul Mal Aceh officers) and academics, the leaders of the muallaf organizations realized the need for more collaborative efforts regarding muallaf issues. Consequently, they recognized the importance of beginning with data collection to guide more effective interventions.[31]

Policies and Interventions on Muallaf: Discursive Practice

An international conference on muallaf called for the entire Muslim community to attend to convert issues seriously.[32] Borrowing Edward Heath Robinson's terminology of government as organizations of people, we argue that the issues of muallaf are issues of the people.[33] This means that both the state and the people must collaborate to solve the problems of muallaf, who are a minority within the majority religion of Aceh and who are also a group of people with double-minority social status.

One of the muallaf interviewed for this study pointed out that there is no reliable system to facilitate conversion for those who wish to pursue it. Instead, conversion relies much on the support of personal initiative from converts' friends who reach out to religious or community leaders. They are very helpful in assisting a conversion process of proclaiming *shahada*, which marks someone as having embraced Islam. For some muallaf, this lack of state support in the conversion process suggests that the implementation of shari`a in Aceh does not cover every single issue. In fact, those muallaf consider that both the government and the Muslim community are not well prepared to welcome their new brothers and sisters. This is quite different from a case in one of the states in Malaysia, Negeri Sembilan. To take just one example, a local law identifies eleven different elements of state involvement in the conversion process. This process ends with a state-supplied certificate of conversion and a thirty-seven-point state guideline detailing the conversion process, including the duties and obligations of muallaf.[34]

There is another new convert issue in Aceh that remains unresolved. It is related to a question of at what point a newly converted Muslim ceases to be considered muallaf. Do they remain muallaf forever? And would the same status of muallaf be applied to their children as well? Is there a known term "muallaf children"? This practice has implications for the assistance new converts receive, both socially and economically. Some of them live in poverty and are jobless, and a few are young widows with children. They remain a marginalized group in Acehnese Muslim society although the term *muallaf* itself has a strong connotation that they are entitled to receive aid or support.

A number of organizations and parties have paid attention to the issues of muallaf. Yet, their efforts are neither consolidated nor integrated. This in part has to do with the fact that there is no existing policy in Aceh to consolidate their varied efforts or program in assisting muallaf

The Uprooted Identity of New Muslim Converts   161

to support one another like in certain states of Malaysia.³⁵ In Malaysia, these states have organized education for Muslim children, health centers, and other aid since the 1960s through Islamic mission (dakwah) organizations such as PERKIM (founded in 1960 by Tunku Abdul Rahman Putera al-Haj, the first Malaysian prime minister) and Harakah Islamiyah (HIKMAH) in Kuching, Sarawak (founded in 1994 by Abdul Taib Mahmud, the head of Menteri Sarawak).³⁶ The management of these organizations was then transferred to the Department of Islamic Affairs and the Islamic Affairs Section of the Prime Minister's Department for zakat distribution to muallaf. Along with PERKIM, the Department of Islamic Affairs had mapped almost twenty issues affecting new converts to Islam that required assistance.³⁷

In Aceh, the Baitul Mal spent Rp1.15 billion for muallaf families who live in poverty in several districts. The data of those poor muallaf families were collected in 2017 by the Baitul Mal with the support of Rumah Zakat, a private organization that has an extensive network in Aceh. With such data that contain names and addresses of the muallaf heads of households, they disbursed some block grants to support small businesses of the muallaf. However, this economic partnership did not last long since there were some serious challenges in the field that could not be mitigated and resolved by both parties.³⁸ In fact, from the beginning, the program relied on trial-and-error methods.

Actions taken by Islamic organizations in Malaysia remind us of the existence of a number of Islamic organizations in Indonesia, among them Nahdlatul Ulama, the Muhammadiyah, Persatuan Tarbiyah Islamiyah, Al-Washliyah, and others, including a number of Islamic political parties. In Aceh, currently there is no Islamic organization paying specific attention to the muallaf problem. Efforts to assist muallaf by some Islamic leaders in eastern Indonesia (such as in Jayapura, Papua) and in other non-Muslim majority provinces are more obvious than anything happening in Aceh. At least when those organizations work well, muallaf can count on having access to a better and more moderate understanding of Islam. This is what happened in Sidrap, one of the districts in South Sulawesi province. As explained by Ramlah Hakim,³⁹ both Nahdlatul Ulama and Muhammadiyah organizations approached muallaf families, visiting them door to door, and taught them about Islam, even in the face of threats from others who disapproved of this action. Another interesting fact is that there have been informal efforts initiated by some individuals at the provincial office of Ministry of

Religion in Jayapura that support muallaf. They established community groups such as Kelompok Kajian Muallaf, Forum Komunikasi Muslim Pegunungan Tengah, Majelis Muslim Papua, and Yayasan Pembinaan Muallaf.[40]

These examples should have challenged the Baitul Mal office in Aceh to do similar things and to act more than business as usual. As this organization expanded from its prior status (a small and poorly funded government agency known as BAZIS) to a well-established office with adequate provincial government support, it should have better programs in providing for muallaf individuals and families in Aceh. Having received billions of rupiah in the form of zakat from the Acehnese people, Baitul Mal has more options to make some effective interventions through zakat distribution to those muallaf.

The question remains: what measures are relevant to enhance the performance of Aceh Baitul Mal? Apparently, no steps have been taken so far to evaluate its programs, and no specific party or agency within the provincial government has initiated such an evaluation. In fact, there are several agencies in Aceh that could work together in dealing with muallaf issues. Those agencies include Baitul Mal, the DSI at the provincial and district levels, and Islamic organizations. As a lesson learned from the other provinces in Indonesia, the problem of Baitul Mal's low performance has something to do with the lack of integrated management, especially by those government offices with the power to intervene.[41]

Given the complex dynamics in different fields and regions in Indonesia, there may be no perfect model for taking care of the new converts. However, it is obvious that assisting muallaf in adjusting to their new religion requires a comprehensive approach. As suggested by Sri Hidayati in her study on muallaf in Singkawang (West Kalimantan), a city with more than 70 percent of its population being non-Muslim Chinese, a well-structured intervention is necessary to cope with social complexities and challenges faced daily by new converts.[42] Her study emphasized that these complexities not only include issues of mobilizing financial contributions but also, more importantly, the challenge of integrating muallaf into a system where government offices, Islamic organizations, and community leaders work together to support those converts.

Despite all the above, it is worth noting that the Baitul Mal of Aceh has a success story of providing a scholarship program to support the education of muallaf children. With data collected on schoolchildren

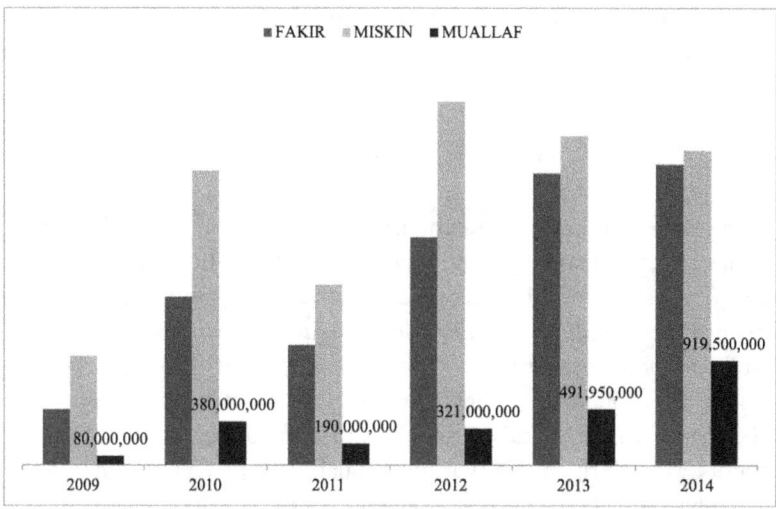

Figure 8.1. Zakat and Allocation for Muallaf, 2009–2014 (in Indonesian rupiah)
Source: Baitul Mal Aceh Office.

from muallaf families, the Baitul Mal funds those children to study at schools in their own areas. It supports not only the basic (twelve-year) level of education but also tertiary education. The scholarship funds are derived from the zakat payment designated especially to support poor families. This scholarship program appears to be sustainable. According to 2015 data, the Baitul Mal supported 141 elementary, junior, and high school students and 550 diploma and undergraduate students through this scholarship program. The office also sent adult muallaf to pesantren to learn more about Islam. Other than this scholarship fund for muallaf, limited financial support was also provided by the government for farming families in the form of homes, farmland, and cash to pay for their basic needs.[43] Figure 8.1 shows six years of zakat allocation by Baitul Mal Aceh, including annual allocation for muallaf needs, which is always less than the other specified allocations—that is, for poor people.[44]

This figure confirms our earlier assumption that most of the support provided to muallaf comes in the form of financial assistance, even though their problems are not always about financial matter but also about integration issues. Their limited access to learning about Islam leaves them lacking confidence and creates psychological barriers to smoothly interact with the Muslim community. The attribute of "muallaf" signifies their difference from others in their adopted religious group, their status as newcomers, and sometimes also their different social and cultural identities.

Conclusion

As the book examines the relationship between minority and majority groups in Aceh through the politics of dominant culture and politics of recognition, muallaf (Muslim convert) has been a specific case. After conversion, their religious identity allows them to be part of the majority, but what about their ethnic or cultural background? Would this ethnic identity be brought into their new religious identity or be discarded? The chapter discussed this ambiguity and defined the stage as uprooting identity as well, the phase that most muallaf occurred especially in the early phases of their conversion when they have found an exit or have been expelled from the group they previously belong to but are not yet integrated well into the newly adopted community.

This uprooting process becomes even more serious when converts' integration into their newly adopted community is unsuccessful or only partially successful. There are several factors behind this, including the limited access they have to learn about their new religion, the host community's lack of social support, and the unsuitable and unsustained assistance, both from government agencies and social religious organizations. A close observation on the muallaf assistance program, especially the one provided by the government, shows a discursive practice and unconsolidated or unintegrated ways. Within this context, a specific minority group like muallaf confirms that identity is quite a complex issue and intersected. Their conversion to Islam does not guarantee their smooth integration and acceptance into the dominant culture, nor does it guarantee they receive equal participation and recognition.

CHAPTER 9

The Limited Agency of Female Religious Minorities

Maintaining a multireligious society has become a special social challenge for Aceh in the postconflict period, especially when the notion of identities, including religious ones, has become stronger and more dominant in the public space. From the civil conflict period in Aceh in the mid-twentieth century until the peace agreement signed in 2005, the politics of identity emerged more publicly in the social and political life of Acehnese society. Admittedly, religion and religious issues are sensitive subjects for most Indonesian communities, let alone Aceh, a region well known as the stronghold Muslim community in Indonesia.

Considering the above context, there has been concern about the possibility of discrimination and intolerance toward religious minority groups in the region. Being part of a minority group can be an uneasy "identity" within the community and, to some extent, can also make individuals or groups within the minority vulnerable. A few of them might even have double minority status. This chapter explores the lives of women, those from religious minority groups in a province like Aceh, where Islam is the religion of the majority population, and the fact that Islamic principles are also applied as positive law through the enacted bylaws. Being a woman and being a believer of a minority religion, this group of people can be regarded as a marginalized minority.

It has been a common perception of how women in many societies are socially and politically marginalized, and their participation is not always fairly recognized. Having a patriarchal culture, Aceh society also faces similar problems and challenges, although Aceh is also known as, according to some observers, a matrifocal society.[1] A few works on Acehnese women have confirmed both sides of women's life: being restricted on the one hand and having relative autonomy and agency in public spaces and roles on the other hand. For most works on women in Aceh, the data available are almost always on Muslim women as majority religion and ethnicity.

This chapter examines the narratives and experiences of women from minority religions in Aceh in dealing with majorities and in the context of the politics of dominant culture as well. The chapter looks at the efforts these women have devoted to building coexistence and gaining recognition for their rights and positions. As in many parts of the world, members of minority religious groups seek public recognition from the dominant culture, to be accepted fairly and to survive socially and politically. To that end, they tend to utilize varied strategies, which are often diverse and contextual.

This chapter begins with a discussion of the normative perspectives of minority religions in Aceh, shedding light on their stories, efforts, and agency in dealing with limitations caused by their minority status. Those of minority religions make use of the public religious sphere, public education, and humanitarian action to maintain their social existence. Two patterns commonly appear in the lives of religious minorities in Aceh. The first is the pattern of Buddhist Chinese descendants, identified in chapter 7, which shows a degree of positive interaction with and acceptance by the Muslim majority. The second is the story of Protestants and Batak Catholics in Aceh, who struggle to attain the same degree of interaction and acceptance. These two groups have different experiences in relation to coexistence and their integration into the host community and culture. This indicates that the plurality of religions in Aceh continue to face some challenges and complexity under a special autonomy status that the Indonesian central government has granted Aceh.

Notably, efforts of women from minority religions to work and build a connection to the majority have been effective through their humanitarian or (semi-)volunteerism-based work as explained later in this chapter. Compared with their male counterparts, these women seem to be very good agents to bridge and bind the relationship with other groups of the community, including the majority. However, as their positions are marginalized, their efforts and roles are mostly unheard or properly known and recognized.

Women of Minority Religions: Textual and Contextual Perspectives

As mentioned earlier, especially within the context of shari`a law enforcement in Aceh, more attention has been paid on how Aceh Muslim women live under shari`a in this province. There is almost no serious intent to explore the life of non-Muslim women within the shari`a context of Aceh society. Although each religion might have specific injunctions and teachings that deal with the life of the believers, the believers are modifying or contextualizing those principles to ensure their relevance to their contextual social environment, survival process, and to be recognized as equal co-citizens.

Our reading of religious teachings suggests the limitations of women's roles in the public sphere, especially in regard to leadership. According to a Buddhist priest, Buddhist women are prohibited from serving as *bhante* (worship leaders). One Buddhist woman we interviewed said that in her sect of Theravada Buddhism, the position of bhante is exclusively for men. In the Mahayana Buddhism, women can achieve the position of *bhikkhuni*,[2] although the term *bhikkhu* refers to a male religious leader. In Aceh, the Buddhist community has only a small number of bhikkhu and no bhikkhuni. One bhikkhuni used to come to Aceh from Medan, North Sumatra.

The situation is similar to those of other religious minority groups in Aceh. Christians, for instance, do not have female religious leaders in Aceh, nor do Catholics or Hindus. A Catholic official (Pembimas)[3] of the Aceh Provincial Ministry of Religion admits the operation of the patriarchal principle in the Catholic religion. Catholic women are not allowed to lead large worship meetings (*eka risti* or *penjamuan kudus*). This congregation can only be led by a priest. Catholic women may serve as nuns or be involved with church management. Women may only take charge of leading worship at home or as informal religious instructors who make "five-minute religious appeals" in between worship day activities.[4]

In Protestantism, especially among Gereja Bethel Indonesia (GBI) disciples, women have more roles available to them. A woman from the GBI said that women may preach to specific congregations in a school or a church. Women may also lead the *pujian* (worship) as long as they show their ability. Christian GBI, which has only a small group of believers in Banda Aceh, today has three women who lead Sunday worship at church. The Banda Aceh GBI's woman leader is also trusted to hold special consultations dealing with children's issues. Other churches of the GBI also have woman pastors.

Compared with other religious minority groups in Aceh, Hinduism has the fewest believers; approximately only thirty-one people in Banda Aceh are Hindu believers. When the tsunami devastated Aceh in 2004, it destroyed Gampong Kedah, where several Hindu families lived. It also killed families of Hindus from the Indian Tamil ethnic group, who still manage a temple in Kedah village. Like Buddhists, Hindus use a different language for worship, namely Sanskrit. Their worship in Banda Aceh is led by Radha, the third generation of a family, who also lead the temple. No other leaders, including women, have a prominent role. Radha received his religious training in Medan. There, many Hindus and leaders supported him. In his roles, he maintains coordination with that larger community, including inviting the higher leader to come to lead Siwa Ratri commemoration day in Banda Aceh.[5]

Women, Domestic Life, and Internalized Values

All the minority religions of Aceh have rules, or teachings, regarding how to respect women and protect their rights. But these rules are always intermingled with traditions, such as Chinese or Batakese tradition. This is also similar to Aceh Muslim society as the majority in which the rules and Islamic teachings of how to treat and respect women are combined with the cultural aspect of the society. One Protestant Chinese woman admitted, for example, that even though her religion teaches that men and women are equal, in the Chinese family tradition a husband has more authority to give instructions or orders to his wife to spend most of her time taking care of the children and the family's needs. This woman did not seem to think this experience was affected by the Acehnese Muslim majority's family culture: "[Male dominance of women] is normal for the Chinese people as well [as for Muslims], even [though] we are hybrid and [have] lived [a long time] in Aceh. It makes us no different [from] other people. It is a man who always receives obedience."[6] The same situation was disclosed by a Batakese woman: even the Catholic teaching orders equity between men and women, all women—even those of a higher social status than their husband—must obey their husband, as it is taught in Batakese families. But for the Chinese and Batakese women, their current family situation allows them to take up certain public roles and activities, such as serving as a humanitarian volunteer, as will be explained later in this chapter.

Both Protestants and Catholics are widely known to oppose polygamy and divorce. Their holy book stipulates the reciprocal rights of husband and wife, providing details on ideal marital relations between the spouses. There is a provision in Protestantism, for instance, that instructs, "Respect your husband and love your wife." One Protestant leader we interviewed argued there is no discrimination against women in the religion, as both men and women have the same duty to respect and love each other. This principle is also found in the Catholic belief. Both Protestants and Catholics see a woman as a partner for her husband in a family, and for Catholics, the husband is considered the leader (*imam*) of his family.

The above values, if observed closely, suggest that women should not be set apart from the public sphere, including from the religious public sphere with its accompanying leadership roles. The interviews confirmed that in various religions and circumstances, women do not take central leadership roles. The situation is considered natural from the common perspective found in the society. The limited public participation of women has partly to do with the values or teaching found in a religion, which is often understood to have an emphasis in women's nature as caring, best suited to child-rearing, and dealing more with the domestic chores of the household. Consequently, this implies the male-female polarization of the public and private spheres dichotomy. Over the time, little has changed regarding this dichotomy, even though some religious reforms and renewal emerged.

Although, generally most religions have some teachings on respecting women's dignity and protecting their rights, some other values found in those religions have been challenged for those virtues. Certain Catholic and Protestant stipulations, such as the prohibition of divorce, have some potential to place women in a difficult position. In a specific case when a requested divorce is not granted, it is women who may suffer the most especially in the case of domestic violence. In general, the church and religious leaders always try to persuade conflicting couples not to divorce. According to a Catholic religious leader, there is a specific mechanism for the divorce process in Catholicism—namely, the Church Tribunal Court. However, most of the time, Catholic religious leaders direct reconciliation between the unhappy spouses in divorce cases. In fact, the emphasis on marriage harmony and reconciliation are also found in the perspective of other religions.

Women's Narratives: Minority Identities and Social Coexistence

People, including women who hold minority identities, are encouraged to integrate with the majority. Such social integration is not always successful and comfortable, however, as those who hold minority identities are more likely to face challenges in their sociopolitical lives. Women from religious minority groups in Banda Aceh hold identities as women first of all, then as Chinese or Batakese, followed by Catholic, Protestant, or Buddhist, and each of these three identities has the potential to generate different treatment from the majority. Aceh women's adaptation to the socioreligious life of the community has been intensified following shari`a law enforcement. As aptly noted by Venelin Terziev, adaptation requires the adjustment of individuals' internal organization to the existing norms of the society.[7] This is an ongoing action that women from minority groups attempt to achieve amid various barriers.

The adjustment process is not simply an effort to resemble the dominant group in all values, beliefs, and behavior,[8] but rather, it is a negotiated domain in which each group has its own strategy that is necessary to the social survival of the group. Although Aceh has for years enforced shari`a law, a public space for other religious minorities remains available. And although Aceh has scored poorly on a national index of tolerance in the past few years, intra-religious violence is relatively rare in the province. Everyone enjoys their own beliefs, but problems can arise in the politics of identity, especially in the post-Suharto era.

Women from religious minority groups, like other minority believers, always strive to maintain their social existence through practices of in-group solidarity and out-group social interaction. The social barriers they face may alter according to changes in their circumstances and contexts. As far as social acceptance is concerned, it is not always easy to create a sincere personal relationship. Humanitarian aid provided by other religious groups, for instance, sometimes prompts suspicions from its recipients regarding the motivations behind such support or assistance. The interviews we conducted made it clear, moreover, that some women from minority religious and ethnic groups, regardless of those barriers, play quite active public roles in health issues within their communities. As an urban area, the city of Banda Aceh welcomes and gives access to opportunities for people of wider-ranging knowledge as well as broader exposure to ideas and agency in their communities. For the minority, being allowed to be active in community-related issues, for instance, is a public recognition as well as social acceptance.

Considering the general story of women's agency in Aceh, the works of women from religious minority groups contribute to a portrait of agency that defies limitations for the sake of social integration. Catherine Lee and Anne Logan have discussed the activism and organization of women in which women need to participate as activists in order to challenge, resist, overthrow, or gain entrance to social structures and institutions that have tended to ignore, exclude, disadvantage, or penalize them.[9] Yet the women's agency we discuss here is primarily an expression of how women, as part of a religious minority group, seek to respond to and connect with the majority group in Aceh. As social agents like their male counterparts, women negotiate their religious and ethnic social existence. On the one hand, they preserve the values of ethnic tradition that attach them to the more private domestic sphere; on the other hand, they engage in wider social activism within society at large. In their religious text such as for Buddhism, most of the values of women are closely attached to their domestic life, stay dominantly with the family, support and nurture the family.

Nevertheless, there is also a narrative that gives women some roles outside the private sphere, as suggested in a work by Lai Suat Yan, which describes three Theravada Buddhist women's identities and roles as spiritual leaders, religious innovators, and ritual specialists. According to Yan, the women's innovation aimed to bring renewal to their faith, which does not recognize bhikkhunis.[10] The roles of Buddhist women in Banda Aceh must be understood as part of the religious innovations Yan discovered in her study in which bhikkhuni became involved in an aid mission to assist survivors of disasters such as the Muslim population affected by the Mount Kelud eruption on Java in 2014.[11]

Although it is different from what the bhikkhuni did, what Buddhist women do in Banda Aceh can be regarded as unusual in the Theravada sect. Their social and humanitarian actions, which will be discussed in the next part of this chapter, are carried out in the name of the ordinary Buddhist. They do not have any special name in their sect, nor do they belong to any special organization for Buddhist women like the organization for Catholic women in Banda Aceh. One woman said her social action to assist the community in Banda Aceh was done in the name of humanity. Nevertheless, like Catholic women's activism, this Buddhist women's activism was not devoted to counter social inequality they face in their life, nor did it use the resistance model of social movements.

Women and Public Agency

Socioreligious Roles and Leadership

Amid limited attention from the government of Aceh toward the educational programs of minority religious groups, all minority religions band together to organize religious education for their own believers. As we have seen, the Aceh politics of shari`a prevents local government from providing formal religious education to non-Muslims as it does to Muslims. Here, women play an important role in both family worship and communal worship activities at churches or temples. Buddhists from the Vihara Sukyamuni, Banda Aceh, for example, utilize the temple as a place for children to learn. Most of the children's education is facilitated by women. It is a woman who takes the children to the vihara for the sake of incorporating Buddhist values, even for very young children. The task of instruction is not easy. One of our informants said that the teachers must be well trained to teach the book, which is written in Sanskrit. Moreover, the teachers must be able to deliver the course in Indonesian or to translate it into the Chinese subethnic language for daily practice.

The GBI Protestant Church also has a special program for children to learn their religion at the church. They have a three-story building with one floor used as a place for children's learning, while the other floors are reserved for adult prayer. For the children's sessions, the learning material includes psychological evaluation. According to a teacher, many children these days become depressed due to their family situations and other factors. Sometimes children experience violence in their families or witness violence between their parents, and parents are not necessarily aware of the serious psychological problems affecting their children. The church calls the psychological evaluation sessions a "retreat" for children. In addition to helping the children with psychological therapy, the women teachers also ask the pastor to talk to the children's parents.

Buddhists also offer this kind of training and consultation session but only when bukkhuni comes to Banda Aceh from Medan to provide the service. This indicates that religious education of children is one site where women from religious minority groups in Aceh play a significant role and make a contribution to their own community.

Social and Humanitarian Action

Women of minority religions also play a role in humanitarian work in the public sphere of Aceh. One Chinese organization in Aceh, Hakka, has engaged intensively in humanitarian work. Hakka is an open organization for the Chinese, who come from many religions, including Buddhism, Protestantism, Catholicism, and Confucianism. Most Hakka members are Buddhist, but there is no domination of Buddhists over the others within the organization. Indeed, Hakka has been active in campaigning for multiculturalism. Its humanitarian action is well known in Banda Aceh. Its programs of blood donation, aid distribution, and even food and mask distribution to anticipate the spread of COVID-19 were publicly welcomed. Women take part in all of these humanitarian activities as volunteers. One of the Buddhist women we interviewed told us proudly that she, together with friends, distributed food and masks to the people during the COVID-19 crisis through Vihara Sukyamuni. Descriptions of such humanitarian actions are published on the group's official social media accounts.[12]

Our interviews revealed that Buddhist women seem to prefer to exercise social agency through volunteer action. One diasporic Chinese Buddhist woman in Peunayong, for instance, took up semi-volunteer work as an activist of Posyandu (a village booth designated for integrated health service). This kind of work gave Buddhist women more time to interact closer with the rest of the village people and to provide a multicultural image of the village. Nevertheless, not all Buddhist women believers choose to do this. Most of them do not wish to be bound to a tight schedule and extreme workload while also engaging in domestic businesses as well as economic activities. Their choice of volunteer work relies on religious values that are applied to them as women, who are responsible for caring for their family and who have less responsibility compared with their male counterparts to take up public religious roles and leadership. Although their humanitarian and volunteer actions are socially useful, they are still not in the position of being decision-makers, and they have less power and control.

Compared with women from other minority religious groups, such as ethnic Batak women, Chinese Buddhist women have an easier sociocultural adaptation to the majority community of Aceh. Because these Chinese women make up a larger population than Batak women, members earn more opportunities derived from their widespread social acceptance by the majority.

A few religious minority figures, including women, do have social or political positions in Aceh. A Catholic state official (Pembimas) confirmed that there is a Catholic woman who became a village head in Muara Situlen, Aceh Tenggara. A few Catholic women have also held the strategic position of village government officer in different districts. Even Hindus, who have the smallest number of religious believers in Aceh or Banda Aceh, nevertheless have one member who holds a strong social position of leadership as a chief of the village football club. Given the small number of women religious minorities, however, they do not have such notable public agency—and male members of religious minorities admitted that they do nothing to promote or encourage women's participation in the public sphere.

Since 2012, Catholic women have taken up expanded roles within Catholic organizations. The Catholic desk officer of the provincial office of the Ministry of Religious Affairs, Baron Pandiangan, encouraged Catholic women to establish the Catholic Women of the Republic of Indonesia (Wanita Katolik Republik Indonesia, WKRI). It complements the three existing non–Catholic Church organizations: Catholic Students of the Republic of Indonesia (Mahasiswa Katolik Republik Indonesia), Catholic Youth of the Republic of Indonesia (Pemuda Katolik Republik Indonesia), and Catholic Merchants Association of the Republic of Indonesia (Ikatan Saudagar Katolik Republik Indonesia). Pandiangan said that women of the Catholic faith need to establish a social movement, as required in Catholic teaching itself. This does not mean all Catholic women are automatically members of the WKRI. The group now has organizational rules, including membership rules and principles. Women who want to be members have to meet certain requirements, including providing their certificate of Catholic baptism.

According to the Aceh WKRI chairwoman, Eliyani Ginting, the organization is dedicated to achieving the mission of the Church. The WKRI stands for the Catholic philosophy *Pro Patria et Ecclesia* (For the state and for the Church). This means that Catholic people, including members of the organization, must devote themselves to both the state and the Catholic Church. The WKRI takes part in public matters as a purely Catholic humanitarian organization. Pandiangan referred this effort to another Catholic basic principle wherein all people are called to be both "light" and "salt." "Light" means people need to shed light for others, while "salt" means making something become good or tasty, as salt makes food taste delicious. He quoted from Matthew 5:13–15.

Pandiangan further acknowledged that he was inspired by local women's organizations such as Solidaritas Perempuan (Women's Solidarity) and Balai Syura Ureung Inong Aceh and by women from Aceh's political party to work on women's issues. He sees an opportunity for Catholic women to manage a similar organization. They have that modality available because so far, Catholic women have visited the church only for worship matters, and all of their activities are under the supervision of the priest. Now they want to become part of the women's solidarity group in Aceh. Today, the WKRI is developing its working strategy. It has divisions of education, entrepreneurship, and social welfare to achieve the organization's mission. The organization has focused its work on the issue of education, including child-rearing and child education. It also considers an opportunity for mobilizing funding to support educational programs in Aceh. The chairwoman of the WKRI was once invited by the Aceh office of the Indonesian Commission of Child Protection to talk about the issue of child protection. For the general election held every five years, the WKRI is also active in conducting voter education programs.

Organizationally, WKRI Aceh remains under the supervision of the WKRI of North Sumatra province. The organization's provisions require Aceh to establish at least two office branches at the district and municipal levels. At the moment, three branches are planned in Aceh Tenggara, Aceh Besar, and Aceh Singkil; these will meet the requirements to establish an autonomous WKRI Aceh. Like Hakka, the WKRI has also coordinated humanitarian blood donation among Catholic believers. These initiatives suggest that Catholic women, though they come from minority religious and ethnic identities, can still contribute to harmonious social life within the larger society. As they have limitations as a minority, Catholic women are eagerly striving to overcome the challenges to their integration and adaptation to the majority, largely through volunteerism and humanitarian actions.

Some Challenges from Social Interaction

Despite limitations, women from religious minorities still attempt to find ways to contribute to the betterment of Aceh society through their actions and programs. It is clear that the primary organizations that facilitate their agency are faith- or ethnicity-based organizations. Their contributions to or participation in these organizations do not automatically solve integration issues, however, or the problem of social acceptance. When two Chinese women from a religious minority group began their social work through Posyandu in their residence area (village of Peunayong), they faced resistance to their involvement. When they distributed food, for instance, people asked questions or showed curiosity about the food they brought. As volunteers, they may continue their work regardless of some people's skepticism. So long as the village leader strongly supports them, these Chinese women are welcome to contribute to and support development within their own villages.

In their social activities, sometimes women of religious minorities in Aceh are required to wear headscarf and long-sleeved dress. Respecting this public decency in Aceh, those women are happy to comply, even if they do not fully cover their bodies. They explained that sometimes they prefer to wear their own dress to be easily identified as non-Muslim people. Such explanation allows Muslim villagers to begin understanding the difference and to gradually accept social diversity in Aceh and to get along quite well with them regardless of differences.

For one of the occasions organized by a well-known Aceh women's organization, a representative from minority groups was invited. She came and participated in the provincial event to elect the leaders for an Aceh women's hub organization. It was a Chinese woman who attended the event, and she was comfortably engaged in that program in which all the other participants were in their headscarf, whereas she was not. Other participants did not mind and respected her faith and her choice to not wear a headscarf. As highlighted by Ansor in his doctoral dissertation,[13] this is one of the situations in which there is a social space where a member of a minority group does not always submit to the dominant majority. Interestingly, women's activism in Aceh and their sisterhood facilitated this model of integration.

On the other hand, living under Muslim majority culture in Aceh makes some Catholics acutely aware of the challenges of missionary work. The sensitive issue of missionary activity in the Acehnese community has made them cautious about how they should act accordingly within the community. A Catholic woman of Batak ethnicity mentioned her strong hope of setting up a small public library so that children from her neighborhood could access books. Yet she was hesitant to do so, wondering if people would visit her library since she comes from a different religion and ethnicity. For this reason, she has put off implementing the idea even though she thinks it would benefit the community, especially children. Her experience suggests that social relations between religious and ethnic minorities and the Muslim majority are not simple in Aceh. Many aspects are included in building trust between people of different backgrounds.

To offer a second example, a Protestant woman from the Batak ethnic group felt she was resisted in most social interactions in her workspace. Her sense was that the resistance was unfair since it resulted from her coworkers not wanting to talk about religion openly and keeping their distance from her instead. Following the example of Catholic leaders, she established communication with a few moderate Muslim women activists and organizations in Aceh. She perceived that being in a minority of religious believers makes her more vulnerable. The case of the 2012 mob, the radical raid, and the local government's action against the GBI community continues to be traumatic for some of her group. Regarding the 2012 mob, as Al Makin has observed, shari`a implementation has created a peculiar new "identity" for most Acehnese, and this left little room for integration and positive social coexistence with the minorities.[14] The tension remains unresolved as a result of the high bar set by the 2016 Aceh qanun on the establishment of worship places for non-Muslims. Today, it is impossible for the GBI sect to meet the standard of having 140 believers before they are allowed to build a new church. Prior to actions of the mob, membership had reached 150 believers, but the incident forced more than half of the diasporic Chinese of the GBI to move to the Huria Kristen Batak Protestan (HKBP) Church, where many of the members are also ethnic Chinese.[15]

To return to the issue of religious agency of women from religious minority groups in Aceh, we found that women continue to serve their churches regardless of past trauma. Yet these women face barriers. To resolve such barriers, they suggested that there should be discussion or consultation among different religious groups to build understanding and avoid conflicts, as well as to gain the support of pro-minority activists, especially women from local civil society organizations in Banda Aceh. One of the women religious minority leaders said that right now, women are in a "wait and see" mode. They do not know what will happen next to their religious groups, given the limitations they currently experience.

An organization of women has been an influential process, giving women the opportunity through activities to establish a positive rapport with the public and recognition from the dominant culture. A number of women's religious groups are active in promoting this rapport, including those who are Catholic and Buddhist. Within the religious groups themselves, women are encouraged to assume an interest in promoting feminine roles, such as child-rearing and the public education of children. Compared with their male counterparts, women are positioned as leaders only in specific spaces or groups. The typical traditional roles of women are preserved. Even within the space of churches and temples, they have to continue negotiating their roles and agency.

Conclusion

This chapter discusses the life of the marginalized group of the minority—namely, women from minority religions. This is not without a purpose, since the limited works available on women in the context of women in Aceh society rarely, or at all, elaborate the life of women from minority religions. In most religions, there are references to how men and women are positioned, where the polarized pattern of public and private dichotomy normally emerges as the model.

Being a double or triple minority has left those women with diverse challenges and complexities. This has much to do with the fact that they live in a society with a strong politics of identity practices. As other chapters highlighted how the minority sought to interact with the majority and the dominant culture, this chapter suggests several efforts and agency models to be adopted, which sometimes defy the normative principles on women outlined in their religion. This study at least demonstrates that those women have been quite flexible in utilizing their social skills to participate in various public roles, and especially through humanitarian work. This has been effective in their integration into the majority and to peaceful coexistence.

The Limited Agency of Female Religious Minorities 179

This study also finds that a few women have quite dynamic agency, especially within the (humanitarian) community and volunteer work to act as agents for social coexistence to bridge and cement their relationship with the Muslim majority. Looking at the agency these women have chosen, it is clear that their social activism is more in the realm of humanitarian action than it is, say, a campaign for equality or resistance against discrimination. Religious and ethnic minority women's humanitarian activities are intended to help with their social integration and create positive interactions with the majority population. Although this humanitarianism through volunteerism is quite successful at fostering social acceptance and building understanding among different social groups, it is still quite challenging for religious minority women in Aceh, with their small numbers, to ensure active social participation being acknowledged. Nevertheless, a few of them have engaged well with other (Muslim) activists from women's organizations, and women activism in Aceh facilitated this space and connection in some ways.

Conclusion

Comparing citizenship in the Netherlands and Aceh, Merry and Milligan argued that ethnicity can be used as a third strategic axis along with civic and religious identity.[1] This is perhaps correct in the context of the relations of Aceh with the Dutch and Japanese colonial forces and Jakarta, even up to today. Yet, this does not apply to the case of dormant citizenship within contemporary Aceh, especially in relation to religious minorities (see chapter 2).

In the context of Aceh's internal dynamics in the postconflict era or 2005 onward, ethnicity is a source of internal tensions. As the largest ethnic group in Aceh, the Acehnese have been trying to predominate almost all aspects of life, from religion to economics and politics, from the issue of governmental leadership and Wali Nanggroe (cultural leader of Aceh) to the so-called Aceh language, Aceh Hymn, and Aceh flag issues. Politicians and leaders whose ethnic backgrounds are non-Indigenous to the region of Aceh, such as Batak and Java, are accepted, not because of their ethnic background but because they are Muslims.

For many decades, Aceh has been inaccurately identified as a unique, singular, and monolithic society. Aceh has its own diversity in terms of ethnicity, language, population, and religion. The last, in fact, has been accounted for being a predominant factor (i.e., Muslims over the others) that led to such typical assumption. Thanks to a number of national laws in the post–New Order period that granted special autonomy to Aceh, the enforcement of shari`a law has largely contributed to generate a strong conclusion that, in tandem with the Aceh ethnic group, Islam is both a majority religion and a dominant culture in Aceh. This book, nevertheless, has shown that Aceh in fact is a plural, ununiformed, and multicultural society, thus it needs to be treated accordingly.

Ethnicities and faiths embraced by the people of Aceh have been key ingredients of this book. By assessing the relationship between the majority and minority groups who live in urban areas as well as in districts around Aceh's provincial border, this study considers that ethnicities and religions are historically and culturally fundamental for the existence of diversity in contemporary Aceh. This study has demonstrated that Aceh's ethnic diversity has been a significant resource, stimulating social changes and shaping the lives of various identity groups within the Aceh communities. Nonetheless, Aceh's ethnic diversity is not the main concern of the ongoing implementation of a special autonomy in Aceh. Ethnic diversity is considered unimportant parts to support the special status of Aceh. In fact, current efforts to implement Aceh's autonomous governance are aimed at strengthening the politics of dominant culture (see chapter 1).

Aceh's Diversity

The politics of dominant culture in Aceh, which has much to do with the formal implementation of shari`a, has pushed a number of ethnic groups away to the edge. Ethnic groups such as Gayo, Alas, Tamiang, Kluet, Aneuk Jamee, Pak Pak Batak, Karo Batak, Chinese, and several others tend to be absorbed into the existing dominant culture. Although some of these minority groups (Pak Pak Batak, Karo Batak, and Chinese) are closely identified with other religions than Islam, they do have a few Muslim believers as well. Each of all these minority groups has specific ways of practicing Islam and observing Islamic values in their own daily life, culture, and tradition.

As a matter of fact, diverse ethnic groups in Aceh have actually made up a significant claim that Aceh society embraces and integrates ethnicities and religions in the present contour of Aceh's social life. However, as the increasing influence of the current politics of dominant culture, minority groups found difficulties in stepping their foot on Aceh's official communal identity. In fact, given the emerging dynamics among various ethnic groups and different faiths in the bordering districts, minority groups have a chance to contest as well as to express demands for equal citizenship.

A comparative perspective between the Chinese people and the Pak Pak Batak people who live in Aceh may help clarify the point above. On the one hand, of the Chinese residents in Aceh whose members adhere to different religions (Buddhist, Christian, Catholic, Confucian, and Islam), none of them sought to resonate a particular representation of the Chinese in the public. On the other hand, the Pak Pak Batak people in the borderland who equally claim to affiliate with either Christianity or Islam were often tacitly competing in making public images of their ethnicity. Whereas Muslim Pak Pak Batak emphasize their close attachment to the dominant culture in Aceh, the Christian Pak Pak Batak aspire to establish their loyalty to national values of citizenship instead. This difference within ethnic groups' public representation in contemporary Aceh has become grounds for minority groups to challenge the politics of dominant culture. And, in fact, the politics of equal recognition that fairly treat all residents of Aceh regardless of their different backgrounds has been overtly and covertly demanded.

The Challenge of Diversity Management

In light of the subnational context of contemporary Indonesia, Aceh has taken a part in managing diversity. Roles of various agencies in Aceh, both government and nongovernmental organizations, have been the center of attention of this book. Unlike other provincial governments across Indonesia that often lack relevant and important partners, Aceh has more than enough to work together to fulfill equal rights between different people. However, as this book unveils in the preceding chapters, diversity management as well as equal citizenship in Aceh remain only a remote possibility. Efforts to strengthen interreligious relationships are increasingly observable in the past two decades in particular. Yet they are not able to achieve the ultimate objective of equal citizenship.

As this book has shown, the extent to which various state institutions have effectively dealt with diversity management in Aceh remains a big challenge. The challenge covers a range of public concerns such as religious services provided by government offices, legal enforcement, religious subjects as well as teachers offered by public schools, uniform of female non-Muslim employees at workplaces, political participation at both legislative and executive bodies, approval for the establishment of worship places, and so on. State offices at provincial as well district levels that engage with all these issues include the Ministry of Religious Affairs, Agency of National Unity, Politics and Community Protection (Kesbangpol Linmas), the Mahkamah Syar`iyah, Civil Service Police Unit and Wilayatul Hisbah (Satpol PP & WH), and provincial/district Offices of Education (Dinas Pendidikan) that supervise public schools at all ranks.

The Ministry of Religious Affairs has a legitimate mandate to serve all believers equally. However, in the provincial border of Aceh, where the number of non-Muslims (i.e., Christian residents) is quite significant, very few are assigned to take a position as community carer or *Pembina Bimbingan Masyarakat* (Pembimas) at the local office of the ministry. The scarcity of a person in charge for this position may have created a public impression that the existence of non-Muslim people as legitimate citizens living in Aceh is not truly important.

Likewise, as discussed in chapter 5, the Forum for the Harmony of Interreligious Communities (FKUB) established at the district level is often dysfunctional. Consisting of local officials from the Ministry of Religious Affairs, Agency of National Unity, Politics, and Community Protection, and the leading figures of different religious communities or denominations, the politics of dominant culture strongly shapes the way this forum works to resolve problems or conflicts that take place between different believers. In certain cases, non-Muslim leaders express their disappointments as well as dissatisfactions for not having an adequate means or chances to openly discuss the underlying troubles and predicaments or to look for the best options that lead to a fair decision for all believers.

The Shari`a Court has relatively the same experience in managing diversity in Aceh. As discussed in chapter 4, the Shari`a Court is incapacitated to aptly recognize diversity in examining Islamic penal cases that involve a non-Muslim offender. Instead of applying the principle of personality like the one in Malaysia, the Aceh's shari`a judges prefer to have a trial based on the combination application with the principle of territory and the principle of subjugation, rendering a liability to non-Muslims being punished by caning. Despite some non-Muslim offenders expressed their willingness to get caned, the application of this particular punishment for them is considered a fait accompli, if not a compulsion. Seen in a larger picture, this is one of many ways to deepen the politics of dominant culture in Aceh's legal sphere.

Punishing non-Muslim offenders by caning has become a controversial issue and is widely criticized. The criticisms stem not only from civil society organizations in Aceh but also from some human rights advocates outside Aceh nationally and globally. They fiercely condemned and questioned why such particular punishment is imposed on non-Muslims while they do not believe in the Islamic faith.

The Impacts of Identity Politics on Diversity

Parts of this book closely discuss the politics of identity as a key driving factor that steers diversity in Aceh. As pointed out in several chapters of this book, a number of ethnic and religious communities in some districts and cities (Aceh Tamiang, Aceh Tenggara, Aceh Singkil, Subulussalam, and Langsa) have been interacting with one another for many decades. Regardless of their different identities, they have experienced together a peaceful coexistence side by side in their respective places. The preexisting social system in this region has enabled them to avoid unnecessary hostilities and conflicts.

It was for the above reason that one should not hastily claim that those areas in the border are more liable to be sites of proselytization, especially by Christian missionaries. In fact, the Provincial Office of Shari`a need not impulsively assert that Muslim residents in the bordering areas are prone to be easily converted into Christian believers so that a special program of mobilizing skilled Muslim preachers from other parts of Aceh to work against Christianization in these areas (*program da'i perbatasan*) is required. An official statement as such is similar to an act of spreading fear and threats from the neighboring province in which it reflects misjudgment or groundless assumption on the part of some Muslim leaders in Aceh. A part in this book has confirmed that the conversion to Christian faith in these areas has not ever taken place on a big scale. On the contrary, it was reported that many non-Muslims have converted to Islam than vice versa (see chapter 8).

Showing a dislike of or prejudice against other people with different religious backgrounds is apparently tolerable in Aceh. This kind of conduct can be traced in fatwa number 8 of 2015 issued by the Ulama Council of Aceh. This fatwa stipulates that Muslim residents in Aceh should not sell or rent their own lands to non-Muslim individuals or institutions. The government of Aceh is also addressed by this fatwa advising that its officials should not facilitate a land purchase transaction, publish a land certificate, or issue any document of land acquisition. In fact, the fatwa went further in recommending that the government must retract land parcels that have been sold or rented to non-Muslim individuals or institutions. Among the reason behind this fatwa was that the Ulama Council of Aceh speculates that a land purchase by non-Muslims (most likely Christians) is motivated by a strategy to support a proposal of establishing a worship place (i.e., church) in particular places. This is because the required proof for accepting the proposal is a sufficient number of households or population who affiliate with the Christian faith and live surrounding the site of proposed worship building.

Despite the above being based on religious grounds as well as political considerations, it demonstrates an increasing trend of identity politics that supports the dominance of a particular culture in one way or another. By intervening in administrative and procedural matters, Aceh's public institutions at some points take sides with the majority's stand. This kind of intervention inevitably influences and convinces members of the majority group to consider themselves having more social recognition and privilege. As a result, although the minority groups may live in Aceh and jointly coexist with their co-citizens in the villages, their chances and public roles are limited.

The Future of Diversity in Aceh: Quo Vadis?

Managing Aceh's diversity is possible only when minority groups are given a chance or support to transform themselves. Supporting minority groups can be carried out by circumventing or terminating the condition of dormant citizenship they have experienced so far (see chapter 2). To fix this dormant citizenship, all sociopolitical elements in Aceh (i.e., the government, the majority, and the minority groups) are expected to work together in providing necessary conditions to fulfill equal citizenship.

Through this study, we envisage a hope to manage diversity better in Aceh by shifting dormant citizenship to actively full citizenship on the part of minority groups. It would mitigate discrimination as well as denial of their particular identity. We learn and suggest some areas to shed light on finding ways toward equal rights between diverse groups in Aceh as below:

Voicing Minority Rights

Minorities can proactively struggle for recognition by establishing institutions and organizations that endorse their active participation in society. So far, most non-Muslim organizations in Aceh are silent. Perhaps they are afraid of provoking tensions within the society. As a matter of fact, their active participation in working for the public good would be seen as a positive contribution.

Almost all minority groups have independent associations or affiliated organizations, whether they be local groups or branches of national organizations. However, most of these are more for accomplishing internal needs. The Roman Catholic organization, for instance, has branches of national organizations and are inwardly oriented. These include Wanita Katolik Republik Indonesia (Catholic Women of the Republic of Indonesia), Mahasiswa Katolik Republik Indonesia (Catholic Students of the Republic of Indonesia), and Pemuda Katolik Republik Indonesia (Catholic Youth of the Republic of Indonesia). Although they are nonchurch organizations, all their works are dedicated to supporting the church's mission.

The only organization so far that is externally oriented is the Forum Cinta Damai Aceh Singkil (Forum for Love of Peace Aceh Singkil, or Forcidas). Founded in Singkil in 2015, Forcidas sought to voice Protestant interests. It is a quite open organization in which cooperation with a Jakarta-based Islamic institution (i.e., the Wahid Institute) was established.[2] Forcidas in the beginning was initiated with a particular aim of dealing with a conflict over the building of churches in Singkil. By and large, it was successful in bringing Christian interests in Singkil to national attention. Nevertheless, whether its campaign has been achieved in promoting local awareness of mutual understanding and coexistence between different believers in Singkil remains uncertain.

Empowering an Interfaith Organization

Despite being established by the Indonesian government at different levels of governance across Indonesia, from the subdistrict to national branches, the existing interfaith organization, FKUB, has been considered a vulnerable institution. The problem is that the majority group controls and dominates this semi-state organization. From time to time, it has frequently become a tool for the majority to maintain social hegemony and to discipline minority groups.

To resolve this problem, the establishment of a bottom-up interfaith organization perhaps is an option to be considered. All religions are invited to send their individual members to join the organization so that all would be equally represented in building equal citizenship in Aceh. This could be an alternative to the existing FKUB, which was established by an initiative of the central government. Being assigned to monitor and resolve religious conflicts that took place across Indonesia, the FKUB however has still much to prepare and to strengthen its organization particularly at the district as well as city levels.

Providing Citizenship Education

Citizenship education is another potential resolution to activate non-Muslims' dormant citizenship in Aceh. Being developed to be contextual to multifaceted situations in many parts of Aceh, citizenship education is considered useful in directing all people of Aceh toward building mutual understanding and achieving equal rights for all citizens. Citizenship education is different to civic education (*pendidikan kewarganegaraan*), an existing subject taught in schools and universities following the collapse of the New Order regime. Civic education is no more than educating students about nationhood in the context of Indonesia. It is thus disconnected to students' day-to-day life in Aceh.

As parts of its content, citizenship education includes both social and cultural citizenship. Citizenship education is intended to direct and encourage students in comprehending a number of values and objectives in social life. Equipped with this knowledge, students would learn how they can take part in ensuring some degree of equality and the right to participate in civic life on an equal footing with others. In addition, students would be taught how they should respect the rights of other people to claim cultural difference, and how they could prevent themselves from making a stigma of difference implying inferiority, even in contexts of inequality.[3]

In fact, the current school curriculum in Aceh in particular and in Indonesia in general does not introduce major theological principles found in respective religions in comparative perspective. Some bureaucrats and academics stated that teaching comparative religions to students is a dangerous thing and therefore should be avoided. With this in mind, no wonder that students in Aceh lack an opportunity to learn about the concept of diversity and to comprehend its application in many ways.

Working toward National Legal Reform

To control and mitigate the possibly excessive impacts of the implementation of shari`a in Aceh for non-Muslim residents in particular, a legal reform at the national level is required. Such legal reform would attract fundamental changes, and it could be introduced as a way to evade or to remove the biased shari`a enforcement in Aceh. Currently, some efforts of legal reform have been made to challenge the primacy given to shari`a in Aceh. It is undertaken by questioning the concordance of shari`a law, as stipulated in the form of qanun, with the 1945 Constitution and Universal Declaration of Human Rights. A woman nongovernmental organization (NGOs), Solidaritas Perempuan, for instance, has filed a petition to review the Qanun Jinayat (Islamic penal law) for applying public caning as a method of punishment. In their view, such punishment discriminates against women, especially in the case of rape.[4]

In 2017, a number of NGOs united under the NGO Network for Advocacy on Qanun Jinayat declared the Qanun Jinayat to be inconsistent with, and in fact against, the Constitution of 1945. It is considered harmful for its discrimination against women. Nonetheless, no progress has yet been made so far in relation to the idea of legal reform. Perhaps it is because legal reform is too costly. Not only that it would create social tension in Aceh if an effort of amending laws on Aceh's special autonomy is taking place but also because it is deployed as a strategy to end prolonged resistance by GAM.

More Inclusive Understanding of Shari`a

A transformation toward a more inclusive and pluralist understanding of shari`a in both the government and society could lead to the reformation of qanun and Islamic thought. There have been progressive voices among young academics, public intellectuals, and NGO activists who are engaged in humanitarian, social, human rights, and women's rights issues. They work on the margins, outside the state boundaries, but their contributions should not be neglected.

An initiative in formulating a program of "Grand Design of Islamic Shari`a" began in 2013. This program was prepared by the Provincial Shari`a Office during the leadership of Syahrizal Abbas (2013–17), who is a professor in law at State Islamic University of Ar-Raniry.[5] The program involved a number of young NGO activists and intellectuals (especially academics). The objective of this program was to promote a "welfare" perspective of shari`a rather than a punishment-oriented one.[6] Apparently, the Grand Design of Islamic Shari`a was formulated on the basis of, or at least in line with, the United Nations Sustainable Development Goals (SDGs).

Despite its ideal and relevant objectives, the program of Grand Design of Islamic Shari`a was terminated. This program received a lot of criticisms. Some groups were challenging and questioning the usefulness of such program. As the program was uncertain, the critics doubted whether such a program would bring positive changes for the current and future implementation of shari`a in Aceh.

Religious Conversion to Islam

Although it is not a desirable path to take for a genuine approach to activate equal citizenship, the conversion to Islam is the fastest way to achieve the goal. Our study of the muallaf group (new converts to Islam) in chapter 8 indicates that as a result of their conversion, these new converts feel more accepted by Acehnese society both emotionally and culturally; they are considered brothers and sisters in Islam. They usually, although not always, change their names by adopting Arabic names. This will not only further their feeling of being more accepted, but they may also have the same rights as other Muslim believers.

The decision to convert to Islam often negatively affects their existing familial and social bonds, business networks, and so on, which put them in vulnerable situations. Without adequate support, their knowledge and practical ability to become (new) Muslims still face a number of constraints. It is for this reason that they can access muallaf funds offered by the Shari`a Office and many philanthropic and empowerment programs run by the Baitul Mal Aceh (Aceh Treasury).[7] Generally speaking, they are now treated more equally than before their conversion.

Nonetheless, for some, whether these people who convert to Islam are motivated by economic interests or something else remains a question. Regardless of any motive behind this conversion, it is quite uncertain if these new Muslim converts would independently exercise equal citizenship. Would they be allowed to claim a difference on their own new "Muslimness" or immediately be absorbed into a big crowd of Muslim community? Due to the lack of or less capacity in Islamic knowledge and practice, it is likely that they cannot refrain from having an inferiority complex, thus leading to unequal citizenship.

Closing Remarks

Finally, in spite of all efforts of diversity management having been suggested to deactivate dormant citizenship of minority groups in Aceh, the politics of dominant culture applied in Aceh has, to use Hefner's words, "pressed all the more firmly for [the realization of] a differentiated, asymmetrical and Muslim supremacist citizenship."[8] So far, minority groups in Aceh have been largely subject to the will of the Muslim majority group in various aspects. This includes issues such as (1) where and when non-Muslim communities could get together for rituals or religious purposes, (2) their access to public jobs at provincial or district offices, and (3) their participation to contribute to the outcome of events and structures that influence their lives culturally, legally, and politically in Aceh.

The nature of equal Indonesian citizenship has been altered by the ongoing dormant citizenship in Aceh. Muslim citizens are given preference at the expense of non-Muslims. Their interests must be prioritized over those of other religious faiths. This has certainly become a constraint in making a well-balanced relationship between majority and minority groups in Aceh in particular and in Indonesia in general. In fact, to cite Hefner again, such "a Muslim-supremacist citizenship is at odds with mainstream understanding of Pancasila nationalism."[9]

It is quite regrettable that the politics of dominant culture as currently practiced in Aceh meets no stern contender. There are a great number of local and national civil society organizations that closely pay attention to the implementation of shari`a and minorities in Aceh—from Lembaga Bantuan Hukum, KONTRAS Aceh, Jaringan Masyarakat Sipil Peduli Syariat Islam, Kaukus Wartawan Peduli Syariat Islam, Laboratorium Pusat Studi Agama of UIN Ar-Raniry, Komunitas Kami Kita, Aceh Art, Gusdurian to Setara Institute. However, their campaign for equal citizenship in Aceh appears to be ineffective. None of these organizations was successful in persuading or appealing to the mass of Aceh people that the recognition of the presence of minority religious communities and their undifferentiated rights is legally and morally mandatory. Living under the current political atmosphere in which minority groups feel marginalized in one way or another, undoubtedly they have a less shared sense of belonging to both territory and identity of Aceh. The formal implementation of shari`a, as a means of the politics of dominant culture, has altered multireligious citizenship and replaced it with a differentiated and asymmetrical citizenship.

Whereas the politics of dominant culture tends to make a demarcation in the interaction between Muslim and non-Muslim citizens, the politics of recognition acknowledges equal rights and accommodates diversities found among the people. The question is, what is the future of the politics of equal recognition in Aceh? Due to the relatively successful mobilization of identity politics in contemporary Aceh that somehow has fundamentally restructured Indonesian national citizenship and the absence of robust civil society leaders who have the courage to resist the politics of dominant culture, the rights of minority groups in Aceh remain disrupted as they continue to be subordinated. It is a long way to struggle for making the politics of equal recognition well established in Aceh. It becomes more challenging if the current unequal citizenship in Aceh is considered a model, or at least an aspiration, for some hardliner Muslim groups at the national level to work for the ideal of Muslim and non-Muslim interactions.

NOTES

Introduction

1. Ahmed et al., "Comparative Study of Zakat and Taxation System for Muslims and Non-Muslims in Malaysia"; Çetinoğlu, "Foundations of Non-Muslim Communities"; Mantran, "Foreign Merchants and Minorities in Istanbul during the Sixteenth and Seventeenth Centuries"; Kuran, "The Economic Ascent of the Middle East's Religious Minorities."

2. Abu-Munshar, "In the Shadow of the 'Arab Spring'"; Emon, "Religious Minorities and Islamic Law"; Fargues, "Demographic Islamization"; Fierro and Tolan, *The Legal Status of Dimmi's in the Islamic West*; Hunwick, "The Rights of Dhimmis to Maintain a Place of Worship"; J. Rehman, "Islam vs the Shari`a"; Zeidan, "The Copts."

3. Kusrin et al., "Legal Provisions and Restrictions on the Propagation of Non-Islamic Religions among Muslims in Malaysia."

4. Pizzo, "The 'Coptic Question' in Post-revolutionary Egypt"; Kymlicka and Pföstl, *Multiculturalism and Minority Rights in the Arab World*; Longva and Roald, *Religious Minorities in the Middle East*; Nielsen, "Contemporary Discussions on Religious Minorities in Muslim Countries"; Saeed, "Rethinking Citizenship Rights of Non-Muslims in an Islamic State"; Stephanous, *Political Islam, Citizenship and Minorities.*

5. Khatab, "Citizenship Rights of Non-Muslims in the Islamic State of Hakimiyya"; Warren and Gilmore, "One Nation under God?"; Shavit, "The Wasatī and Salafī Approaches to the Religious Law of Muslim Minorities."

6. See, for example, Safrilsyah, "Non-Muslim under the Regulation of Islamic Law in Aceh Province"; Ansor, "We Are from the Same Ancestors"; Ansor et al., "Under the Shadow of Sharia."

7. Fadhilah and Mahara, "The Sharia on Non-Muslims."

8. Uddin, "Religious Freedom Implications of Sharia Implementation in Aceh, Indonesia."

9. Makin, "Islamic Acehnese Identity, Sharia, and Christianization Rumor."

10. Ansor, "Agensi Perempuan Kristen dalam Ruang Publik Islam Aceh."

11. Ichwan, "Forbidden Visibility."
12. C. Taylor, *Multiculturalism*, 36.
13. C. Taylor, *Multiculturalism*, 37.
14. Yuval-Davis, "Multi-layered Citizenship in the Age of 'Glocalization'"; Yuval-Davis, "Intersectionality, Citizenship and Contemporary Politics of Belonging."
15. Van Klinken and Berenschot, "Everyday Citizenship in Democratizing Indonesia."
16. Kivisto and Faist, *Citizenship*; Kivisto, "Citizenship."
17. Delanty, *Citizenship in a Global Age*, 9; Joppke, "Transformation of Citizenship."
18. Hefner, *The Politics of Multiculturalism*; Hefner, "Shariah Formalism or Democratic Communitarianism?"
19. Van Klinken and Berenschot, "Everyday Citizenship in Democratizing Indonesia."
20. Marshall, *Class, Citizenship, and Social Development*.
21. Isin and Nyers, *Routledge Handbook of Global Citizenship Studies*, 4.
22. Dominelli, "Problematising Concepts of Citizenship and Citizenship Practices," 17.
23. Lister, *Citizenship*.
24. Lewis, *Citizenship*.
25. Moosa-Mitha, "Exclusionary and Inclusionary Citizenship Practices around Faith-Based Communities."
26. Metcalf, "Islam in Contemporary Southeast Asia," 309.
27. Hefner, *The Politics of Multiculturalism*; Hefner, "Christians, Conflict, and Citizenship in Muslim-Majority Indonesia."
28. Hefner, "Christians, Conflict, and Citizenship in Muslim-Majority Indonesia"; Chaplin, "Salafi Islamic Piety as Civic Activism."
29. Kloos and Berenschot, "Citizenship and Islam in Malaysia and Indonesia."
30. Salim, "The Special Status of Islamic Aceh."
31. Salim, "Shari`a from below in Aceh."
32. Syamsuddin, *The Republican Revolt*.
33. Fukuyama, *Identity*.
34. Fukuyama, *Identity*, 39.
35. Fukuyama, *Identity*, 41.
36. Fukuyama, *Identity*, 163.
37. Fukuyama, *Identity*, 9–10.
38. Fukuyama, *Identity*, 59.
39. Fukuyama, *Identity*, 56–58.
40. An-Na'im, "Political Islam in National Politics and International Relations," 103.

41. Fukuyama, *Identity*, xiii.
42. Hughes, *Identity, Law and Politics*.
43. Benda, "South-East Asian Islam in the Twentieth Century."
44. Morris, "Aceh."
45. Salim, "Shari`a from below in Aceh."
46. Ghanea, "Human Rights of Religious Minorities and of Women in the Middle East."
47. Fukuyama, *Identity*.
48. Fukuyama, *Identity*, 18–20.
49. Ansor, "We Are from the Same Ancestors," 21.

Chapter 1

1. Sila, "Kerukunan Umat Beragama di Indonesia"; Tumanggor and Muallim, *Perspektif Kehidupan Keberagamaan non-Muslim di Nanggroe Aceh Darussalam dengan Diberlakukannya Syariat Islam*.
2. Suparlan, "Kemajemukan, Hipotesis Kebudayaan Dominan dan Kesukubangsaan."
3. Bruner, "The Expression of Ethnicity in Indonesia."
4. Lamont and Molnár, "The Study of Boundaries in the Social Sciences."
5. Bowen, *Islam, Law and Equality in Indonesia*; Schröter, "Acehnese Culture(s)."
6. Schwedler, "Islamic Identity."
7. Salim, "Shari`a from below in Aceh."
8. Morris, "Aceh," 87.
9. Syamsuddin, *The Republican Revolt*, 111.
10. The first governor of Aceh, appointed in 1949, was the chairman of the ulama association, Teungku Daud Beureueh, who had served as the military governor of Aceh for various periods between 1946 and 1949. In 1950, the province of Aceh was dissolved and merged with the province of North Sumatra, a region with plural sociocultural life and a strong Protestant population. As the province of Aceh was incorporated into North Sumatra, the ulama's objective of maintaining Islamic domination in the region and their plans to apply Islamic law in Aceh came to a halt. The presence of non-Acehnese officials in some cities in Aceh alarmed the ulama, who perceived a serious danger to Acehnese religious values, as these "outsiders" brought with them habits prohibited by Islam, including drinking, gambling, and other forms of moral laxity (Syamsuddin, *The Republican Revolt*, 113).
11. Syamsuddin, *The Republican Revolt*, 113.
12. Kell, *The Roots of Acehnese Rebellion*.
13. McGibbon, "Local Leadership and the Aceh Conflict."

14. Salim, "Epilogue."
15. Pratt, *Identity and Interaction*, 7–11.
16. Feener, *Shari`a and Social Engineering*.
17. Gozdecka, "Religious Pluralism as a Legal Principle."
18. Gupta and Ferguson, "Space, Identity, and the Politics of Difference."
19. Wilmsen, *Land Filled with Flies*.
20. Al Fairusy, *Singkel*; Al Fairusy, "Menjadi Singkel Menjadi Aceh, Menjadi Aceh Menjadi Islam."
21. Lombard, *Kerajaan Aceh*; Ito and Reid, "From Harbour Autocracies to Feudal Diffusion in Seventeenth-Century Indonesia."
22. Kloos, "Foreword."
23. Al Fairusy, *Singkel*, 285.
24. Al Fairusy, *Singkel*, 284–85.
25. Sahlins, *Boundaries*.
26. Al Fairusy, *Singkel*.
27. Viner and Kaplan, "The Changing Pakpak Batak."
28. Konrad, "Borders and Culture."
29. Interview with Boas Tumangger, Banda Aceh, August 13, 2016.
30. Birchok, "Sojourning on Mecca's Verandah."
31. Ansor, "We Are from the Same Ancestors."
32. Mujiburrahman, *Feeling Threatened*.
33. On the FPI presence in Aceh, see Afriko, "Syariat Islam dan radikalisme massa."
34. Al Fairusy, *Singkel*, 293.
35. Ansor, "We Are from the Same Ancestors."
36. Al Fairusy, *Singkel*; Ansor, "We Are from the Same Ancestors."

Chapter 2

1. Casanova, *Public Religions in the Modern World*; Rosenblum, *Obligations of Citizenship and Demands of Faith*; Hefner, "Islamism and the Struggle for Inclusive Citizenship in Democratic Indonesia," 14-37; Hefner, "Christians, Conflict, and Citizenship in Muslim-Majority Indonesia"; Moosa-Mitha, "Exclusionary and Inclusionary Citizenship Practices around Faith-Based Communities."
2. Hefner, *The Politics of Multiculturalism*; Rosaldo, *Cultural Citizenship in Southeast Asia*; Berenschot et al., *Citizenship and Democratization in Southeast Asia*.
3. Berenschot et al., *Citizenship and Democratization in Southeast Asia*; Hiariel and Stokke, *Politics of Citizenship in Indonesia*; Van Klinken, "Citizenship and Local Practices of Rule in Indonesia"; Van Klinken and Berenschot, "Everyday Citizenship in Democratizing Indonesia"; Hefner, *Islam and Citizenship in Indonesia*; Berenschot and Van Klinken, "Informality and Citizenship."

4. Reid, *Verandah of Violence*; Kingsbury, "The Free Aceh Movement"; Aspinall, *Islam and Nation*; Feener, *Shari'a and Social Engineering*; Kloos, "Becoming Better Muslims"; Kloos et al., *Islam and the Limits of the State*.

5. Rahmawati et al., "The Negotiation of Political Identity."

6. Merry and Milligan, "Complexities of Belonging in Democratic and Democratizing Societies."

7. Hefner, *The Politics of Multiculturalism*.

8. Isin and Turner, "Citizenship Studies," 4; Van Klinken and Berenschot, "Everyday Citizenship in Democratizing Indonesia."

9. Faist, "Dual Citizenship as Overlapping Membership," 37.

10. Yuval-Davis, "Multi-layered Citizenship in the Age of 'Glocalization'"; Yuval-Davis, "Intersectionality, Citizenship and Contemporary Politics of Belonging."

11. Lister, "Citizenship on the Margins."

12. Boland, *The Struggle of Islam in Modern Indonesia*, 69.

13. McCarty, "The Demonstration Effect"; Aspinall, *Islam and Nation*.

14. Aspinall, *Islam and Nation*.

15. Feener, *Shari'a and Social Engineering*.

16. Sulaiman and Van Klinken, "From Autonomy to Periphery," 135; Afriko, "Syariat Islam dan radikalisme massa," 28–29.

17. Focus group discussion, Langsa, December 22, 2016.

18. Anderson, *Imagined Communities*; see also Metcalf, "Islam in Contemporary Southeast Asia."

19. Berenschot and Van Klinken, "Informality and Citizenship."

20. As Brown, *Contending Nationalisms in Southeast Asia*, 2.

21. Talsya, "Atjeh tidak pernah menjerahkan kedaulatan kepada Belanda"; Boland, *The Struggle of Islam in Modern Indonesia*, 69.

22. Boland, *The Struggle of Islam in Modern Indonesia*, 69.

23. El Ibrahimy, *Peran Tgk. M. Daud Beureueh dalam Pergolakan Aceh*, 77–79.

24. Van Dijk, *Rebellion under the Banner of Islam*; Reid, "War, Peace and the Burden of History in Aceh"; Formichi, *Islam and the Making of the Nation*.

25. Tiro, *The Price of Freedom*, 15–17.

26. Hamzah, *Hasan Tiro*, 510–13; Sulaiman and Van Klinken, "From Autonomy to Periphery," 135.

27. Reid, "War, Peace and the Burden of History in Aceh"; Schulze, *The Free Aceh Movement (GAM)*; Kingsbury, "The Free Aceh Movement"; Aspinall, *Islam and Nation*.

28. Miller, *Rebellion and Reform in Indonesia*, 32–90.

29. See Abubakar, *Syariat Islam di Provinsi Nanggroe Aceh Darussalam*; Feener, *Shari'a and Social Engineering*; Salim, *Contemporary Islamic Law in Indonesia*.

30. Ichwan, "The Politics of Shari'atisation."

31. Muhammad, *Revitalisasi Syariat islam di Aceh*.

32. An-Na'im, "Beyond Dhimmihood"; Müller, "Non-Muslims as Part of Islamic Law."

33. Interview with Tgk Tu Bulqaini, adviser of Front Islamic Defender (FPI) Banda Aceh, October 7, 2018; with Abu Haris Naufal, a Salafi scholar, October 6, 2018; and with Tgk Faisal Ali, vice chairperson of the Deliberative Council of Ulama (MPU) and chairperson of the Nahdlatul Ulama of Aceh, October 3, 2018.

34. Hidayatullah, "Warga Non-Muslim Aceh Ahlul Dzimmah."

35. The proverb is quoted in the Elucidation of the Qanun No. 11/2002 on the Implementation of Shari`a in the Fields of Belief (Aqīdah), Devotion (Ibādah), and Symbols (Shi'ār). Dinas Syariat Islam, *Himpunan Undang-undang*, 7.

36. Syaikh 'Abd al-Ra'uf al-Sinkili, known as "Syiah Kuala," was Shaykh al-Islam of the Aceh sultanate during Sulṭāna Taj ul-'Alam Safiatuddin Shah (r. February 18, 1641–October 23, 1675), the daughter of Iskandar Muda, and the wife of his successor, Iskandar Thani, and the next two sultanas, until his death in 1693. See Azra, *The Origin of Islamic Reformist in Southeast Asia*, 71. On the Aceh sultanates, see Khan, "The Sultanahs of Aceh; Khan, *Sovereign Women in a Muslim Kingdom*; Khan, "The Sultanahs of Aceh, 1641–1699."

37. Sultan Iskandar Muda's wife was the princess of Pahang. This indicates that she was given an important role in maintaining civil law. In today's Aceh, qanun is used as civil bylaw pertaining to shari`a and general affairs. See Clavé-Çelik, "Silenced Fighters," 280.

38. This indicates that the admiral, who was in charge of maritime security, held an important position in the Aceh sultanate. The admiral was Keumalahayati or Malahayati, a female fighter of the Aceh sultanate. See Clavé-Çelik, "Silenced Fighters," 280.

39. Mohammad Akbar, "Larangan Berjilbab Melanggar HAM," March 29, 2014, https://khazanah.republika.co.id/berita/n372uu/larangan-berjilbab-melanggar-ham-2.

40. Bastoni, *Serambi Makkah dihempas tsunami diterjang Kristenisasi*.

41. "Umat Islam dan Kristen di Aceh Investigasi Bersama Kasus Pemurtadan," https://www.merdeka.com/peristiwa/umat-islam-dan-kristen-di-aceh-investigasi-bersamakasus-pemurtadan.html.

42. "Perempuan/wanita asal aceh Cut Fitri handayani pindah agama," Philokalia Official, June 16, 2020, https://www.youtube.com/watch?v=3mUbGP_0dhA.

43. Ansor, "We Are from the Same Ancestors"; Ansor et al., "Under the Shadow of Sharia"; Makin, "Islamic Acehnese Identity, Sharia, and Christianization Rumor."

44. Interviews with Ustadh Hambali Sinaga, local leader of Front of Islamic Defence (FPI) of Singkil, April 21, 2016, and with Suriadi, the head of Singkil

Islamic Youth, Yogyakarta, July 12, 2016. After the church-burning accident, Suriadi fled to Yogyakarta.

45. Al Fairusy, *Singkel*.

46. Ansor, "We Are from the Same Ancestors."

47. Tgk Faisal Ali and Tgk Tu Bulqaini, two representatives of the dayah leaders, said that this had nothing to do with such a conflict; rather, the conflict was caused by a violation of local consensus based on the Shāfiʿī ruling that there should be only one *jāmiʿ* mosque (a mosque used for Friday prayer) in a village, except when there was a new consensus to add another mosque because of the large number of attendees. In both the cases referred to here, according to the dayah representative, there was no such consensus. However, Professor Alyasa' Abubakar, former Muhammadiyah provincial chairperson, said this argument was irrelevant because the local communities of these two regions belonged in the past mostly to the modernist All-Acehnese Ulama Association (Persatuan Ulama Seluruh Aceh). Interviews with Tgk Faisal Ali, September 6, 2018, with Tgk Tu Bulqaini, September 7, 2018, and with Professor Alyasa' Abu Bakar, October 6, 2018.

48. Usman, *Etnis Cina Perantauan di Aceh*, 150–51.

49. Disnak Aceh, "Data Peternakan Provinsi Aceh."

50. This regulation authorizes the subdistrict head, subdistrict police head, and subdistrict military commander to conduct surveillance of pig livestock in Southeast Aceh in the form of guidance and counseling.

51. Serambi Indonesia, "Babi Bebas Diternakkan di Agara."

52. Lintas Gayo, "Babi Berkeliaran, Tuak Marak."

53. Interviews with Baharuddin Pinem, head of FKUB of Kutacane, Kutacane, March 30, 2016; Qarnain Musra, head of the Islamic Center of Kutacane, Kutacane, March 29, 2016; and Agus Nurjamil, a border preacher of Kutacane, Kutacane, April 1, 2016.

54. Interview with Sabar Andreas Simbolon, a *panatua* (minister) of HKBP, Langsa, December 25, 2016.

55. Interview with Bondan Tarigan, head of the Catholic Church's Parish Council, Takengon, December 27, 2017.

56. Ansor, "Menjadi Seperti Beragama Lain."

57. Interviews with Bondan Tarigan, Takengon, December 27, 2017; and with Christian local people, Tamiang, December 23, 2016.

58. Kompas, "Panglima TNI." See Safira Mustaqilla, Irwan Abdullah, Moch. Nur Ichwan, and Lailatussaadah Lailatussaadah, "The Existence of Non-Muslim Minorities in Aceh Indonesia: A Study of Civil and Police Institutions," *Samarah*, 8, no. 1 (2024): 628–45.

59. Lembong, "Indonesian Government Policies and the Ethnic Chinese."

60. Interview with Akim, leader the Chinese community Persatuan Tolong Menolong, Tamiang, December 27, 2016. See also Srimulyani et al., "Diasporic

Chinese Community in Post-conflict Aceh." On Chinese communities in Aceh, see Usman, *Etnis Cina Perantauan di Aceh*.

61. Interview with Boas Tumangger, head of Forum Cinta Damai Aceh Singkil (Forcidas), Banda Aceh, August 13, 2016.

62. Tim Investigasi, "Menelusuri Polemik Pendidikan Agama di Aceh Singkil."

63. Interview with Boas Tumangger, Banda Aceh, August 13, 2016.

64. Marwanto, "Menjadi Garam dan Terang Lewat Pendidikan."

Chapter 3

1. See Feener, *Shari`a and Social Engineering*.
2. See, for example, Salim, *Challenging the Secular State*; Salim, *Contemporary Islamic Law in Indonesia*; Feener, *Shari`a and Social Engineering*.
3. Rehman and Askari, "How Islamic Are Islamic Countries?"
4. Abubakar, *Syariat Islam di Provinsi Nanggroe Aceh Darussalam*, 19.
5. Afadhal, *Dinamika Birokrasi Lokal Era Otonomi Daerah*.
6. Santos, "A Theory of Bureaucratic Authority."
7. Abubakar, *Syariat Islam di Provinsi Nanggroe Aceh Darussalam*, 93.
8. Sulaiman and Van Klinken, "The Rise and Fall of Governor Puteh."
9. Juwana, *Penyusunan Naskah Akademik sebagai Prasyarat dalam Perencanaan Pembentukan RUU*, 175.
10. Azizy, *Change Management dalam Reformasi Birokrasi*; Künkler, "Law, Legitimacy, and Equality."
11. Abubakar, *Syariat Islam di Provinsi Nanggroe Aceh Darussalam*, 94.
12. Etzioni, "Authority Structure and Organizational Effectiveness."
13. Afriko, "Syariat Islam dan radikalisme massa."
14. Personal communication with the head of Aceh Sharia Office, Banda Aceh, August 6, 2017.
15. Afriko, "Syariat Islam dan radikalisme massa."
16. Human Rights Watch, *Menegakkan Moralitas*; Ichwan, "Alternatives to Shariatism."
17. Santos, "A Theory of Bureaucratic Authority," 252.
18. See, for example, Afadhal, *Dinamika Birokrasi Lokal Era Otonomi Daerah*.
19. Knowledge Sector Initiative, *Catatan Kebijakan Meninjau Ulang Standar Kompetensi Jabatan Pimpinan Tinggi*.
20. Interview with Aceh Sharia Office staff, Banda Aceh, June 11, 2018.
21. Santos, "A Theory of Bureaucratic Authority."
22. Personal communication with the head of Law Development Sector at the Aceh Sharia Office, Banda Aceh, November 11, 2017.

23. In the past few years, the DSI leadership situation seems to have improved less despite the recruitment of two PhD-bearing department heads. One of them, Munawar A. Djalil, eventually became DSI head. The appointment of these scholars created some problems within the DSI: one subordinate, Syukri, who is older than the director, felt that he would have been able to plan DSI activities better than the new head. He expressed his disagreement with the head's decision on the 2017 Rakornis draft, which should have been discussed with him since he was the section head and the person in charge of planning activities. Lower-level staff later decided they needed to comply with orders and directives from the two different figures to keep operations running. Personal communication with the head of the Law Development Sector at the Aceh Sharia Office, Banda Aceh, November 11, 2017.

24. Bolton and Dewatripont, "Authority in Organizations."

25. Interview with the head of the Organization and Governance Bureau, Office of the Governor of Aceh, Banda Aceh, May 16, 2018.

Chapter 4

1. Warner and Wegrich, "Theories of the Policy Cycle," 31.
2. Al-Mawardi, *Al-Ahkamu al-Shulthaniyya*.
3. Salim, "Epilogue."
4. See, for example, Salsabila, *Pertimbangan Hakim dalam Memutus Hukuman Cambuk bagi Non-Muslim sebagai Pelaku Jarimah Khamar*; Multazam, "Penerapan Asas-Asas Hukum Pidana dalam Kasus `Uqubat Takzir terhadap Non-Muslim." Whereas the former analyzed caning as being appropriate to the regulations, the latter convinced that non-Muslims in Aceh are positioned as dhimmi.
5. See An-Na'im, *Islam and the Secular State*.
6. Cammack and Feener, "The Islamic Legal System in Indonesia."
7. The latest compilation of qanun jinaya, Qanun 6/2014, added ikhtilath (intimacy prior to adultery), zina (adultery), *pelecehan seksual* (sexual harassment), *pemerkosaan* (rape), qadhaf (false accusation for adultery), liwath (sodomy), and musahaqah (lesbianism).
8. Mahkamah Syar`iyah Aceh, Jumlah SDM Hakim Mahkamah Syar`iyah Aceh dan Mahkamah Syar`iyah Kabupaten/Kota se Aceh, https://ms-aceh.go.id/transparansi-kesekretariatan/data-statistik-kepegawaian/2689-jumlah-sdm-hakim-mahkamah-syar-iyah-se-wilayah-aceh-per-31-oktober-2018.html.
9. Interview with Ansharullah, subhead of employee affairs at Mahkamah Syar`iyah Aceh, Banda Aceh, August 19, 2019.
10. Qanun 10/2002 specified in verse 5a that the advancement of the Islamic court was supported by the Supreme Court of Indonesia (Mahkamah

Agung), and its organization, administration, and financial matters were to be facilitated by a minister or governor. Thus, in doing this task, the DSI operates on behalf of the governor of Aceh.

11. Shuaib, "The Islamic Legal System in Malaysia"; Hung, *The Politics of Hudud Law Implementation in Malaysia.*

12. See Hotli Simanjuntak, "'Qanun Jinayat' Becomes Official for All People in Aceh," *Jakarta Post*, October 23, 2015, https://www.thejakartapost.com/news/2015/10/23/qanun-jinayat-becomes-official-all-people-aceh.html.

13. A close proximity between a male and female adult who have no marriage or kin relationship, in a place or situation where intimate contact is possible.

14. From 2016 to 2017, at least thirteen non-Muslim cases have been handled by the Sharī`a Court. There must be some non-Muslim cases remaining in the Jinaya Directory, for instance from both the Sharī`a Court of Jantho and Meulaboh, as reported by media, but we cannot read the details due to limited publication. See Satu Harapan, "2 Umat Buddha Dihukum Cambuk di Aceh karena Adu Ayam," March 11, 2017, http://www.satuharapan.com/read-detail/read/2-umat-buddha-dihukum-cambuk-di-aceh-karena-adu-ayam, and Darmansyah Muda, "Lapas Meulaboh Gelar Cambuk Perdana terhadap Warga Non Muslim," AJNN (Aceh Journal National Network), May 15, 2018, http://www.ajnn.net/news/lapas-meulaboh-gelar-cambuk-perdana-terhadap-warga-non-muslim/index.html.

15. Adji, *Sistem Hukum Pidana dan Keadilan Restoratif.*

16. Cribb, "Legal Pluralism and Criminal Law in Dutch Colonial Order."

17. DSI head of Aceh Tamiang district confirms that non-Muslim offenders would be punished by caning should they violate the qanun on jinaya. Interview, Kuala Simpang, December 23, 2016.

18. Governor's Regulation 5/2018, article 7, specifies detention in prison (*rumah tahanan*) under terms of rehabilitation (*pembinaan*). But several Satpol PP-WH offices have that kind of prison; so, for example, in Banda Aceh, prisoners are held in Satpol PP-WH prison.

19. This declaration is crucial to determining which court is authorized to examine the case and what law should be referred to throughout the adjudication process.

20. Interview with "M," Satpol PP-Wilayatul Hisbah officer, Banda Aceh, August 28, 2019.

21. Salim, *Challenging the Secular State.*

22. Interview with Catholic, Protestant, and Buddhist religious leaders and observations of the socioreligious conditions of Central Aceh, Takengon, December 23, 2018.

23. Arzia Tivany Wargadiredja, "Kenapa Nonmuslim di Aceh Kembali Dihukum Cambuk Sesuai Syariat Islam?" https://www.vice.com/id_id/article/d7edbq/kenapa-nonmuslim-di-aceh-kembali-dihukum-cambuk-sesuai-syariat-islam.

24. One case of faith blasphemy occurred in Pidie district, where Diana, a Protestant woman from Central Java, was sentenced to two years' imprisonment. This case did not attract media attention due to the nonviolent nature of the sentence. The verdict, number 6/JN/2018/MS.Sgi, notes that Diana was sentenced for having torn pages out of the Qur'an, violating an article about developing and protecting the faith. Had the media known of this case, it would no doubt have attracted the same attention as those of the leader and followers of Gafatar in Indonesia and Aceh. They were similarly sentenced to imprisonment by the Civil Court due to violating article 156a of the national criminal code (KUHP) regarding religious blasphemy. The chronology and analysis of this case can be found in Mawa Kresna, "Memenjarakan Gafatar," Tirto, March 8, 2017, https://tirto.id/memenjarakan-gafatar-ckkq.

25. Rafki Hidayat, "Cambuk perempuan Non-Muslim, Pusat diminta tegur Aceh," BBC News Indonesia, April 15, 2016, https://www.bbc.com/indonesia/berita_indonesia/2016/04/160414_indonesia_aceh_qanun_hakim.

26. See, for example, Hidayat, "Cambuk perempuan Non-Muslim, Pusat diminta tegur Aceh."

27. Redaksi, "Eksekusi Cambuk Penjual Miras Non Muslim Dipertanyakan," KBA One, August 29, 2018, https://www.kba.one/news/eksekusi-cambuk-penjual-miras-non-muslim-dipertanyakan/index.html.

28. For instance, Halim, "Non-Muslims in the Qanun Jinayat and the Choice of Law in Sharia Courts in Aceh."

29. ICJR, "Setahun Qanun Jinayat: Penggunaan Hukuman Cambuk yang Semakin Eksesif di Aceh," October 22, 2016, http://icjr.or.id/setahun-qanun-jinayat-penggunaan-hukuman-cambuk-yang-semakin-eksesif-di-aceh/print.

30. Nurdin Hasan, "Pemuda Budha Dicambuk Bersama 10 Warga Aceh," Benar News, January 8, 2019, https://www.benarnews.org/indonesian/berita/budha-cambuk-aceh-08012019123136.html.

Chapter 5

1. Abubakar, *Syariat Islam di Provinsi Nanggroe Aceh Darussalam*; Ichwan, "The Politics of Shari'atisation"; Salim, *Challenging the Secular State*; Feener, *Shari`ah and Social Engineering*.

2. Chambert-Loir, "Islamic Law in 17th Century Aceh."

3. Personal communication with Ustadz Qusayen Aly, senior teacher at Dayah Darul Ihsan, Siem Village, Aceh Besar District, May 22, 2020.

4. Ichwan, "Faith, Ethnicity, and Illiberal Citizenship"; Ansor et al., "Under the Shadow of Sharia."

5. Srimulyani, "Islamic Schooling in Aceh."

6. "200 Guru SMA Ikuti Pelatihan Kurikulum Aceh Islami," Aceh Trend, May 18, 2019, https://www.acehtrend.com/2019/05/18/200-guru-sma-ikuti-pelatihan-kurikulum-aceh-islami/.

7. "Salafiyah" here does not refer to "Salafism" as Wahhabism but to traditional orientation, which is based on classical *madhhab* (Islamic law schools) and also adaptable to local culture.

8. "DSI Aceh Adakan TOT Syariat Islam Bagi Guru," Dinas Syariat Islam, March 12, 2020, https://dsi.acehprov.go.id/dsi-aceh-adakan-tot-syariat-islam-bagi-guru-2/.

9. Interview with Dr. Sri Suyanta, lecturer of Tarbiyah and Teaching Faculty, UIN Ar-Raniry, May 2019.

10. Agus Lukman, "Siswa Kristen Terpaksa Belajar Agama Islam di Aceh Singkil ini Sikap PGI," KBR, March 26, 2016, https://kbr.id/nasional/03-2016/siswa_kristen_terpaksa_belajar_agama_islam_di_aceh_singkil__ini_sikap_pgi_/79810.html.

11. Tim Investigasi, "Menelusuri Polemik Pendidikan Agama di Aceh Singkil," *Media Indonesia*, April 4, 2016, https://mediaindonesia.com/read/detail/38091-menelusuri-polemik-pendidikan-agama-di-aceh-singkil.

12. Before Joko Widodo's first term, the name of the ministry was the Ministry of Education and Culture. During his first term (2014–19), the name was changed to the Ministry of Research, Technology, and Higher Education, and during his second term (2019–24), it adopted the first name. Due to these changes, we simply call it the Ministry of Education.

13. See "Aceh Target Misionaris," *Serambi Indonesia*, January 28, 2015, https://aceh.tribunnews.com/2015/01/28/aceh-taget-misionaris.

14. The Da'wah and Communication Faculty conducted research on Da'i Perbatasan in 2018.

15. Quipper Blog, "Ini Dia Sebaran Pekerjaan Alumni UIN Ar-Raniry," March 29, 2017, https://www.quipper.com/id/blog/quipper-campus/campus-life/ini-dia-sebaran-pekerjaan-alumni-uin-ar-raniry/.

16. M. Marzuki, "Penguatan Materi PAI bagi Mahasiswa Bidikmisi di Universitas Syiah Kuala (USK) Banda Aceh," https://acied.pp-paiindonesia.org/index.php/acied/article/view/18

17. Herman Fithra et al., *Modul Mata Kuliah Kemalikussalehan*, Universitas Malukussaleh, 2020, 7–8.

18. Erlina, "Membangun Karakter Keindonesiaan Pancasila Melalui Pendidikan Kewarganegaraan di Era Global."

19. "Unsyiah Gelar Konferensi Internasional Kewarganegaraan," https://usk.ac.id/unsyiah-gelar-konferensi-internasional-kewarganegaraan/.

20. The original essay is now not accessible, but a reprint is available. See Redaski, "Belajar di Australia Dosen IAIN Ajak Mahasiswa ke Gereja di Banda

Aceh," Sejuk, January 8, 2015, http://sejuk.org/2015/01/08/belajar-di-australia-dosen-iain-ajak-mahasiswa-ke-gereja-di-banda-aceh/.

21. Andreas Harsono, "Rosnida Sari: Saya Mau Tunjukkan Aceh yang Toleran Namun Disalahmengerti," February 12, 2015, http://www.andreasharsono.net/2015/02/rosnida-sari-saya-mau-tunjukkan-aceh.html.

22. Personal communication with Rosnida Sari, April 5, 2020.

23. Arabiyani Abubakar, Facebook post, January 6, 2015, https://www.facebook.com/arabiyani.abubakar/posts/10152627495432058.

24. "Statemen Fuad Mardhatillah (Direktur Aceh Institute) Terkait Kasus Rosnida Sari," Aceh Institute, January 6, 2015, https://acehinstitute.org/ruang-berita/press-rilis/statemen-pak-fuad-mardhatillah-terkait-rosnida-sari.html.

25. Usman, *Etnis Cina Perantauan di Aceh*.

26. On FPI, see Afriko, "Syariat Islam dan radikalisme massa."

27. "Mujahidin Aceh Siap Perang Jihad Melawan Buddha Tzu Chi," Independensi, February 15, 2018, https://independensi.com/2018/02/15/mujahidin-aceh-siap-perang-jihad-melawan-buddha-tzu-chi/.

28. "FPI Tolak Keterlibatan Yayasan Buddha Tsu Chi dan Minta Pemkab Pijay Hentikan Pembangunan Gedung AKN," StatusAceh, http://www.statusaceh.net/2018/02/fpi-tolak-keterlibatan-yayasan-budha.html.

29. "Ulama: Bantuan Buddha Tzu Chi tak Ada Kaitan dengan Agama," Serambinews, February 14, 2018, https://aceh.tribunnews.com/2018/02/14/ulama-bantuan-buddha-tzu-chi-tak-ada-kaitan-dengan-agama.

30. Personal communication with Fuad Mardhatillah, academic of UIN Ar-Raniry and public intellectual, April 4, 2020.

31. "Press Release: Indeks Kota Toleran IKT Tahun 2018," Setara Institute, December 7, 2018, http://setara-institute.org/indeks-kota-toleran-ikt-tahun-2018/.

32. "Disebut Kota Intoleran Pemkot Banda Aceh Siap Tuntut Setara Institute," Kumparan, December 11, 2018, https://kumparan.com/kumparannews/disebut-kota-intoleran-pemkot-banda-aceh-siap-tuntut-setara-institute-1544507296838992719/full.

33. The survey was conducted by the Center of Research and Development of the Guidance of Religious Communities (Pusat Penelitian dan Pengembangan Bimbingan Masyarakat Agama dan Layanan Keagamaan), Agency of Research, Development, Education and Training, Ministry of Religious Affairs.

34. Haris Prabowo, "Daftar Skor Indeks Kerukunan Beragama versi Kemenag 2019," Tirto, December 11, 2019, https://tirto.id/engH.

35. "Indeks Kerukunan di Aceh Paling Rendah FKUB Pertanyakan Indikator Survei," Detik, December 11, 2019, https://news.detik.com/berita/d-4818650/indeks-kerukunan-di-aceh-paling-rendah-fkub-pertanyakan-indikator-survei.

36. "Survei Kemenag Tempatkan Aceh Rangking Terbawah Toleransi Beragama, Begini Reaksi Pendeta Idaman," Serambi Indonesia, December 17, 2019, https://aceh.tribunnews.com/2019/12/16/survei-kemenag-tempatkan-aceh-rangking-terbawah-toleransi-beragama-begini-reaksi-pendeta-idaman.

37. Al Fairusy, "Menjadi Singkel Menjadi Aceh, Menjadi Aceh Menjadi Islam."

38. Regional Office of the Ministry of Religion, Aceh Province, "FKUB dan Tokoh Lintas Agama di Aceh Bahas Hasil Survei Indeks Kerukunan 2019," December 24, 2019, https://aceh.kemenag.go.id/berita/508793/fkub-dan-tokoh-lintas-agama-di-aceh-bahas-hasil-survei-indeks-kerukunan-2019.

39. We borrow and adapt the concept of "negative tolerance" from Johan Galtung's (Galtung, "An Editorial") concept of "negative peace," which refers to "the absence of violence, the absence of war," whereas "positive peace" refers to "the integration of human society."

Chapter 6

1. Although Governor's Decree 54/2014 was issued in 2014, the border da'i program was created in 2002, based on Qanun 11/2002 on Islamic Shariah in the field of Belief ('aqidah), Devotion ('ibadah), and Symbols (syiar). Interview with Prof. Rusydi Ali Muhammad, Banda Aceh, 2017.

2. Tamiang was part of Aceh Timur and not separated as an independent district until 2002. Singkil was part of Aceh Tenggara until 2002, when the former became an independent district. Subulussalam was part of Singkil until 2007, when the former became an independent municipality. This information is important for interpreting statistics about the number of religious adherents and places of worship, as well as the local politics of religion.

3. See Article 1:7 and 1:8 of Governor's Decree 54/2014.

4. Although most Javanese embrace Islam, some embrace Protestantism and Catholicism.

5. Castles, "The Political Life of a Sumatran Residency"; Kloos, Foreword to *Singkel*.

6. BPS Aceh 2015, 111.

7. BPS Aceh 2015, 111.

8. "Situasi Membaik, Pengamanan 4 Gereja di Subulussalam Dikurangi," Kompas, October 19, 2015, https://regional.kompas.com/read/2015/10/19/13553461/Situasi.Membaik.Pengamanan.4.Gereja.di.Subulussalam.Dikurangi.

9. Interview with Akim, chairperson of Buddhist foundation Yayasan Tolong Menolong Kemalangan Setempat, Tamiang, December 27, 2016. Langsa has one Buddhist temple, which is shared with Hindus.

10. Al Fairusy, *Singkel*, 265–70; see also Sembiring, *Tradisi Masyarakat Parmalim di Toba Samosir*.
11. Tripa, *Setelah Tsunami Usai*, 63.
12. Febriandi, "Menyiasati Politik 'Kerukunan Agama' di Bawah Qanun Aceh."
13. Van der Ven, *Human Rights or Religious Rules?* 292.
14. Chabry and Chabry, *Politique et minorités au Proche-Orient*; quoted in Berger, "Public Policy and Islamic Law," 91.
15. The Setara Institute rated Banda Aceh the third most intolerant city in Indonesia in 2018 (Yudhistra, "10 kota toleran vs 10 kota intoleran di Indonesia," *Tagar*, November 19, 2019, https://www.tagar.id/10-kota-toleran-vs-10-kota-intoleran-di-indonesia), while the Ministry of Religious Affairs in its survey of Religious Harmony in 2019 put Banda Aceh in the lowest place (Prabowo, "Daftar skor indeks kerukunan beragama versi kemenag 2019").
16. For regulation about *da'i perbatasan*, see Gubernatorial Regulation No. 54 year 2014, issued on September 30, 2014. Peraturan Gubernur Aceh Nomor 54 Tahun 2014 tentang Petunjuk Teknis Pelaksanaan Kegiatan Da'i Wilayah Perbatasan dan Daerah Terpencil.
17. Hatta et al., *Strategi Dakwah Islamiyah di Aceh*.
18. Gubernatorial Decree No. 54/2014 1: 9-15.
19. On pesantren, see Dofier, *Tradisi Pesantren, Studi tentang Pandangan Hidup Kiyai*; Ziemek, *Pesantren dalam Perubahan Sosial*.
20. On dayah and ulama, see Amiruddin, "The Response of Ulama Dayah to Modernization of Islamic Law in Aceh."
21. See Zulkarnain, "Dinamika Madzhab Shafi'i dengan Cara Aceh."
22. See Bylaw No. 6/2000 on Education (Articles 1:17 and 15:3) and Qanun No. 23/2002 on Education in Aceh, especially article 16; Qanun No. 5/2008 on Education, article 1: 29, 30, 31 and article 32.
23. "Profil Dayah Safinatussalamah," *Dinas Pendidikan Provinsi Aceh*, http://dpd.acehprov.go.id.
24. Qanun Aceh Nomor 12 Tahun 2013 Tentang Rencana Pembangunan Jangka Menengah Aceh Tahun 2012–17.
25. See Mulyono, "Bantuan Sosial Kementerian Agama RI bagi Rumah Ibadat dan Ormas Keagamaan di Provinsi Aceh."
26. Interview with an official for Protestant and Catholic Affairs, District Office of Religious Affairs, Aceh Tenggara, April 5, 2016.
27. Interview with Drs. Ramlan, chairperson of FKUB of Singkil, April 3, 2016.
28. In the media, only Pemuda Peduli Islam was assigned responsibility for the action. Interviews with Ust. Hambali Syah Sinaga, chairperson of the Islamic Defense Front of Singkil, April 21, 2016 and Suriadi, head of Pemuda Peduli Islam of Singkil, Yogyakarta, June 3, 2016.

29. Interview with Suriadi, June 3, 2016.

30. Regional Office of the Ministry of Religion, Aceh Province, "FKUB Dan Tokoh Lintas Agama di Aceh Bahas Hasil Survei Indeks Kerukunan 2019," December 24, 2019, https://aceh.kemenag.go.id/berita/508793/fkub-dan-tokoh-lintas-agama-di-aceh-bahas-hasil-survei-indeks-kerukunan-2019.

Chapter 7

1. The Badan Rehabilitasi dan Rekonstruksi Aceh-Nias has a ministerial-level governance structure. It is the national agency that coordinated all of the incoming aid to Aceh for post-tsunami and postconflict rehabilitation over the period 2005–8. The Badan Reintegrasi Aceh is an Aceh provincial board established after the peace agreement was signed in 2005, mandated to deal with reintegration matters and sustain peace building in Aceh. It operated as an ad hoc office from 2005 through 2016 and then became a permanent government office.

2. Sulaiman and Van Klinken, "The Rise and Fall of Governor Puteh," 333.

3. The fieldwork for this study was conducted in Banda Aceh, the capital of Aceh province. Banda Aceh has the largest Chinese population in the province. While most of the data for this chapter derive from interviews, the chapter also relies on observation notes and other relevant documents.

4. R. Taylor, "Sharia as Heterotopia," 567.

5. Tan, "The Ethnic Chinese in Indonesia"; Tan, *Etnis Tionghoa di Indonesia*; Suryadinata, *Ethnic Chinese as Southeast Asians*; Suryadinata, *Political Thinking of the Indonesian Chinese*; Suryadinata, Arifin, and Ananta, "The Ethnic Chinese"; Suryadinata, "Chinese Indonesians in an Era of Globalization"; Suryadinata, *Ethnic Chinese in Contemporary Indonesia*; Suryadinata, "Ethnic Groups and the Indonesian Nation-State," 43–53; Godley and Lloyd, *Perspectives on the Chinese Indonesians*; Giblin, "Overcoming Stereotypes?"; Hoon, *Chinese Identity in Post-Suharto Indonesia*; Coppel, *Studying Ethnic Chinese in Indonesia*; Dawis, *The Chinese of Indonesia and Their Search for Identity*; Dieleman, Konig, and Post, *Chinese Indonesians and Regime Change*; Lindsey and Pausaker, *Chinese Indonesians*; Koning, "Chinese Indonesian."

6. Ananta, Arifin, and Bakhtiar, "Chinese Indonesians in Indonesia."

7. Tsai and Kammen, "Anti-Communist Violence and the Ethnic Chinese in Medan."

8. Hui, *Strangers at Home*.

9. Arifin, Hasbullah, and Pramono, "Chinese Indonesians."

10. Ahok, *Kembalinya Pengusaha Tionghoa di Banda Aceh*; Sulaiman, *Pengusaha Aceh dan Pengusaha Cina di Kotamadya Banda Aceh*; Rusdi, *Strategi Adaptasi Masyarakat Tionghoa Pasca Tsunami*; Ananta, "The Population and Conflict"; Usman, *Etnis Cina Perantauan di Aceh*.

11. Hooker, *Indonesian Islam*; An-Na'im, *Islam and the Secular State*.
12. Most of the Chinese are Buddhist or Christian; only a few converted to Islam or become Muslim.
13. Indonesian National Census, 2010.
14. Usman, *Etnis Cina Perantauan di Aceh*, 43.
15. Sulaiman, *Pengusaha Aceh dan Pengusaha Cina di Kotamadya Banda Aceh*, 1.
16. Suryadinata, *Ethnic Chinese as Southeast Asians*, 2.
17. These laborers came during the colonial period to work on the reconstruction projects in Dutch-colonized areas of the archipelago. A number of bridges, roads, and buildings were built with the technical skills of the Chinese; their work featured the use of big stone (*batu besar*) as a primary material. These projects survived the 2004 earthquake and currently exist.
18. Rusdi, *Strategi Adaptasi Masyarakat Tionghoa Pasca Tsunami*, 16.
19. Interview with Keuchik of Gampong Laksana, Banda Aceh, May 30, 2016.
20. During the colonial period, the Chinese usually rented their houses and shops *Cak Te*, meaning they had a right to rental over their lifetimes. When this special right was taken from them, they began to purchase the shops instead of renting them.
21. Interview with Chinese local leader in Banda Aceh, January 12, 2018.
22. Field, *Social Capital*.
23. Usman, *Etnis Cina Perantauan di Aceh*.
24. On the New Order's policy on the Chinese, see Aizawa, "Assimilation, Differentiation, and Depoliticization."
25. Interview with Ko Khie Siong, chief of HAKKA, Banda Aceh, April 26, 2016, and interview with Willy, leader of Vihara Dharma Bhakti-Peunayong, Banda Aceh, January 21, 2021.
26. "Mereka itu lebih berat, kita tidak terlalu berat, karena Cina kalau dia kawin dengan orang kita mereka kan tidak sekedar berubah agama, mereka juga harus berubah budaya juga" (It is harder for them [the Chinese], but the Acehnese, when a Chinese marry our people, they do not only change their religion, but also the culture). Interview with a Keuchik of Gampong Laksana, Banda Aceh, May 30, 2016.
27. Jujuk Ernawati and Dani Randi, "Gadis Berjilbab Jadi Tim Barongsai di Aceh," Viva, February 16, 2018, https://www.viva.co.id/gaya-hidup/inspirasi-unik/1007946-gadis-berjilbab-jadi-tim-barongsai-di-aceh.
28. "Selama Ramadan, kebutuhan pokok biasanya lebih banyak, maka kita bantu dengan membagikan sembako untuk mengurangi beban mereka.... Melalui kegiatan ini diharapkan persaudaraan antara warga etnis Tionghoa dan warga Muslim terus berlanjut" (During Ramadan, [Muslim's] basic needs are usually increased, so we [Hakka] help them by distributing food and other needs to ease their burden. We hope this activity will maintain the brotherhood between

the Tionghoa ethnic [as non-Muslim] and Muslim). Interview with Ko Khie Siong, chief of HAKKA, Banda Aceh, April 26, 2016.

29. Sulaiman, *Pengusaha Aceh dan Pengusaha Cina di Kotamadya Banda Aceh*, 4–11.

30. "Mereka tidak mau sembarangan melakukan tindakan-tindakan yang memicu kemarahan pribumi, karena mungkin mereka masih trauma dengan insiden demon China pada tahun 1980an itu" (They [Chinese] are always aware of actions that may trigger the Indigenous people's anger because there is still possibly trauma with the anti-Chinese demonstration in the 1980s). Interview with a village head of Gampong Laksana, Banda Aceh, May 30, 2016.

31. Keuchik is the Acehnese ethnic predicate for village head. But for some other ethnic groups, they have a different predicate; Datok Penghulu for the Tamiang ethnic, Reje for the Gayo ethnic, and in some Acehnese ethnic areas have different spelling with Geuchik.

32. "Kalau orang kita warisan itu ada yang dijual, dan yang sanggup membeli adalah China, meskipun tiga juta satu meter, mereka beli" (Our people [the Acehnese] tend to sell the inherited land parcels, and the Chinese usually afford the price [to buy], even though 3 millions rupiah per square meter, they will take it. Interview with a village head of Gampong Laksana, Banda Aceh, May 30, 2016.

33. Aspinall, *Islam and Nation*.

34. In 2018, as a Chinese community leader, Ko Khie Siong became a member of Forum Pembauran Kebangsaan. The forum was officially inaugurated by the governor of Aceh. According the Governor's Decree No. 300/669/2018, this Forum Pembauran Kebangsaan aims to preserve the harmony among the diversity of Aceh.

35. G30S, widely known as the biggest communist uprising during the Indonesian independence period, is still widely considered as *pengkhianatan* (betrayal) by many Indonesians. This event resulted in the kidnapping and murder of nine military high-ranked officers. In response, the Indonesian military and civilian groups engaged in widespread purges of suspected thousands of Indonesian Communist Party members across the country, leading to one of the largest genocides in Indonesia's history during the Suharto era.

36. Ahok, *Kembalinya Pengusaha Tionghoa di Banda Aceh*, 5.

37. Mevlin, *"Why Not Genocide?"* 67.

38. Suryadinata, *Political Thinking of the Indonesian Chinese*, 8.

39. Aspinall, *The Helsinki Agreement*, 8.

40. Sutrisno, "Konflik Etnisitas di Aceh Masa Reformasi, 1998–2005."

41. Hedman, "Aceh under Martial Law," 18.

42. Purdey, *Anti-Chinese Violence in Indonesia*.

43. Weng, *Negotiating Ethnicity and Religiosity*, 71.

44. Interview with Chinese local leader in Banda Aceh, January 12, 2018.

45. Sulaiman and Van Klinken, "The Rise and fall of Governor Puteh," 333; Salim, "Epilogue."

46. Senin, "Barongsai dan Liong Dilarang Tampil di Aceh," Berita Satu, August 13, 2012, https://www.beritasatu.com/nasional/65779/barongsai-dan-liong-dilarang-tampil-di-aceh.

47. Interview with Ko Khie Siong, chief of HAKKA, Banda Aceh, April 26, 2016.

48. Interview with a Chinese woman, a teacher, Banda Aceh, May 7, 2016.

49. "Kalau kita diam, jurang pemisah ini semakin melebar. Dulu tidak terpikir sama sekali kita bisa kerjasama sama orang NU, dengan teman-teman Muhammadiyah. Kalau dulu orang Tionghoa ini nggak peduli dengan hal-hal itu" (When we are passive, the gap will be widened. We used to think that we might not be able to collaborate with people from NU and Muhammadiyah. Chinese people used to never care about this kind of thing). Interview with Ko Khie Siong, chief of HAKKA, Banda Aceh, April 26, 2016.

50. Interview with Ko Khie Siong, chief of HAKKA, Banda Aceh, April 26, 2016.

51. "Di pihak agama Anda di sini [Muslim], dan di pihak etnis Anda di sini [Tionghoa]" (From the religious side, you are here [as Muslim], and from the ethnic side you are here [as Tionghoa]). Interview with Ko Khie Siong, chief of HAKKA, Banda Aceh, April 26, 2016. In daily conversation, Acehnese Muslims refer to those Chinese who have converted to Islam as *Cina muallaf*.

Chapter 8

1. Qardhawi, *Fiqhuz-Zakat*, 563–66.

2. Kasim, Abdullah, and Baba, "A Survey of Problems Faced by Converts Islam in Malaysia"; Johari, Ali, and Aziz, "The Role of Zakat and Success Factor for Muallaf Conditions"; Sahad, Nizam, and Abdullah, "Malaysian News Report on Muslim Converts Issues"; Nurish, "Religious Conversion in Northeast Thailand."

3. Jannah, "Gambaran Kebermaknaan Hidup oleh Muallaf di Aceh Besar."

4. Guleng and Muhamat, "Adaptation of Muallaf Youth in the Community."

5. Interview with a female muallaf from the Toraja ethnic group in Sulawesi, Banda Aceh, April 29, 2016.

6. Siegel, *The Rope of God*, 39.

7. Weng, *Negotiating Ethnicity and Religiosity*.

8. Some of them would go door to door asking for donations.

9. Interview with the Baitul Mal Banda Aceh commission member, Banda Aceh, February 16, 2017.

10. Interview with Muhammad Rasyid, the leader of FORMULA, Banda Aceh, April 28, 2016.

11. Interview with Soenwardi, Buddhist community leader in Banda Aceh, and his wife, Lily Tan, Banda Aceh, April 20, 2016.

12. Interview with a Keuchik of Gampong Laksana, Banda Aceh, May 30, 2016.

13. "Malu kalau dilihat orang. Antar sesama kita saja tidak beres [konflik]" (We are ashamed when people look at us. We even could not unite, always in conflict). Interview with Ko Khie Siong, chief of HAKKA, Banda Aceh, April 26, 2016.

14. Interview with an old woman muallaf, the Gampong Mulia resident, Banda Aceh, February 19, 2017.

15. Interview with some women muallaf during the observation of PMAS's Qur'anic reading course, Banda Aceh, April 29, 2016.

16. Interview with Fatimah Azzahra, head of PMAS, Banda Aceh, October 31, 2018.

17. Observation of PMAS's Qur'anic reading course, Banda Aceh, April 29, 2016.

18. Observation of a muallaf religious congregation at the musholla of Banda Aceh Municipal Office, February 19, 2017. The students were provided a course on worship practice by reading *Fardhu 'Ain* and *Masa'ila Al-Muhtadi*, both standard books for basic students in traditional Islamic boarding schools (dayah).

19. Weng, *Chinese Ways of Being Muslim*.

20. Interview with Fatimah, chief of PMAS, Banda Aceh, August 24, 2016.

21. Muhamat and Puteh, "Chinese Muallaf Background in Malaysia."

22. Muhamat and Puteh's study explains that the word *muallaf* was used in the Administration of Islamic Law Enactment of Malaysia, 1992, and the Law Reform (Marriage and Divorce) Act, 1976. It is also used in Article 11(1) and Article 12(3) and (4) of the Federal Constitution of Malaysia.

23. A joint focus group discussion held by the Contending Modernities Aceh researchers and the Pusat Penelitian Ilmu Sosial Budaya of Syiah Kuala University on "Muallaf Empowerment in Aceh," Banda Aceh, April 29, 2017.

24. Alyasa' Abubakar serves as adviser for the Baitul Mal office. He is professor of Islamic jurisprudence at the State University of Ar-Raniry, Banda Aceh. He also served as head of the Aceh Dinas Syariat Islam (Aceh Shari`a Office) from 2002 until 2007. This office, inaugurated in 2000, manages local Islamic religious issues.

25. Focus group discussion on muallaf in Aceh, Banda Aceh, May 1, 2017.

26. Siegel, *The Rope of God*, 3.

27. Hugrontje, *The Achehnese*.

28. There are seven other of zakat beneficiaries: *fuqara*, *masakin*, *riqab*, *gharim*, *ibnu sabil*, *amil*, and *fi sabilillah*.

29. https://baitulmal.acehprov.go.id/sejarah-bma/.

30. Interview with Ilyas, border da'i, Southeast Aceh, July 14, 2016.
31. Focus group discussion on muallaf in Aceh, Banda Aceh, May 1, 2017.
32. Prosiding Persidangan Antarabangsa Pembangunan Mualaf, "Kemaslahatan Muallaf Tanggungjawab Ummah."
33. Robinson, "The Distinction between State Government."
34. https://www.islam.gov.my/images/garis-panduan/Garis-Panduan-Pengurusan-Saudara-Baru.pdf. Jabatan Kemajuan Islam Malaysia. *Garis Panduan Pengurusan Saudara Baru (Mualaf)*. Lengkapnya; Jabatan Kemajuan Islam Malaysia. *Garis Panduan Pengurusan Saudara Baru (Mualaf)*. Kuala Lumpur: iTilmiz Network Sdn. Bhd., 2010.
35. See Zahrah et al., "Pengajaran Pendidikan Islam terhadap Muallaf."
36. Razali, "Pembinaan Saudara Baru (Muallaf) at Harakah Islamiyah (HIKMAH) Kuching, Sarawak."
37. Sahad, Nizam, and Abdullah, "Malaysian News Report on Muslim Converts Issues," 224–25.
38. Interview with Armiadi, head of Baitul Mal Aceh Office, Banda Aceh, August 5, 2016.
39. Hakim, *The Pattern of Muslim Convert Guidance in Sidrap Regency, South Sulawesi Province*, 85–95.
40. Balai Litbang Agama Makassar, "Pola Pembinaan Muallaf di Kota Jayapura." 193
41. Hakim, *The Pattern of Muslim Convert Guidance*, 91–92.
42. Hidayati, "Problematika Pembinaan Muallaf di Kota Singkawang dan Solusinya melalui Program Konseling Komprehensif."
43. Interview with Armiadi, head of Provincial Baitul Mal of Aceh, Banda Aceh, August 5, 2016.
44. http://baitulmal.acehprov.go.id/?page_id=2238.

Chapter 9

1. Siegel, *The Rope of God*; Siapno, *Gender, Islam, Nationalism and the State in Aceh*; Srimulyani, Salim, and Ichwan, "Islam, Adat and the State."
2. A short explanation on the lives of bhikkhuni appears in Mary Talbot, "Bhikkhuni Ordination: Buddhism's Glass Ceiling," *Tricycle* (Fall 2016), https://tricycle.org/magazine/bhikkhuni-ordination-modern-buddhism/.
3. The Indonesian Ministry of Religious Affairs assigns one official to each religion. This official is responsible for managing religious issues in the region. The ministry's directorate, with a derivative position at the provincial office, deals with religions and believers from different religions in Indonesia.
4. Interview with Eliyani Ginting, Catholic religious instructor at Kementerian Agama, Aceh province, Banda Aceh, April 10, 2020.

5. Interview with Radha, Hindu leader in Banda Aceh temple, Banda Aceh, March 11, 2020.

6. Interview with Christie (pseudonym), Chinese woman in Banda Aceh, February 19, 2020.

7. Terziev, "Conceptual Framework of Social Adaptation."

8. Spielberg, *Encyclopedia of Applied Psychology*, 615.

9. Lee and Logan, "Women's Agency, Activism and Organisation."

10. Yan, "Buddhist Women as Agents of Change."

11. Yan, "Buddhist Women as Agents of Change."

12. Many arts, cultural, worship, and humanitarian activities of Vihara Sukyamurni can be reviewed on their Facebook page, https://web.facebook.com/VBSBandaAceh/?__tn__=%2Cd%2CP-R&eid=ARA-5Cbnbi5Cw7XlRRMP_FMMqpPENK_NJS0G1KNjNDCYNYhi2DhxBfuFtGye3kjMNFaigIl7XAHEqAkb, as well as on their Instagram account, https://www.instagram.com/vbsbandaaceh/?igshid=ssu63g2x0vx.

13. Ansor, "Agensi Perempuan Kristen dalam Ruang Publik Islam Aceh."

14. Makin, "Islamic Acehnese Identity, Sharia, and Christianization Rumor."

15. Interview with Margaret (pseudonym), GBI mentor, Banda Aceh, February 20, 2020.

Conclusion

1. Merry and Milligan, "Complexities of Belonging in Democratic and Democratizing Societies."

2. Interview with Boas Tumangger, Banda Aceh, August 13, 2016.

3. Marshall, *Class, Citizenship, and Social Development*, 104; Rosaldo, *Cultural Citizenship in Southeast Asia*, 7.

4. Artharini, "Penerapan perda syariat Islam di Aceh diminta dikaji ulang."

5. Interview with Prof. Syahrizal Abbas, Banda Aceh, September 25, 2018.

6. Djalil, "Apa kabar 'Grand Design' syariat Islam Aceh?"

7. Interview with Fatimah, chief of Persatuan Muallaf Aceh Sejahtera (Association of Prosperous Aceh Muslim Converts), Banda Aceh, August 24, 2016; and interview with Muhammad Rasyid, leader of Formula (a muallaf organization), Banda Aceh, April 28, 2016.

8. Hefner, "Islamism and the Struggle for Inclusive Citizenship in Democratic Indonesia," 17.

9. Hefner, "Islamism and the Struggle for Inclusive Citizenship in Democratic Indonesia," 27.

WORKS CITED

Abdul Ghani, Yusra Habib, Nordin Hussin, and Azlizan Mohd. Enh. *Strategi Belanda Mengepung Aceh, 1873–1945*. Banda Aceh: Bandar, 2016.

Abubakar, Alyasa'. *Syariat Islam di Provinsi Nanggroe Aceh Darussalam: Paradigma, kebijakan, dan kegiatan* [Shariah in Nanggore Aceh Darussalam Province: Paradigm, policy, and activity]. 5th ed. Banda Aceh: Dinas Syariat Islam Provinsi Nanggroe Aceh Darussalam, 2008.

———. *The Academic Script of the Qanun Jinayat Aceh Draft*. Aceh: Government of Aceh, 2008.

Abu-Munshar, M. "In the Shadow of the 'Arab Spring': The Fate of Non-Muslims under Islamist Rule." *Islam and Christian-Muslim Relations* 23 (2012): 487–503.

Adan, Hasanuddin Yusuf. *Tamaddun dan sejarah etnologi kekerasan di Aceh*. Yogyakarta: Ar-Ruzz Media, 2003.

Adji, Indriyanto Seno. *Sistem Hukum Pidana dan Keadilan Restoratif*. Paper presented in a focus group discussion at BPHN Building, Indonesia, December 1, 2016.

Afadhal, ed. *Dinamika Birokrasi Lokal Era Otonomi Daerah* [The dynamics of local bureaucracy in the era of autonomy]. Jakarta: Pusat Penelitian Politik (P2P) LIPI, 2003.

Afriko, Marzi. "Syariat Islam dan radikalisme massa: Melacak jejak awal kehadiran FPI di Aceh." In *Serambi Mekkah yang berubah: Views from Within*, edited by Arskal Salim and Adlin Sila, 19–55. Jakarta: Alvabet and Aceh Research Training Institute (ARTI), 2010.

Ahmed, E. R., M. A. Islam, and S. B. Yahya. "Comparative Study of Zakat and Taxation System for Muslims and Non-Muslims in Malaysia." *Advances in Environmental Biology* 8, no. 9 (2014): 549–53.

Ahok, Pasifikus. *Kembalinya Pengusaha Tionghoa di Banda Aceh*. Working paper. Banda Aceh: Pusat Latihan Ilmu-ilmu Sosial-PLPIIS, 1976.

Aizawa, N. "Assimilation, Differentiation, and Depoliticization: Chinese Indonesians and the Ministry of Home Affairs in Suharto's Indonesia." In

Chinese Indonesians and Regime Change, edited by M. Dieleman, J. Koning, and P. Post, 47–64. Leiden: Brill, 2010.

Al Fairusy, Muhajir. "Menjadi Singkel Menjadi Aceh, Menjadi Aceh Menjadi Islam." *Jurnal Sosiologi USK* 9, no. 1 (June 2016): 17–33.

———. *Singkel: Sejarah, Etnisitas dan Dinamika Sosial*. Yogyakarta: Pustaka Larasan, 2016.

Al-Maududi, Abu al-A`la. *Huquq ahl al-dhimma fi'l-Dawla al-Islamiyya*. Cairo: Dar al-Fikr, 1948.

Al-Mawardi, Abu Hasan. *Al-Ahkamu al-Shulthaniyya: The Laws of Islamic Governance*. Translated by Asadullah Yate. London: Ta-Ha, 1996.

Amiruddin, M. Hasbi. "The Response of Ulama Dayah to Modernization of Islamic Law in Aceh." MA thesis, McGill University, 1994.

Ananta, Aris. "The Population and Conflict." In *A New Dawn*, 15–33. Singapore: ISEAS, 2007.

Ananta, Aris, E. N. Arifin, and Bakhtiar. "Chinese Indonesians in Indonesia and the Province of Riau Archipelago: A Demographic Analysis." In *Ethnic Chinese in Contemporary Indonesia*, edited by Leo Suryadinata, 17–47. Singapore: ISEAS, 2008.

Anderson, Benedict. 1983. *Imagined Communities*. London: Verso, 1983.

An-Na'im, Abdullahi Ahmed. "Beyond Dhimmihood: Citizenship and Human Rights." In *Muslims and Modernity: Culture and Society since 1800*. Vol. 6 of *The New Cambridge History of Islam*, edited by Robert W. Hefner, 314–34. Cambridge: Cambridge University Press, 2011.

———. *Islam and the Secular State: Negotiating the Future of Sharia*. Cambridge, MA: Harvard University Press, 2008.

———. "Political Islam in National Politics and International Relations." In *The Desecularization of the World: Resurgent Religion and World Politics*, edited by Peter L. Berger, 103–22. Washington, DC: Ethics and Public Policy Center, 1999.

Ansor, Muhammad. "Agensi Perempuan Kristen dalam Ruang Publik Islam Aceh." PhD diss., State Islamic University of Syarif Hidayatullah Jakarta, 2019.

———. "Menjadi Seperti Beragama Lain: Jilbab dan Identitas Hibrid Mahasiswi Kristen Aceh." *Jurnal Penamas* 29, no. 1 (2016): 11–30.

———. "We Are from the Same Ancestors: Christian-Muslim Relations in Contemporary Aceh Singkil." *AL ALBAB—Borneo Journal of Religious Studies* 3, no. 1 (2014): 3–24.

Ansor, Muhammad, Y. Amri, and I. F. Arrauf. "Under the Shadow of Sharia: Christian Muslim Relations from Acehnese Christian Experience." *Komunitas* 8, no. 1 (2016): 25–134.

Arifin, Evi Nurvidya, M. Sairi Hasbullah, and Agus Pramono. "Chinese Indonesians: How Many, Who and Where?" *Journal of Asian Ethnicity*, September 13, 2016, 1–20.

Artharini, Isyana. "Penerapan perda syariat Islam di Aceh diminta dikaji ulang." BBC, October 24, 2016. https://www.bbc.com/indonesia/indonesia/2016/10/161023_indonesia_setahun_qanun_jinayah.

Aspinall, Edward. "Combatant to Contractors: The Political Economy of Peace in Aceh." *Indonesia* 87 (April 2009): 1–34.

———. *Islam and Nation: Separatist Rebellion in Aceh, Indonesia*. Stanford: Stanford University Press, 2009.

———. *The Helsinki Agreement: A More Promising Basis for Peace in Aceh?* Washington, DC: East West Center, 2005.

Azizy, Qodri A. *Change Management dalam Reformasi Birokrasi*. Jakarta: Gramedia Pustaka Utama, 2007.

Azra, Azyumardi. *The Origin of Islamic Reformist in Southeast Asia: Networks of Malay-Indonesian and Middle Eastern 'Ulama' in the Seventeenth and Eighteenth Centuries*. Honolulu: University of Hawai'i Press, 2004.

Balai Litbang Agama Makassar. "Pola Pembinaan Muallaf di Kota Jayapura." *Al-Qalam* 18, no. 2 (July–December 2012): 188–97.

Bastoni, Hepi Andi. *Eman mulyatman and artawijaya, Serambi Makkah dihempas tsunami diterjang Kristenisasi*. Jakarta: Qalammas, 2006.

Benda, H. J. "South-East Asian Islam in the Twentieth Century." In *The Cambridge History of Islam*, edited by P. M. Holt, Ann K. S. Lambton, and Bernard Lewis, 2a:182–208. Cambridge: Cambridge University Press, 1970.

Berenschot, Ward, Henk Schulte Nordholt, and Laurens Bakker, eds. *Citizenship and Democratization in Southeast Asia*. Leiden: Brill, 2016.

Berenschot, Ward, and Gerry van Klinken. "Informality and Citizenship: The Everyday State in Indonesia." *Citizenship Studies* 22, no. 2 (2018): 95–111.

Berger, Maurits. "Public Policy and Islamic Law: The Modern Dhimmī in Contemporary Egyptian Family Law." *Islamic Law and Society* 8, no. 1 (2001): 88–136.

Birchok, Daniel Andrew. "Imagining a Nation Divided." *Inside Indonesia*, April 18, 2016. http://www.insideindonesia.org/imagining-a-nation-divided.

———. "Sojourning on Mecca's Verandah: Place, Temporality, and Islam in an Indonesian Province." PhD diss., University of Michigan, 2013.

Boland, B. J. *The Struggle of Islam in Modern Indonesia*. Dordrecht: Springer, 1982.

Bolton, P., and M. Dewatripont. "Authority in Organizations." In *Handbook of Organizational Economics*, edited by R. Gibbons and J. Roberts, 1–59. Princeton: Princeton University Press, 2013.

Bowen, John. *Islam, Law and Equality in Indonesia: An Anthropology of Public Reasoning*. Cambridge: Cambridge University Press, 2003.

BPS Aceh. *Aceh dalam Angka 2015*. Banda Aceh: BPS, 2015.

Brown, D. *Contending Nationalisms in Southeast Asia*. Working Paper 117, Asia Research Centre. Perth: Murdoch University, 2005.

Bruner, E. M. "The Expression of Ethnicity in Indonesia." In *Urban Ethnicity*, edited by Abner Cohen, 251–88. London: Tavistock, 1974.

Buehler, Michael. "The Rise of Sharia Bylaws in Indonesian Districts: An Indication for Changing Patterns of Power Accumulation and Political Corruption." *South East Asia Research* 16, no. 2 (2008): 255–85.

———. *The Politics of Sharî a: Islamist Activists and the State in Democratizing Indonesia*. Cambridge: Cambridge University Press, 2016.

Bush, Robin. "Regional Sharia Regulations in Indonesia: Anomaly or Symptom?" In *Expressing Islam: Religious Life and Politics in Indonesia*, edited by G. Fealy and S. White, 174–91. Singapore: ISEAS, 2008.

Cammack, Mark E., and Michael R. Feener. "The Islamic Legal System in Indonesia." *Pacific Rim Law and Policy Journal* 21, no. 1 (2012): 13–42.

Casanova, José. *Public Religions in the Modern World*. Chicago: University of Chicago Press, 1994.

Castles, Lance. "The Political Life of a Sumatran Residency: Tapanuli, 1915–1940." PhD diss., Yale University, 1972.

Çetinoğlu, S. "Foundations of Non-Muslim Communities: The Last Object of Confiscation." *International Criminal Law Review* 14, no. 2 (2014): 396–406.

Chabry, Laurent, and Annie Chabry. *Politique et minorités au Proche-Orient*. Paris: Maison-neuve and Larousse, 1984.

Chambert-Loir, Henri. "Islamic Law in 17th Century Aceh." *Archipel* 94 (2017): 51–96.

Chaplin, Chris. "Salafi Islamic Piety as Civic Activism: Wahdah Islamiyah and Differentiated Citizenship in Indonesia." *Citizenship Studies* 22, no. 2 (2017): 208–23.

Clavé-Çelik, Elsa. "Silenced Fighters: An Insight into Women Combatants' History in Aceh (17th–20th c.)." *Archipel* 87 (2014): 273–306.

Coppel, Charles A. *Indonesian Chinese in Crisis*. Kuala Lumpur: Oxford University Press, 1983.

———. *Studying Ethnic Chinese in Indonesia*. Singapore: Singapore Society of Asian Studies, 2002.

Cribb, Robert. "Legal Pluralism and Criminal Law in Dutch Colonial Order." *Indonesia 90*, October 2010, 47–66.

Crouch, M. "Religious Regulations in Indonesia: Failing Vulnerable Groups." *Review of Indonesian and Malaysian Affairs* 43, no. 2 (2009): 53–103.

Dawis, A. *The Chinese of Indonesia and Their Search for Identity: The Relationship between Collective Memory and the Media*. Amherst, NY: Cambria Press, 2009.

Delanty, Gerard. *Citizenship in a Global Age: Society, Culture, Politics*. Buckingham: Open University Press, 2000.

Dieleman, M., J. Koning, and P. Post, eds. *Chinese Indonesians and Regime Change*. Leiden: Brill, 2011.

Dinas Kebudayaan dan Pariwisata Aceh. *Data Kebudayaan dan Pariwisata Aceh* [Aceh cultural and tourism data]. Banda Aceh: Dinas Kebudayaan dan Pariwisata, 2015.
Dinas Peternakan Aceh. "Data Peternakan Provinsi Aceh." 2017. http://disnak.acehprov.go.id/wp-content/uploads/DATA_PETERNAKAN_UPDATED_Produksi_Daging.pdf.
Dinas Syariat Islam. *Himpunan Undang-undang, Keputusan Presiden, Peraturan Daerah/Qanun, Instruksi Gubernur, Edaran Gubernur Berkaitan Pelaksanaan Syariat Islam*. 7th ed. Banda Aceh: Dinas Syariat Islam Aceh, 2009.
Djalil, Munawar A. "Apa kabar 'Grand Design' syariat Islam Aceh?" *Serambinews*, November 30, 2018. https://aceh.tribunnews.com/2018/11/30/apa-kabar-grand-design-syariat-islam-aceh.
Dofier, Zamakhsyari. *Tradisi Pesantren, Studi tentang Pandangan Hidup Kiyai*. Jakarta: LP3ES, 1984.
Dominelli, Lena. "Problematising Concepts of Citizenship and Citizenship Practices." In *Reconfiguring Citizenship: Social Exclusion and Diversity within Inclusive Citizenship Practices*, edited by Lena Dominelli and Mehmoona Moosa-Mitha, 13–22. Farnham: Ashgate, 2014.
Dominelli, Lena, and Mehmoona Moosa-Mitha, eds. *Reconfiguring Citizenship: Social Exclusion and Diversity within Inclusive Citizenship Practices*. Farnham: Ashgate, 2014.
El Ibrahimy, M. Nur. *Peran Tgk. M. Daud Beureueh dalam Pergolakan Aceh*. Rev. ed. Jakarta: Media Dakwah, 2001.
Emon, A. M. "Religious Minorities and Islamic Law: Accommodation and the Limits of Tolerance." In *Islamic Law and International Human Rights Law*, edited by A. M. Emon, M. Ellis, and B. Glahn, 323–43. Oxford: Oxford University Press, 2012.
Erlina, Terra. "Membangun Karakter Keindonesiaan Pancasila Melalui Pendidikan Kewarganegaraan di Era Global." *Factum* 8, no. 2 (October 2019): 154.
Etzioni, A. "Authority Structure and Organizational Effectiveness." *Administrative Science Quarterly* 4, no. 1 (June 1959): 43–67.
Fadhilah, H., and F. Mahara. "The Sharia on Non-Muslims: Should They Follow?" *Jurnal Lektur Keagamaan* 15, no. 2 (2017): 334–44.
Faist, Thomas. "Dual Citizenship as Overlapping Membership." Willy Brandt Series of Working Papers in International Migration and Ethnic Relations. Malmö: School of International Migration and Ethnic Relations, Malmö University, November 3, 2001.
Fanani, Ahmad Fuad. "Shari'ah Bylaws in Indonesia and Their Implications for Religious Minorities." *Journal of Indonesian Islam* 5, no. 1 (June 2011): 17–34.
Fargues, P. "Demographic Islamization: Non-Muslims in Muslim Countries." *SAIS Review* 21, no. 2 (2001): 103–16.

Febriandi, Yogi. "Menyiasati Politik 'Kerukunan Agama' di Bawah Qanun Aceh." *CRCS UGM*, August 25, 2017. https://crcs.ugm.ac.id/news/11332/menyiasati-politik-kerukunan-agama-di-bawah-qanun-aceh.html.
Feener, R. Michael. *Shari`a and Social Engineering: The Implementation of Islamic Law in Contemporary Aceh, Indonesia*. New York: Oxford University Press, 2013.
Field, John, *Social Capital*. New York: Routledge, 2003.
Fierro, M., and J. Tolan, eds. *The Legal Status of Dimmi's in the Islamic West*. Turnhout: Brepols, 2013.
Formichi, Chiara. *Islam and the Making of the Nation: Kartosuwiryo and Political Islam in Twentieth Century Indonesia*. Leiden: KITLV, 2012.
Fukuyama, Francis. *Identity: Contemporary Identity Politics and the Struggle for Recognition*. London: Profile Books, 2018.
Galtung, Johan. "An Editorial." *Journal of Peace Research* 1, no. 1 (1964): 1–4.
Garis Panduan Pengurusan Saudara Baru (Muallaf) [The guidance for the new converts]. February 20, 2009. https://www.islam.gov.my/images/garis-panduan/Garis-Panduan-Pengurusan-Saudara-Baru.pdf.
Geertz, Clifford. "The Javanese Kijaji: The Changing Role of a Cultural Broker." *Comparative Studies in Society and History* 2, no. 2 (1962): 228–49.
Ghanea, N. "Human Rights of Religious Minorities and of Women in the Middle East." *Human Rights Quarterly* 26, no. 3 (2004): 705–29.
Giblin. "Overcoming Stereotypes? Chinese Indonesian Civil Society Groups in Post-Suharto Indonesia." *Asian Ethnicity* 4, no. 3 (2003): 353–68.
Godley, M. R., and G. J. Lloyd, eds. *Perspectives on the Chinese Indonesians*. Adelaide: Crawford House, 2001.
Good, Mary-Jo DelVecchio, and Byron J. Good. "Perspectives on the Politics of Peace in Aceh, Indonesia." In *Radical Egalitarianism: Local Realities, Global Relations*, edited by Felicity Aulino, Miriam Goheen, and Stanley J. Tambiah, 191–208. New York: Fordham University Press, 2013.
Gozdecka, Dorota A. "Religious Pluralism as a Legal Principle." In *Religion and Legal Pluralism*, edited by Russell Sandberg, 179–95. Cambridge: Cambridge University Press, 2015.
Guleng, Marlop P., and Razaleight Muhamat. "Adaptation of Muallaf Youth in the Community." Unpublished paper. N.d.
Gupta, A., and J. Ferguson. "Space, Identity, and the Politics of Difference." *Cultural Anthropology* 7, no. 1 (1992): 6–24.
Handayaningrat, Suwarno. *Administrasi pemerintahan dalam pembangunan nasional* [The governmental administration in the national development]. Jakarta: Gunung Agung, 2001.
Hakim, Ramlah. *The Pattern of Muslim Convert Guidance in Sidrap Regency, South Sulawesi Province*. Makassar, Indonesia: Balai Penelitian dan Pengembangan Agama, 2013.

Halim, Abdul. "Non-Muslims in the Qanun Jinayat and the Choice of Law in Sharia Courts in Aceh." *Human Rights Review* 23 (2022): 265–88.
Hamzah, Murizal. *Hasan Tiro: Jalan panjang menuju damai Aceh*. Banda Aceh: Bandar Publishing, 2014.
Hatta, Kusmawati, Jauhari Jasafat, A. R. Baharuddin, Aburizal M. Yati, and Syahril Furqany. *Strategi Dakwah Islamiyah di Aceh (Studi Deskriptif Kinerja Da`i Perbatasan)*. Banda Aceh: Dinas Syariat Islam Provinsi Aceh, 2017.
Hedman, Eva-Lotta E., ed. "Aceh under Martial Law: Conflict, Violence and Displacement." RSC Working Paper no. 24, Queen Elizabeth House Department of International Development, University of Oxford, July 2005.
Hefner, Robert W. "Christians, Conflict, and Citizenship in Muslim-Majority Indonesia." *Review of Faith & International Affairs* 15, no. 1 (2017): 91–101.
———. *Islam and Citizenship in Indonesia: Democracy and the Quest for an Inclusive Public Ethics*. London and New York: Routledge, 2024.
———. "Islamism and the Struggle for Inclusive Citizenship in Democratic Indonesia." In *Religious Pluralism in Indonesia: Threats and Opportunities for Democracy*, edited by Chiara Formichi, 14–37. Ithaca: Cornell University Press, 2021.
———. "Shariah Formalism or Democratic Communitarianism? The Islamic Resurgence and Political Theory." In *Communitarian Politics in Asia*, edited by Chua Beng Huat, 122–47. London: RoutledgeCurzon, 2004.
Hefner, Robert W., ed. *The Politics of Multiculturalism: Pluralism and Citizenship in Malaysia, Singapore, and Indonesia*. Honolulu: University of Hawai'i Press, 2001.
Hiariel, Eric, and Kristian Stokke, eds. *Politics of Citizenship in Indonesia*. Jakarta: Yayasan Obor Indonesia in Cooperation with PalGov UGM and University of Oslo, 2017.
Hidayati, Sri. "Problematika Pembinaan Muallaf di Kota Singkawang dan Solusinya melalui Program Konseling Komprehensif." *Jurnal Dakwah* 15, no. 1 (2014): 111–36.
Hidayatullah. "Warga Non-Muslim Aceh Ahlul Dzimmah, Diperlakukan Sama dengan Muslim." *Hidayatullah*, September 13, 2014. http://hidayatullah.com/berita/nasional/read/2014/09/13/29400/warga-non-muslim-aceh-ahlul-dzimmah-diperlakukan-sama-dengan-muslim.html.
Hooker, M. B. *Indonesian Islam: Social Change through Contemporary Fatwa*. Honolulu: University of Hawai'i Press, 2003.
Hoon, C. Y. *Chinese Identity in Post-Suharto Indonesia: Culture, Politics and Media*. Brighton: Sussex Academic Press, 2008.
Hughes, R. A. *Identity, Law and Politics*. Armidale, Australia: University of New England Press, 1995.
Hui, Y. F. *Strangers at Home: History and Subjectivity among the Chinese Communities of West Kalimantan, Indonesia*. Leiden: Brill, 2011.

Human Rights Watch. *Menegakkan Moralitas: Pelanggaran dalam Penerapan Syariah Islam di Aceh, Indonesia*. New York: Human Rights Watch, 2010.
Hung, Helen Ting Mu. *The Politics of Hudud Law Implementation in Malaysia*. ISEAS Working Paper Series. Singapore: ISEAS Yusof Ishak Institute, 2016.
Hunwick, J. O. "The Rights of Dhimmis to Maintain a Place of Worship: A Fifteenth Century Fatwa from Tlemcen." *Al-Qantara* 12, no. 1 (1991): 133–56.
Hurgronje, C. Snouck. *The Achehnese*. Vol. 2. Leiden: Brill, 1906.
Ichwan, M. N. "'Alternatives to Shariatism: Progressive Muslim Intellectuals, Feminists, Queers and Sufis in Contemporary Aceh.' In *Regime Change, Democracy and Islam: The Case of Indonesia*. Final report, Islam Research Programme, Jakarta, 2013." *International Criminal Law Review* 14, no. 2 (2013): 396–406.
———. "Faith, Ethnicity, and Illiberal Citizenship: Authority, Identity, and Religious 'Others' in Aceh's Border Areas." *Contending Modernities*, February 27, 2017. http://sites.nd.edu/contendingmodernities/2017/02/22/Faith-Ethnicity-and-Illiberal-Citizenship.
———. "Forbidden Visibility: Queer Activism, Shari`a Sphere and Politics of Sexuality in Aceh." *Studia Islamika* 28, no. 2 (2021): 283–317.
———. "The Politics of Shari`atisation: Central Governmental and Regional Discourses of Shari`a Implementation in Aceh." In *Islamic Law in Modern Indonesia*, edited by Michael Feener and Mark E. Cammack, 193–215. Cambridge, MA: Islamic Legal Studies Program, Harvard University, 2007.
Isin, Engin F., and Peter Nyers, eds. *Routledge Handbook of Global Citizenship Studies*. New York: Routledge, 2014.
Isin, Engin F., and Bryan S. Turner. "Citizenship Studies: An Introduction." In *Handbook of Citizenship Studies*, edited by Engin F. Isin and Bryan S. Turner, 1–10. London: Sage, 2003.
Ito, Takeshi, and Anthony Reid. "From Harbour Autocracies to Feudal Diffusion in Seventeenth-Century Indonesia: The Case of Aceh." *Sydney Studies in Society and Culture* 2 (1985): 197–213.
Jann, Warner, and Kai Wegrich. "Theories of the Policy Cycle." In *A Handbook of Public Policy Analysis: Theory, Politics and Methods*, edited by Frank Fischer, 43–62. West Palm Beach, FL: CRC Press, 2007.
Jannah, Rauzatul. "Gambaran Kebermaknaan Hidup oleh Muallaf di Aceh Besar." BA thesis, State Islamic University of Ar-Raniry, 2019.
Johari, Fuadah, Ahmad Fahme Mohd Ali, and Muhammad Ridhwan Ab Aziz. "The Role of Zakat and Success Factor for Muallaf Conditions: An Analysis in Selangor, Malaysia." *Ulum Islamiyyah: The Malaysian Journal of Islamic Sciences* 24, no. 1 (2018): 11–23.
Joppke, Christian. "Transformation of Citizenship: Status, Rights, Identity." *Citizenship Studies* 11, no. 1 (2007): 37–48.

Juwana, H. *Penyusunan Naskah Akademik sebagai Prasyarat dalam Perencanaan Pembentukan RUU.* Jakarta: Departemen Hukum dan HAM, 2006.
Kasim, Sayed Buhar Musal, Mohd Syukri Yeoh Abdullah, and Zawiyah Baba. "A Survey of Problems Faced by Converts Islam in Malaysia." *Journal of Social Science and Humanity* 8, no. 1 (2013): 85–97.
Kell, Tim. *The Roots of Acehnese Rebellion, 1989–1992.* Ithaca: Cornell Modern Indonesia Project, 1995.
Khan, Sher Banu A. L. *Sovereign Women in a Muslim Kingdom: The Sultanahs of Aceh, 1641–1699.* Singapore: NUS Press, 2017.
———. "The Sultanahs of Aceh, 1641–1699." In *Aceh: History, Politics and Culture*, edited by Arndt Graaf, Susanne Schroter, and Edwin P. Wieringa, 3–25. Singapore: ISEAS, 2010.
Khatab, S. "Citizenship Rights of Non-Muslims in the Islamic State of Hakimiyya Espoused by Sayyid Qutób." *Islam and Christian-Muslim Relations* 13, no. 2 (2002): 163–87.
Kingsbury, Damien. "The Free Aceh Movement: Islam and Democratization." *Journal of Contemporary Asia* 37, no. 2 (2007): 166–89.
Kivisto, Peter. "Citizenship." In *International Encyclopedia of the Social Sciences*, 2nd ed., edited by William A. Darity Jr., 542–44. Detroit: Macmillan Reference, 2008.
Kivisto, Peter, and Thomas Faist. *Citizenship: Discourse, Theory, and Transnational Prospects.* Malden, MA: Blackwell, 2007.
Kloos, David. "Becoming Better Muslims: Religious Authority and Ethical Improvement in Aceh, Indonesia." PhD diss., Vrije Universiteit Amsterdam, 2013.
———. Foreword to *Singkel: Sejarah, Etnisitas, dan Dinamika Sosial*, by Muhajir Al Fairusy, vi–ix. Denpasar: Pustaka Larasan, 2016.
Kloos, David, and Ward Berenschot. "Citizenship and Islam in Malaysia and Indonesia." In *Citizenship and Democratization in Southeast Asia*, edited by Ward Berenschot, Henk Schulte Nordholt, and Laurens Bakker, 178–207. Leiden: Brill, 2017.
Kloos, David, R. Michael Feener, and Annemarie Samuels, eds. *Islam and the Limits of the State: Reconfigurations of Practices, Community and Authority in Contemporary Aceh.* Leiden: Brill, 2015.
Knowledge Sector Initiative. *Catatan Kebijakan Meninjau Ulang Standar Kompetensi Jabatan Pimpinan Tinggi.* Jakarta: KSI, 2017.
Kompas. "Panglima TNI: Jilbab Hanya untuk Anggota TNI Perempuan di Aceh." *Kompas*, May 29, 2015. http://regional.kompas.com.
Koning, Juliette. "Chinese Indonesian: Business, Ethnicity, and Religion." In *Routledge Handbook of Contemporary Indonesia*, edited by Robert W. Hefner, 177–86. New York: Routledge, 2018.

Konrad, V. "Borders and Culture: Zones of Transition, Interaction and Identity." *Eurasia Border Review* 5, no. 1 (2014): 41–57.
Künkler, M. "Law, Legitimacy, and Equality: The Bureaucratization of Religion and Conditions of Belief in Indonesia." In *A Secular Age beyond the West: Religion, Law and the State in Asia, the Middle East and North Africa*, edited by Mirjam Künkler, John Madeley, and Shylashri Shankar, 107–27. New York: Cambridge University Press, 2018.
Kuran, T. "The Economic Ascent of the Middle East's Religious Minorities: The Role of Islamic Legal Pluralism." *Journal of Legal Studies* 33, no. 2 (2004): 475–515.
Kusrin, Zuliza Mohd, Zaini Nasohah, Mohd al-Adib Samuri, and Mat Noor Mat Zain. "Legal Provisions and Restrictions on the Propagation of Non-Islamic Religions among Muslims in Malaysia." *Kajian Malaysia* 31, no. 2 (2013): 1–18.
Kymlicka, W., and E. Pföstl. *Multiculturalism and Minority Rights in the Arab World*. Oxford: Oxford University Press, 2014.
Lamont, Michèle, and Virág Molnár. 2002. "The Study of Boundaries in the Social Sciences." *Annual Review of Sociology* 28 (2002): 167–95.
Lee, Catherine, and Anne Logan. "Women's Agency, Activism and Organisation." *Women's History Review* 28, no. 6 (2019): 831–34.
Lembong, Eddie. "Indonesian Government Policies and the Ethnic Chinese: Some Recent Development." In *Ethnic Chinese in Contemporary Indonesia*, edited by Leo Suryadinata, 48–56. Singapore: Chinese Heritage Centre and ISEAS, 2008.
Lev, Daniel. *Islamic Courts in Indonesia: A Study in the Political Bases of Legal Institutions*. Berkeley: University of California Press, 1972.
Lewis, G. *Citizenship: Personal Lives and Social Policy*. Bristol: Policy Press, 2004.
Lindsey, T., and H. Pausacker, eds. *Chinese Indonesians: Remembering, Distorting, Forgetting*. Singapore: ISEAS, 2015.
Lintas Gayo. "Babi Berkeliaran, Tuak Marak: HMI Agara Pertanyakan Qanun Syari'at." Lintas Gayo, September 2, 2016. http://lintasgayo.co/2016/09/29/babi-berkeliaran-tuak-marak-hmi-agara-pertanyakan-qanun-syariat.
Lister, R. *Citizenship: Feminist Perspectives*. New York: New York University Press, 1997.
———. "Citizenship on the Margins: Citizenship, Social Work and Social Action." *European Journal of Social Work* 1, no. 1 (1998): 5–18.
Lombard, Denys. *Kerajaan Aceh: Zaman Sultan Iskandar Muda (1607–1636)*. Jakarta: Kepustakan Populer Gramedia, 2006.
Longva, A. N., and A. S. Roald. *Religious Minorities in the Middle East: Domination, Self-Empowerment, Accommodation*. Leiden: Brill, 2012.

Makin, Al. "Islamic Acehnese Identity, Sharia, and Christianization Rumor: A Study of the Narratives of the Attack on the Bethel Church in Penauyong Banda Aceh." *Journal of Indonesian Islam* 10, no. 1 (2016): 1–35.

Mantran, R. "Foreign Merchants and Minorities in Istanbul during the Sixteenth and Seventeenth Centuries." In *Christians and Jews in the Ottoman Empire: The Functioning of a Plural Society*, edited by Benyamin Braude and Bernard Lewis, 1:127–28. New York: Holmes and Meier, 1982.

Marshall, T. H. *Class, Citizenship, and Social Development*. Garden City: Doubleday, 1964.

Marwanto, Yanuari. "Menjadi Garam dan Terang Lewat Pendidikan." Hidup Katolik, December 21, 1964. http://hidupkatolik.com.

McCarthy, John. "The Demonstration Effect: Natural Resources, Ethnonationalism and the Aceh Conflict." *Singapore Journal of Tropical Geography* 23, no. 3 (2007): 314–33.

McGibbon, Rodd. "Local Leadership and the Aceh Conflict." In *Verandah of Violence: The Background to the Aceh Problem*, edited by Anthony Reid, 38–51. Singapore: NUS Press, 2006.

Menchik, Jeremy. *Islam and Democracy in Indonesia: Tolerance without Liberalism*. New York: Cambridge University Press, 2016.

Merdeka. "Umat Islam dan Kristen di Aceh Investigasi Bersama Kasus Pemurtadan." April 9, 2015. http://merdeka.com.

Merry, Michael S., and Jeffrey A. Milligan. "Complexities of Belonging in Democratic and Democratizing Societies: Islamic Identity, Ethnicity and Citizenship in the Netherlands and Aceh." *Journal of Muslim Minority Affairs* 29, no. 3 (2009): 311–23.

Metcalf, Barbara D. 1997. "Islam in Contemporary Southeast Asia: History, Community, Morality." In *Politics and Religious Renewal in Muslim Southeast Asia*, edited by Robert W. Hefner and Patricia Horvatich, 309–20. Honolulu: University of Hawai'i Press, 1997.

Mevlin, Jess. "Why Not Genocide? Anti-Chinese Violence in Aceh, 1965–1966." *Journal of Current Southeast Asian Affairs* 32, no. 3 (2013): 63–91.

Miller, Michelle Ann. *Rebellion and Reform in Indonesia: Jakarta's Security and Autonomy Polices in Aceh*. London: Routledge, 2009.

Moosa-Mitha, Mehmoona. "Exclusionary and Inclusionary Citizenship Practices around Faith-Based Communities." In *Reconfiguring Citizenship: Social Exclusion and Diversity within Inclusive Citizenship Practices*, edited by Lena Dominelli and Mehmoona Moosa-Mitha, 23–32. Farnham: Ashgate, 2014.

Morris, Eric. "Aceh: Social Revolution and the Islamic Vision." In *Regional Dynamics of the Indonesian Revolution: Unity from Diversity*, edited by Audrey R. Kahin, 83–110. Honolulu: University of Hawai'i Press, 1985.

Muhamat, Razaleigh Muhamat, and Anuar Puteh. "Chinese Muallaf Background in Malaysia." Unpublished paper. N.d.

Muhammad, Rusjdi Ali. *Revitalisasi Syariat islam di Aceh: Problem, Solusi, dan Implementasi.* Jakarta: Logos, 2003.

Mujiburrahman. *Feeling Threatened: Muslim-Christian Relations in Indonesia's New Order.* Leiden: Amsterdam University Press, 2006.

Müller, Christian. "Non-Muslims as Part of Islamic Law: Juridical Casuistry in a Fifth/Eleventh-Century Law Manual." In *The Legal Status of Dimmis in the Islamic West*, edited by Maribel Fierro and John Tolan, 21–64. Turnhout: Brepols, 2013.

Multazam, Moh. Arief. "Penerapan Asas-Asas Hukum Pidana dalam Kasus ʽUqubat Takzir terhadap Non-Muslim; Perbandingan Fiqh Jinayat dan Qanun No. 6 Tahun 2014 Tentang Hukum Jinayat." BA thesis, State Islamic University of Ar-Raniry, 2017.

Mulyono, Agus. "Bantuan Sosial Kementerian Agama RI bagi Rumah Ibadat dan Ormas Keagamaan di Provinsi Aceh." In *Bantuan Sosial Kementerian Agama RI bagi Rumah Ibadat dan Ormas Keagamaan*, edited by Muchit A. Karim, 137–62. Jakarta: Kementerian Agama RI Badan Litbang dan Diklat Puslitbang Kehidupan Keagamaan, 2011.

Nielsen, J. "Contemporary Discussions on Religious Minorities in Muslim Countries." *BYU Law Review* 2 (2002): 353–70.

Nurish, Amanah. "Religious Conversion in Northeast Thailand: The Baha'i Movement in Contemporary Southeast Asia." Paper presented for the SEASREP twentieth anniversary and international conference at Gadjah Mada University, Yogyakarta, Indonesia, November 3–5, 2015.

Pizzo, P. "The 'Coptic Question' in Post-revolutionary Egypt: Citizenship, Democracy, Religion." *Ethnic and Racial Studies* 38, no. 14 (2015): 2598–613.

Prabowo, Haris. "Daftar skor indeks kerukunan beragama versi kemenag 2019." *Tirto*, December 11, 2019. https://tirto.id/daftar-skor-indeks-kerukunan-beragama-versi-kemenag-2019-engH.

Pratt, Douglas. *Identity and Interaction: Islam and the Challenge of Interreligious Dialogue.* Sydney: Charles Strong Memorial Trust, 1999.

Prosiding Persidangan Antarabangsa Pembangunan Mualaf. "Kemaslahatan Muallaf Tanggungjawab Ummah." Paper presented at an international meeting at College University Islam Antar Bangsa, Selangor, Malaysia, September 7–8, 2013.

Purdey, Jemma. *Anti-Chinese Violence in Indonesia, 1996–1999.* Singapore: NUS Press, 2005.

Qardhawi, Yusuf. *Fiqhuz-Zakat.* Translated by Salman Harun, Didin Hafidhuddin, and Hasanuddin. Jakarta: Pustaka Lentera Nusa, 1973.

Rahmawati, Arifah, Dewi H Susilastuti, Mohtar Mas'oed, and Muhadjir Darwin. "The Negotiation of Political Identity and Rise of Social Citizenship: A Study of the Former Female Combatants in Aceh since the Helsinki Peace Accord." *Humaniora* 30, no. 3 (2018): 237–47.

Razali, Ardika bin. "Pembinaan Saudara Baru (Muallaf) at Harakah Islamiyah (HIKMAH) Kuching, Sarawak, 1994–2017." BA thesis, State Islamic University Sunan Ampel, Indonesia, 2018.
Rehman, J. "Islam vs the Shari'a: Minority Protection within Islamic and International Legal Traditions." In *Islamic Law and International Human Rights Law*, edited by Anver M. Emon, Mark Ellis, and Benjamin Glahn, 371–78. Oxford: Oxford University Press, 2013.
Rehman, S. S., and Askari, H. "How Islamic Are Islamic Countries?" *Global Economy Journal* 10, no. 2 (2010): 185–98.
Reid, Anthony. *Verandah of Violence: The Background to the Aceh Problem*. Singapore: NUS Press, 2006.
———. "War, Peace and the Burden of History in Aceh." Asia Research Institute Working Paper Series 1. Singapore: Asia Research Institute, 2003.
Reid, Anthony, ed. *Witnesses to Sumatra: A Travellers' Anthology*. Oxford: Oxford University Press, 1995.
Riddell, Peter G. "Aceh in the Sixteenth and Seventeenth Centuries: 'Serambi Mekkah' and Identity." In *Verandah of Violence*, edited by Anthony Reid, 38–51. Singapore: NUS Press, 2006.
Robinson, Edward Heath. "The Distinction between State Government." *Geography Compass* 7/8 (2013): 556–66.
Rosaldo, Renato, ed. *Cultural Citizenship in Southeast Asia: Nation and Belonging in the Hinterlands*. Berkeley: University of California Press, 2003.
Rosenblum, Nancy L., ed. *Obligations of Citizenship and Demands of Faith: Religious Accommodation in Pluralist Democracies*. Princeton: Princeton University Press, 2000.
Rusdi, Piet. *Strategi Adaptasi Masyarakat Tionghoa Pasca Tsunami: Studi Kasus Barak Peunayong, Kecamatan Kuta Alam, Banda Aceh*. Banda Aceh: Pusat Penelitian Ilmu Sosial dan Budaya-PPISB, 2005.
Saeed, A. "Rethinking Citizenship Rights of Non-Muslims in an Islamic State: Rashid Al-Ghannūshi's Contribution to the Evolving Debate." *Islam and Christian-Muslim Relations* 10, no. 3 (1999): 307–23.
Safrilsyah. "Non Muslim under the Regulation of Islamic Law in Aceh Province." In *Conference Proceeding Annual International Conference on Islamic Studies*, 544–53. Surabaya, Indonesia: UIN Sunan Ampel Surabaya, 2012.
Sahad, Mohd, Siti Aishah Chu Abdullah Nizam, and Suhaila Abdullah. "Malaysian News Report on Muslim Converts Issues: A Study on Malaysiakini." *International Journal of Humanities and Social Science* 3, no. 13 (July 2013): 219–30.
Sahlins, P. *Boundaries: The Making of France and Spain in the Pyrenees*. Berkeley: University of California Press, 1989.
Salim, Arskal. *Challenging the Secular State: The Islamization of Law in Modern Indonesia*. Honolulu: University of Hawai'i Press, 2008.

———. *Contemporary Islamic Law in Indonesia: Shariah and Legal Pluralism*. Edinburgh: Edinburgh University Press, 2015.

———. "Epilogue: Shari`a in Indonesia's Current Transition; An Update." In *Shari`a and Politics in Modern Indonesia*, edited by Arskal Salim and Azyumardi Azra, 213–32. Singapore: ISEAS, 2003.

———. "Shari`a from below in Aceh (1930s–1960s): Islamic Identity and the Right to Self Determination with Comparative Reference to the Moro Islamic Liberation Front (MILF)." *Indonesia and Malay World* 32, no. 92 (March 2004): 80–99.

———. "The Special Status of Islamic Aceh." In *Routledge Handbook of Contemporary Indonesia*, edited by Robert W. Hefner, 237–45. Boston: Routledge, 2018.

Salsabila, Aina. "Pertimbangan Hakim dalam Memutus Hukuman Cambuk bagi Non-Muslim sebagai Pelaku Jarimah Khamar: Analisis Terhadap Putusan Mahkamah Syar'iyah Takengon Aceh Tengah Nomor 01/JN/2016/MS-TKN." BA thesis, State Islamic University of Sumatera Utara, 2017.

Santos, Conrado R. "A Theory of Bureaucratic Authority." *Canadian Public Administration* 21, no. 2 (1978): 243–67.

Sarkissian. Ani. *The Varieties of Religious Repression: Why Governments Restrict Religion*. Oxford: Oxford University Press, 2015.

Schröter, Susanne. "Acehnese Culture(s): Plurality and Homogeneity." In *Aceh: History, Politics and Culture*, edited by A. Graf, S. Schröter, and E. Wieringa, 157–79. Singapore: ISEAS, 2010.

Schulze, Kirsten E. *The Free Aceh Movement (GAM): Anatomy of a Separatist Organization*. Policy Studies 2. Washington, DC: East-West Center, 2004.

Schwedler, Jillian. "Islamic Identity: Myth, Menace, or Mobilizer?" *SAIS Review* 21, no. 2 (2001): 1–17.

Sembiring, Sri Alem Br. *Tradisi Masyarakat Parmalim di Toba Samosir*. Banda Aceh: Balai Pelestarian Nilai Budaya Banda Aceh, 2012.

Serambi Indonesia. "Babi Bebas Diternakkan di Agara." *Serambi Indonesia*, September 27, 2014. http://aceh.tribunnews.com/2014/09/27/babi-bebas-diternakkan-di-agara.

Shavit, U. "The Wasatī and Salafī Approaches to the Religious Law of Muslim Minorities." *Islamic Law and Society* 19, no. 1 (2012): 416–57.

Shuaib, Farid Sufian. "The Islamic Legal System in Malaysia." *Pacific Rim Law and Policy Journal* 21, no. 1 (January 2012): 85–113.

Siapno, Jacqueline Aquino. *Gender, Islam, Nationalism and the State in Aceh: The Paradox of Power, Co-optation and Existence*. London: RoutledgeCurzon, 2002.

Siegel, James T. *The Rope of God*. Berkeley: University of California Press, 1969.

Sila, Adlin. "Kerukunan Umat Beragama di Indonesia: Mengelola Kerukunan Dari Dalam." In *Kebebasan, Toleransi dan Terorisme: Riset dan Kebijakan Agama*

di Indonesia, edited by Ali-Fauzi, Zainal Abidin Bagir, and Irsyad Rafsadi, 117–58. Jakarta: PUSAD Yayasan Paramadina, 2017.
Spielberg, Charles. *Encyclopedia of Applied Psychology*. New York: Academic Press, 2004.
Srimulyani, Eka "Islam, Adat, and the State: Matrifocality in Aceh Revisited." *Al-Jami'ah: Journal of Islamic Studies* 48, no. 2 (2010): 321–42.
———. "Islamic Schooling in Aceh: Change, Reform, and Local Context." *Studia Islamika* 20, no. 3 (2013): 467–88.
Srimulyani, Eka, Marzi Afriko, Arskal Salim, and Moch Nur Ichwan. "Diasporic Chinese Community in Post-conflict Aceh: Socio-cultural Identities, and Social Relations with Acehnese Muslim Majority." *Al-Jami`ah Journal of Islamic Studies* 56, no. 2 (2018): 395–420.
Stephanous, A. *Political Islam, Citizenship and Minorities: The Future of Arab Christians in the Islamic Middle East*. Lanham, MD: University Press of America, 2010.
Sufi, Rusdi. *Peranan tokoh agama dalam perjuangan kemerdekaan 1945–1950 di Aceh*. Jakarta: Departemen Pendidikan dan Kebudayaan, Direktorat Jenderal Kebudayaan. Direktorat Sejarah dan Nilai Tradisional. Proyek Inventarisasi dan Dokumentasi Kebudayaan Daerah, 1997.
Sulaiman, Irchamni. *Pengusaha Aceh dan Pengusaha Cina di Kotamadya Banda Aceh*. Banda Aceh: Pusat Latihan dan Penelitian Ilmu Sosial dan Budaya Unsyiah, 1983.
Sulaiman, M. Isa, and Gerry van Klinken. "From Autonomy to Periphery: A Critical Evaluation of Acehnese Nationalist Movement." In *The Veranda of Violence: The Background to the Aceh Problem*, edited by Anthony Reid, 121–48. Singapore: NUS Press, 2006.
———. "The Rise and Fall of Governor Puteh." In *Renegotiating Boundaries: Local Politics in Post-Suharto Indonesia*, edited by Henk Schulte Nordholt and Gerry van Klinken, 225–53. Leiden: KITLV Press, 2007.
Suparlan, Parsudi. "Kemajemukan, Hipotesis Kebudayaan Dominan dan Kesukubangsaan." *Antropologi Indonesia* 30, no. 3 (2006): 229–36.
Suryadinata, Leo. "Chinese Indonesians in an Era of Globalization: Some Major Characteristics." In *Ethnic Chinese in Contemporary Indonesia*, edited by Leo Suryadinata, 1–16. Singapore: ISEAS, 2008.
———. *Ethnic Chinese in Contemporary Indonesia*. Singapore: ISEAS, 2008.
———. "Ethnic Groups and the Indonesian Nation-State: With Special Reference to Ethnic Chinese." In *Routledge Handbook of Contemporary Indonesia*, edited by Robert W. Hefner, 43–53. New York: Routledge, 2018.
———. "Indonesian State Policy towards Ethnic Chinese: From Assimilation to Multiculturalism?" In *Chinese Indonesians: State, Policy, Monoculture and Multiculture*, edited by Leo Suryadinata, 1–16. Singapore: Eastern University Press, 2004.

Suryadinata, Leo, ed. *Ethnic Chinese as Southeast Asians*. Singapore: ISEAS, 1997.
———. *Political Thinking of the Indonesian Chinese, 1900–1995: A Sourcebook*. 2nd ed. Singapore: Singapore University Press, 1997.
Suryadinata, Leo, Evi Nurvidya Arifin, and Aris Ananta. "The Ethnic Chinese: A Declining Percentage." In *Indonesia's Population: Ethnicity and Religion in a Changing Political Landscape*, 1–16. Indonesia's Population Series. Singapore: ISEAS, 2003.
Sutrisno, Imam H. "Konflik Etnisitas di Aceh Masa Reformasi, 1998–2005." *Journal of Indonesian Historical Studies* 2, no. 1 (2018): 1–12.
Syamsuddin, Nazaruddin. *The Republican Revolt: A Study of the Acehnese Rebellion*. Singapore: ISEAS, 1985.
Talsya, T. Alibasjah. "Atjeh Tidak Pernah Menjerahkan Kedaulatan kepada Belanda." *Sinar Darussalam: Madjallah Pengetahuan dan Kebudajaan* 12 (March–April 1969): 59–65.
Tan, Mely G. *Etnis Tionghoa di Indonesia: Kumpulan Tulisan* [Ethnic Chinese in Indonesia: Collected writings] [in English and Indonesian]. Jakarta: Yayasan Obor Indonesia, 2008.
———. "The Ethnic Chinese in Indonesia: Issues of Identity." In *Ethnic Chinese as Southeast Asians*, edited by Leo Suryadinata, 33–66. Singapore: ISEAS, 1997.
Taylor, Charles, *Multiculturalism: Examining the Politics of Recognitions*. Edited by Amy Guttman. Princeton: Princeton University Press, 1994.
Taylor, Reed. "Sharia as Heterotopia: Responses from Muslim Women in Aceh Indonesia." *Religions* 6 (2015): 566–93.
Terziev, Venelin. "Conceptual Framework of Social Adaptation." In Proceedings of INTCESS 2019—6th International Conference on Education and Social Sciences, February 4–6, 2019, Dubai, UAE.
Tim Investigasi. "Menelusuri Polemik Pendidikan Agama di Aceh Singkil." Media Indonesia, April 4, 2016. https://mediaindonesia.com/read/detail/38091-menelusuripolemik-pendidikan-agama-di-aceh-singkil.
Tiro, Hasan Di. *The Price of Freedom: The Unfinished Diary of Tengku Hasan di Tiro*. London: National Liberation Front of Aceh Sumatra, 1984.
Tripa, Sulaiman, and Murizal Hamzah. *Setelah Tsunami Usai*. Banda Aceh: Bandar Publishing, 2009.
Tsai, Y. L., and D. Kammen. "Anti-Communist Violence and the Ethnic Chinese in Medan, North Sumatra." In *The Contours of Mass Violence in Indonesia*, edited by D. Kammen and K. McGregor, 1965–68. Singapore: NUS Press, 2012.
Tumanggor, Rusmin, and Edwar Muallim. *Perspektif Kehidupan Keberagamaan non-Muslim di Nanggroe Aceh Darussalam dengan Diberlakukannya Syariat Islam*. Jakarta: Puslitpen UIN Syarif Hidayatullah, 2016.
Uddin, A. T. "Religious Freedom Implications of Sharia Implementation in Aceh, Indonesia." *University of St. Thomas Law Journal* 7, no. 3 (2010): 603–48.

Umar, Muhammad. *Peradaban Aceh (Tamaddun) 1.* Banda Aceh: CV. Boebon Jaya, 2008.
Usman, Abdul Rani. *Etnis Cina Perantauan di Aceh.* Jakarta: Yayasan Obor, 2009.
———. *Sejarah Peradaban Aceh: Suatu analisis interaksionis, integrasi, dan konflik.* Jakarta: Yayasan Obor, 2003.
Van der Ven, Johannes A. *Human Rights or Religious Rules?* Leiden: Brill, 2010.
Van Dijk, Kees. *Rebellion under the Banner of Islam: The Darul Islam in Indonesia.* The Hague: Nijhoff, 1981.
van Klinken, Gerry. "Citizenship and Local Practices of Rule in Indonesia." *Citizenship Studies* 22, no. 2 (2018): 112–28.
van Klinken, Gerry, and Ward Berenschot. "Everyday Citizenship in Democratizing Indonesia." In *Routledge Handbook of Contemporary Indonesia*, edited by Robert W. Hefner, 151–62. New York: Routledge, 2018.
Viner, A. C., and E. L. Kaplan. "The Changing Pakpak Batak." *Journal of the Malaysian Branch, Royal Asiatic Society* 54, no. 1 (1981): 93–105.
Warner, Bill. *Shari`a Law for the Non-Muslim.* Brno: Center for the Study of Political Islam, 2010.
Warren, David H., and Christine Gilmore. "One Nation under God? Yusuf al-Qaradawi's Changing Fiqh of Citizenship in the Light of the Islamic Legal Tradition." *Contemporary Islam* 8, no. 3 (2014): 217–37.
Weng, Hew Wei. *Chinese Ways of Being Muslim: Negotiating Ethnicity and Religiosity in Indonesia.* Copenhagen: Nordic Institute of Asian Studies, 2018.
———. "Negotiating Ethnicity and Religiosity: Chinese Muslim Identities in Post–New Order Indonesia." PhD diss., Australian National University, 2011.
Wilmsen, Edwin N. *Land Filled with Flies: A Political Economy of the Kalahari.* Chicago: University of Chicago Press, 1989.
Yan, Lai Suat. "Buddhist Women as Agents of Change: Case Studies from Thailand and Indonesia." *Kyoto Review of South East Asia*, no. 16 (2015). https://kyotoreview.org/yav/buddhist-women-as-agents-of-change/.
Yudhistra, Rommy. "10 kota toleran vs 10 kota intoleran di Indonesia." *Tagar*, November 19, 2019. https://www.tagar.id/10-kota-toleran-vs-10-kota-intoleran-di-indonesia.
Yuval-Davis, Nira. "Intersectionality, Citizenship and Contemporary Politics of Belonging." *Critical Review of International Social and Political Philosophy* 10, no. 4 (2007): 561–74.
———. "Multi-layered Citizenship in the Age of 'Glocalization.'" *International Feminist Journal of Politics* 1, no. 1 (1999): 119–37.
———. *The Politics of Belonging: Intersectional Contestations.* London: Sage, 2011.
Zahrah, Siti Fathimatul binti Yusri, A'thiroh Masyaa'il Tan binti Abdullah, and Tan Ai Pow. "Pengajaran Pendidikan Islam terhadap Muallaf: Satu Tinjauan Literatur." In *Prosiding Seminar Pengurusan Islam: Ke Arah Pemantapan Ummah*, 1–17. Bangi: Universiti Kebangsaan Malaysia, 2015.

Zeidan, D. "The Copts—Equal, Protected or Persecuted? The Impact of Islamization on Muslim-Christian Relations in Modern Egypt." *Islam and Christian-Muslim Relations* 10, no. 1 (1999): 53–76.

Ziemek, Manfred. *Pesantren dalam Perubahan Sosial.* Jakarta: P3M, 1986.

Zulkarnain. "Dinamika Madzhab Shafi'i dengan Cara Aceh: Studi tentang Praktik Mazhab di Kalangan Tokoh Agama." *Ijtihad: Jurnal Wacana Hukum Islam dan Kemanusiaan* 15, no. 2 (2015): 159–76.

ABOUT THE AUTHORS

Arskal Salim is professor of politics of Islamic law at UIN Jakarta, Indonesia, and adjunct fellow of Western Sydney University, Australia. He obtained a PhD in 2006 from Melbourne Law School, University of Melbourne, Australia. His initial publication was a coedited volume, *Shari`a and Politics in Modern Indonesia* (ISEAS 2003). His dissertation, *Challenging the Secular State: The Islamization of Laws in Modern Indonesia*, was published by University of Hawai'i Press (2008). He was a postdoctoral fellow (2006–9) at the Max Planck Institute for Social Anthropology, Germany, where he accomplished an ethnographic work, *Contemporary Islamic Law in Indonesia: Sharia and Legal Pluralism*, published by Edinburgh University Press (2015). Salim co-edited with John R. Bowen, *Women and Property Rights in Indonesian Islamic Legal Contexts*, which was published by Brill (2019).

Moch. Nur Ichwan is professor of Islamic social and political sciences at the School of Graduate Studies, UIN Sunan Kalijaga Yogyakarta, Indonesia. He earned his PhD in religious studies from Tilburg University (2006). He was a research fellow of the International Institute of Asia Studies, Leiden (2001–5) and a postdoctoral fellow of the Royal Netherlands Academy of Arts and Sciences in the framework of Scientific Program Indonesia Netherlands (2008–9), and the Islam Research Programme, Leiden University (2010–12). His journal articles appear in *Islamic Law and Society*; *Islam and Christian-Muslim Relations*; *Journal of Islamic Studies*; *Politics, Religion and Ideology*; *Bijdragen tot de taal-, land- en volkenkunde*; *Al-Jami`ah Journal of Islamic Studies*; *Studia Islamika*; and *Journal of Indonesian Islam*.

Eka Srimulyani is professor of sociology at Ar-Raniry State Islamic University (UIN) in Banda Aceh, Indonesia. She is also a senior researcher at the International Centre for Aceh and Indian Ocean Studies. Her recent publications include "Analysing the Spectrum of Female Education Leaders' Agency in Islamic Boarding Schools in Post-conflict Aceh, Indonesia," *Gender and Education* (Routledge, 2018) and "Diasporic Chinese Community in Post-conflict Aceh: Socio-cultural Identities, and Social Relations with Acehnese Muslim Majority," *Al-Jami'ah Journal of Islamic Studies* 56, no. 2 (2018).

Marzi Afriko received his master's degree from the Faculty of Law at the University of North Sumatra in 2004. Since his undergraduate study in 2001 in the Department of Comparative Law at the Islamic University of Ar-Raniry, Banda Aceh, he has been actively involved in governance studies, particularly related to the issue of social and religion development. Marzi has much experience in collaborative work with policymakers and has often been requested to provide technical assistance to the provincial and district governments of Aceh. He has worked for the World Bank and Australian Aid projects for more than ten years in a variety of programs. In his policymaking work, he actively supports the Aceh Researcher Forum network of researchers.

INDEX

A
Aceh Barongsai, 143
Aceh Hymn, 180
Aceh Institute, 107, 109
adat, 49
agency, 6, 65, 69, 71, 111, 131, 165, 167, 169, 171, 172, 173, 175, 177, 179, 183
Ahmadiyyah, 116
Akhlāq li al-banīn, 100
Al-Washliyah, 107, 161
Aneuk Jamee, 181

B
Baapo, 34
Baitul Mal, 11, 157, 159, 161, 162, 163, 189, 212n24
Balai Syura Ureung Inong Aceh, 109, 175
Barongsai, 137, 142, 143
Batak, 10, 30, 31, 34, 35, 36, 54, 92, 108, 116, 117, 118, 119, 134, 145, 149, 166, 174, 177, 180, 181, 182
Batak Catholics, 166
Batak Islam, 149
bhikkhuni, 213n2
Bina Peradilan, 66
border areas, 9, 116, 117, 157
Buddha Zuchi, 51
Buddhists, 10, 26, 34, 54, 82, 92, 118, 119, 133, 137, 142, 144, 146, 168, 172, 173

C
caning, 90, 92
Catholics, 9, 12, 11, 26, 34, 50, 57, 58, 82, 119, 126, 133, 167, 169, 177
"Character Building I and II" course, 104
Chinatown, 11, 134
Chinese Buddhists, 30, 142, 173, 174
Chinese communities, 6, 131, 133, 135, 137, 139, 141, 143, 145, 199n60
Christianization, 33, 36, 55, 115, 120, 125, 126, 184
Christian mission, 116–20
Christian Pakpak, 34
Christian symbols, 37
churches, 108, 120, 169, 172, 174, 175, 177, 198n44
Church Tribunal Court, 169
Cina muallaf, 149, 211n51
citizenship, 1, 13, 5, 6, 41, 47, 58, 105, 187
City of Tolerance Index, 110
civic education, 104, 105
Civil Court, 88, 89, 90, 203n24
Confucians, 11, 10, 26, 119, 137
coordination, 68
Council of Young Indonesian Intellectuals and Ulama (MIUMI), 48
courts, 203n24
COVID-19, 173

D

Daerah Operasi Militer, 132
dakwah, 107, 157
Darul Islam, 5, 43, 45, 46, 105
Darussalam, 28, 44, 46, 47, 67, 121, 135
dayah, 107, 124, 125, 207n20
Dayah Darul Amin, 125
Dayah Manarul Islam, 124
Dayah Minhajus Salam, 124
Dayah Safinatussalamah, 125
development planning, 69, 70, 71
Devotion, 55, 206n1
Dinas Dayah, 11
discrimination, 36–37
districts, 9, 54, 57, 117
Dutch East Indies, 133

E

education, 57, 58, 98, 99, 100, 102, 105, 111, 113, 114, 119, 183, 187, 204n12, 207n22
equality, 18
erasure, 50
ethnicity, 209n28, 210n31, 211n51
ethnonationalism, 43
Europeans, 32, 42
Executive Office, 67

F

Flower Aceh, 109
Forum Islam Rahmatan Lil 'Alamin, 109
Forum Komunikasi Muslim Pegunungan Tengah, 162

G

Gafatar, 203n24
Gampong, 134, 135, 136, 137, 139, 145, 151, 168
Gayo Muslims, 92
Gerakan 30 September, 140

Gereja, 120, 167

H

Hadith, 100
HAKKA, 209n28
Helsinki Peace Agreement, 28
Hindus, 10, 26, 34, 82, 133, 167, 168, 174, 206n9
Hizbut Tahrir, 108, 153
hudud, 88
human rights, 188

I

Ikatan Pembina Gelanggang Anak-anak Buddhis Indonesia, 108
Ikatan Saudagar Katolik Republik Indonesia, 174
Imlek, 134, 137, 154, 155
Indian people, 32, 148, 168
Indigenous people, 85, 180, 210n30
Indische Staatsregeling, 85
Indonesian citizens, 29, 41, 80, 141, 190
Islamic Acehnese, 2, 8
Islamic state, 45

J

Jaringan Masyarakat Sipil Peduli Syariat, 109, 190
Jaringan Pemantau 231, 109
Javanese, 25, 28, 92, 117, 141, 142, 206n4
Jawi, 99
Jinayat, 3, 97, 188
justice, 93

K

Katolik, 108, 174, 186
Kejaksaan Negeri, 11
Kelompok Kajian Muallaf, 162
Keluarga Buddhayana Indonesia, 108
Kemalikussalehan, 104

Kesatuan Aksi Mahasiswa Indonesia, 140
keuchik, 139, 210n31
Keuskupan Agung, 118
kitab, 87, 153
Kitab Jawi, 153
Kitāb Matn taqrīb, 100
Koalisi NGO HAM Aceh, 109
Konferensi Waligereja, 120
KONTRAS, 109, 190
Kristen, 108, 177
Kristenisasi, 50, 100
Kurikulum Aceh yang Islami, 99

L
Laboratory of Socioreligious Development, 103
local government offices, 56

M
madrasaization, 99–100
Mahasiswa Katolik Republik Indonesia, 108, 186
Mahkamah Syar'iyah, 9, 66, 80, 94
Majelis Buddhayana Indonesia, 108
Majelis Muslim Papua, 162
Majelis Pendidikan Aceh, 99
Majelis Taklim, 156
majority, 13, 140
Masa Orientasi Siswa, 101
Masāil al-muhtadī, 100
Medium-Term Development Plan, 71
Millata Abraham, 116
Minangkabau, 32
Ministry of Religious Affairs, 12, 9, 64, 101, 102, 103, 110, 111, 119, 122, 123, 126, 174, 183, 207n15, 213n3
minorities, 9, 50, 154, 167, 170, 186
Modul Wawasan Ke-Islaman, 101
mosques, 66
muallaf, 7, 145, 149, 150, 154, 159, 160, 163, 211n51, 212n22

N
National Book of Criminal Acts, 84
national criminal code, 80, 203n24
National Education System, 98, 99, 105
Negara Islam Indonesia (Islamic State of Indonesia), 8
New Order regime, 8, 13, 28, 141, 142, 143, 187
non-Muslims, 9, 10, 30, 31, 56, 59, 79–94, 104

P
Pakpak, 10, 30, 34, 35, 36, 117, 118, 119
Pak Pak Muslims, 149
Pancasila, 27, 40, 46, 104, 105, 113, 190
peace, 108, 186
Pembimas, 167, 174, 183
Pemuda Peduli Islam, 126, 207n28
Pendidikan Agama, 104
Pendidikan Kewargaan Negara, 105
Perbatasan, 204n14
performance, 72
Persatuan Ulama Seluruh Aceh, 199n47
pesantren, 207n19
places of worship, 52, 122, 127
politics, 11, 44, 139, 183, 184
populations, 57, 208n3
pork, 9, 54
Pos Bantuan Hukum dan Hak Asasi Manusia, 109
Posyandu, 173, 176
prosecution process, 87
Protestants, 9, 10, 11, 30, 34, 50, 57, 58, 92, 117, 119, 126, 158, 166, 169

Q
qanun, 3, 29, 48, 52, 53, 55, 56, 57, 65, 66, 67, 80, 85, 88, 90, 97, 98, 99, 100, 101, 102, 113, 122, 127, 142, 188, 198n37, 201n7, 201n10, 202n17, 206n1

R

recognition, 13, 118
regional government, 67
religious education, 57, 104
Religious Harmony Index, 110
religious life, 157
research and development, 70
restrictions, 52

S

Salafism, 108, 204n7
Satpol, 65, 71, 72, 77, 86, 183, 202n18
Sustainable Development Goals (SDGs), 189
Serambi Mekkah, 37, 44
service, 67
Setara Institute, 110, 123, 190, 207n15
Seudati, 3, 143
Shari`a instruction, 102
Shi'i, 116
singularized identity, 28–29
social interactions, 176–78
Solidaritas Perempuan, 109, 175, 188
special autonomy, 46, 113, 121
special status, 109, 113
structural problems, 69
Studi Syariat Islam di Aceh, 103
subjugation principle, 85–86
Sultan Iskandar Muda, 32, 49, 198n37
Sunna, 29, 104
Sunni, 99, 116, 124
Syariah dan Adat, 103

T

Technical Coordination Meeting, 69
territory principle, 84–85
Teungku, 27, 45, 102, 136, 195n10
transgender, 3

U

ulama, 48, 81, 107, 108, 109, 120, 125, 127, 144, 161, 184, 185, 207n20

V

Vihara, 108, 172, 173
violence, 36

W

Wali Nanggroe, 180
Wanita Katolik Republik Indonesia, 108, 174, 186
war, 44
Western tradition, 48
Wilayatul Hisbah, 11, 9, 55, 63, 65, 69, 71, 72, 77, 81, 86, 93, 183

Y

Yayasan Pembinaan Muallaf, 162

www.ingramcontent.com/pod-product-compliance
Lightning Source LLC
Chambersburg PA
CBHW050440240426
43661CB00055B/2458